Contents

		Page
Preface		vii
Quick view of votes by cluster (49 resolutions and 3 decisions)		viii

Resolutions

62/13	Objective information on military matters, including transparency of military expenditures	1
62/14	Implementation of the Declaration of the Indian Ocean as a Zone of Peace	5
62/15	African Nuclear-Weapon-Free Zone Treaty	8
62/16	Consolidation of the regime established by the Treaty for the Prohibition of Nuclear Weapons in Latin America and the Caribbean (Treaty of Tlatelolco)	10
62/17	Developments in the field of information and telecommunications in the context of international security	12
62/18	Establishment of a nuclear-weapon-free zone in the region of the Middle East	16
62/19	Conclusion of effective international arrangements to assure non-nuclear-weapon States against the use or threat of use of nuclear weapons	20
62/20	Prevention of an arms race in outer space	25
62/21	Verification in all its aspects, including the role of the United Nations in the field of verification	30
62/22	Assistance to States for curbing the illicit traffic in small arms and light weapons and collecting them	32
62/23	Implementation of the Convention on the Prohibition of the Development, Production, Stockpiling and Use of Chemical Weapons and on Their Destruction	35
62/24	Follow-up to nuclear disarmament obligations agreed to at the 1995 and 2000 Review Conferences of the Parties to the Treaty on the Non-Proliferation of Nuclear Weapons	38
62/25	Towards a nuclear-weapon-free world: accelerating the implementation of nuclear disarmament commitments	43
62/26	National legislation on transfer of arms, military equipment and dual-use goods and technology	47
62/27	Promotion of multilateralism in the area of disarmament and non-proliferation	49

62/28	Observance of environmental norms in the drafting and implementation of agreements on disarmament and arms control.	53
62/29	Convening of the fourth special session of the General Assembly devoted to disarmament	56
62/30	Effects of the use of armaments and ammunitions containing depleted uranium.	60
62/31	Treaty on the South-East Asia Nuclear-Weapon-Free Zone (Bangkok Treaty)	62
62/32	Reducing nuclear danger.	65
62/33	Measures to prevent terrorists from acquiring weapons of mass destruction	68
62/34	Prohibition of the dumping of radioactive wastes	71
62/35	Nuclear-weapon-free southern hemisphere and adjacent areas	74
62/36	Decreasing the operational readiness of nuclear weapons systems	80
62/37	Renewed determination towards the total elimination of nuclear weapons	83
62/38	Regional disarmament.	88
62/39	Follow-up to the Advisory Opinion of the International Court of Justice on the *Legality of the Threat or Use of Nuclear Weapons*	90
62/40	Prevention of the illicit transfer and unauthorized access to and use of man-portable air defence systems	94
62/41	Implementation of the Convention on the Prohibition of the Use, Stockpiling, Production and Transfer of Anti-personnel Mines and on Their Destruction	97
62/42	Nuclear disarmament	101
62/43	Transparency and confidence-building measures in outer space activities	108
62/44	Conventional arms control at the regional and subregional levels.	111
62/45	Confidence-building measures in the regional and subregional context	114
62/46	Preventing the acquisition by terrorists of radioactive materials and sources	117

Office for Disarmament Affairs
New York, 2008

The United Nations
DISARMAMENT
YEARBOOK

Volume 32 (Part I): 2007

*Disarmament Resolutions and Decisions
of the Sixty-second Session
of the United Nations General Assembly*

Guide to the user

To facilitate early analysis of the resolutions and decisions on disarmament adopted at the sixty-second session of the General Assembly, UNODA offers Part I of the *Yearbook* as a handy, concise reference tool, containing the full texts of all the resolutions and decisions adopted at the sixty-second session of the General Assembly, the date of adoption by the Assembly and the First Committee, the agenda item number, the symbol number of the Report of the Rapporteur, the main sponsors and the voting patterns in the Assembly. For a snapshot of this information in a convenient chart, see "Quick view of votes by cluster". For a list of agenda items and their corresponding reports, see Annex.

Bold type in the list of sponsors indicates the State that introduced the draft resolution or decision. Throughout the book, any deviation in introducing and/or voting on resolutions is asterisked, and explained in a corresponding footnote.

Electronically available in PDF or HTML format at
http://disarmament.un.org

UNITED NATIONS PUBLICATION
Sales No. E.08.IX.1

ISBN 978-92-1-142260-3

Copyright © United Nations, 2008
All rights reserved
Printed in United Nations, New York

62/47	The illicit trade in small arms and light weapons in all its aspects.	121
62/48	Relationship between disarmament and development	126
62/49	United Nations Regional Centre for Peace, Disarmament and Development in Latin America and the Caribbean	130
62/50	United Nations regional centres for peace and disarmament	133
62/51	Convention on the Prohibition of the Use of Nuclear Weapons	135
62/52	United Nations Regional Centre for Peace and Disarmament in Asia and the Pacific.	138
62/53	Regional confidence-building measures: activities of the United Nations Standing Advisory Committee on Security Questions in Central Africa.	141
62/54	Report of the Disarmament Commission.	145
62/55	Report of the Conference on Disarmament	147
62/56	The risk of nuclear proliferation in the Middle East	149
62/57	Convention on Prohibitions or Restrictions on the Use of Certain Conventional Weapons Which May Be Deemed to Be Excessively Injurious or to Have Indiscriminate Effects.	154
62/58	Strengthening of security and cooperation in the Mediterranean region	158
62/59	Comprehensive Nuclear-Test-Ban Treaty	161
62/60	Convention on the Prohibition of the Development, Production and Stockpiling of Bacteriological (Biological) and Toxin Weapons and on Their Destruction	164
62/216	United Nations Regional Centre for Peace and Disarmament in Africa.	167

Decisions

62/512	Review of the implementation of the Declaration on the Strengthening of International Security.	171
62/513	United Nations conference to identify appropriate ways of eliminating nuclear dangers in the context of nuclear disarmament	172
62/514	Missiles.	174

Annex

List of reports and notes of the Secretary-General 176

Preface

In February of 2007, Secretary-General Ban Ki-moon outlined for the General Assembly his intentions with regard to strengthening the capacity of the Organization to manage and sustain peace and security operations and to advance the disarmament agenda (see A/61/749 of 15 February 2007). He concluded that what was needed was an office headed by a High Representative so as to maximize the flexibility, agility and proximity to the Secretary-General required to facilitate ongoing and new disarmament and non-proliferation efforts, and that the arrangement would allow for more systematic interaction between the Secretary-General and the High Representative.

The Office would continue to fulfil the mandates of the former Department, while the High Representative would take on increased functions in the area of policy development and coordination and advocacy of disarmament and non-proliferation issues with Member States and civil society, as well as promotion and support of multilateral efforts on disarmament and non-proliferation of weapons of mass destruction and on conventional disarmament.

On 1 April 2007, the Department for Disarmament Affairs was designated the *United Nations Office for Disarmament Affairs (UNODA)* and on 2 July 2007 Mr. Sergio de Queiroz Duarte of Brazil was appointed as the High Representative for Disarmament Affairs.

Following a survey in 2007 of the readership of its flagship publication, *The United Nations Disarmament Yearbook* (now in its thirty-second year of publication), UNODA was encouraged by its findings to maintain the *Yearbook* in print and electronic format, as a handy, consolidated research and reference tool covering a wide variety of disarmament-related security issues of the international community.

However, in an effort to better meet the needs of our prime users and the demands of productivity and streamlining, we decided to revamp the *Yearbook* in the following way. The 2007 *Yearbook* has been produced in two parts. Part I replaces the *Disarmament Resolutions and Decisions Booklet* and contains all the resolutions and decisions of the previous General Assembly. Each year, it will be published in early spring.

Part II will be divided as usual among the main issues of multilateral consideration during the year, and will present developments and trends, with convenient issue-oriented timelines, short summaries of First Committee and General Assembly action taken on resolutions and decisions, the full texts of principal multilateral agreements reached during the year and declarations adopted by treaty review conferences. The chart of submissions to the United Nations Register of Conventional Arms will continue to appear, and a graph giving regional participation in the Register. The reader will notice other changes such as the size of *Yearbook* (Parts I and II will be the same size.), and its more appealing presentation.

We hope this improved format will be useful to the Member States and other readers of the *Yearbook*.

Ed.

Quick view of votes by cluster (49 resolutions and 3 decisions)

No.	Title	First Com. action (vote, date)	GA action, 5 Dec. (vote)
Cluster 1: Nuclear weapons			
62/15	African Nuclear-Weapon-Free Zone Treaty	w/o vote 30 Oct.	w/o vote
62/16	Consolidation of the regime established by the Treaty for the Prohibition of Nuclear Weapons in Latin America and the Caribbean (Treaty of Tlatelolco)	w/o vote 30 Oct.	w/o vote
62/18	Establishment of a nuclear-weapon-free zone in the region of the Middle East	w/o vote 30 Oct.	w/o vote
62/19	Conclusion of effective international arrangements to assure non-nuclear-weapon States against the use or threat of use of nuclear weapons	120-1-54 30 Oct.	121-1-56
62/24	Follow-up to nuclear disarmament obligations agreed to at the 1995 and 2000 Review Conferences of the Parties to the Treaty on the Non-Proliferation of Nuclear Weapons	103-53-15 102-48-11, p.p. 6 30 Oct.	109-55-15 114-50-10, p.p. 6
62/25	Towards a nuclear-weapon-free world: accelerating the implementation of nuclear disarmament commitments	151-5-13 155-4-2, o.p. 6 31 Oct.	156-5-14 165-4-2, o.p. 6
62/31	Treaty on the South-East Asia Nuclear-Weapon-Free Zone (Bangkok Treaty)	161-1-4 1 Nov.	174-1-5
62/32	Reducing nuclear danger	113-50-13 30 Oct.	117-52-12
62/34	Prohibition of the dumping of radioactive wastes	w/o vote 30 Oct.	w/o vote
62/35	Nuclear-weapon-free southern hemisphere and adjacent areas	162-3-7 156-1-8, o.p. 6 154-2-9, last 3 words, o.p. 6 31 Oct.	169-3-8 163-1-8, o.p. 6 163-1-9, last 3 words, o.p. 6
62/36	Decreasing the operational readiness of nuclear weapons systems	124-3-34 1 Nov.	139-3-36
62/37	Renewed determination towards the total elimination of nuclear weapons	165-3-10 30 Oct.	170-3-9

No.	Title	First Com. action (vote, date)	GA action, 5 Dec. (vote)
62/39	Follow-up to the Advisory Opinion of the International Court of Justice on the *Legality of the Threat or Use of Nuclear Weapons*	121-25-29 30 Oct.	127-27-27
62/42	Nuclear disarmament	113-45-17 30 Oct.	117-47-17
62/46	Preventing the acquisition by terrorists of radioactive materials and sources	w/o vote 2 Nov.	w/o vote
62/51	Convention on the Prohibition of the Use of Nuclear Weapons	115-50-11 30 Oct.	120-52-10
62/56	The risk of nuclear proliferation in the Middle East	164-3-6 161-3-6, p.p. 6 30 Oct.	170-5-7 166-3-6, p.p. 6
62/59	Comprehensive Nuclear-Test-Ban Treaty	166-1-4 31 Oct.	176-1-4
62/513	United Nations conference to identify appropriate ways of eliminating nuclear dangers in the context of nuclear disarmament (decision)	123-3-44 30 Oct.	133-3-43
62/514	Missiles (decision)	117-6-51 30 Oct.	123-7-51
Cluster 2: Other weapons of mass destruction			
62/23	Implementation of the Convention on the Prohibition of the Development, Production, Stockpiling and Use of Chemical Weapons and on Their Destruction	w/o vote 30 Oct.	w/o vote
62/33	Measures to prevent terrorists from acquiring weapons of mass destruction	w/o vote 30 Oct.	w/o vote
62/60	Convention on the Prohibition of the Development, Production and Stockpiling of Bacteriological (Biological) and Toxin Weapons and on Their Destruction	w/o vote 31 Oct.	w/o vote

No.	Title	First Com. action (vote, date)	GA action, 5 Dec. (vote)

Cluster 3: Outer space (disarmament aspects)

62/20	Prevention of an arms race in outer space	170-1-1 30 Oct.	178-1-1
62/43	Transparency and confidence-building measures in outer space activities	168-1-1 31 Oct.	179-1-1

Cluster 4: Conventional weapons

62/22	Assistance to States for curbing the illicit traffic in small arms and light weapons and collecting them	w/o vote 30 Oct.	w/o vote
62/40	Prevention of the illicit transfer and unauthorized access to and use of man-portable air defence systems	w/o vote 1 Nov.	w/o vote
62/41	Implementation of the Convention on the Prohibition of the Use, Stockpiling, Production and Transfer of Anti-personnel Mines and on Their Destruction	154-0-18 31 Oct.	164-0-18
62/47	The illicit trade in small arms and light weapons in all its aspects	165-1-0 1 Nov.	179-1-0
62/57	Convention on Prohibitions or Restrictions on the Use of Certain Conventional Weapons Which May Be Deemed to Be Excessively Injurious or to Have Indiscriminate Effects	w/o vote 31 Oct.	w/o vote

Cluster 5: Regional disarmament and security

62/38	Regional disarmament	w/o vote 30 Oct.	w/o vote
62/44	Conventional arms control at the regional and subregional levels	167-1-1 30 Oct.	177-1-1
62/53	Regional confidence-building measures: activities of the United Nations Standing Advisory Committee on Security Questions in Central Africa	w/o vote 2 Nov.	w/o vote
62/58	Strengthening of security and cooperation in the Mediterranean region	w/o vote 30 Oct.	w/o vote

No.	Title	First Com. action (vote, date)	GA action, 5 Dec. (vote)
Cluster 6: Other disarmament measures and international security			
62/13	Objective information on military matters, including transparency of military expenditures	w/o vote 31 Oct.	w/o vote
62/14	Implementation of the Declaration of the Indian Ocean as a Zone of Peace	120-3-45 1 Nov.	130-3-47
62/17	Developments in the field of information and telecommunications in the context of international security	168-1-0 1 Nov.	179-1-0
62/21	Verification in all its aspects, including the role of the United Nations in the field of verification	w/o vote 31 Oct.	w/o vote
62/26	National legislation on transfer of arms, military equipment and dual-use goods and technology	w/o vote 31 Oct.	w/o vote
62/27	Promotion of multilateralism in the area of disarmament and non-proliferation	112-4-51 1 Nov.	123-6-51
62/28	Observance of environmental norms in the drafting and implementation of agreements on disarmament and arms control	162-1-3 1 Nov.	175-1-3
62/30	Effects of the use of armaments and ammunitions containing depleted uranium	122-6-35 1 Nov.	136-5-36
62/45	Confidence-building measures in the regional and subregional context	w/o vote 31 Oct.	w/o vote
62/48	Relationship between disarmament and development	166-1-2 1 Nov.	179-1-2
62/512	Review of the implementation of the Declaration on the Strengthening of International Security (decision)	w/o vote 1 Nov.	w/o vote
Cluster 7: Disarmament machinery			
62/29	Convening of the fourth special session of the General Assembly devoted to disarmament	166-1-0 1 Nov.	179-1-1
62/49	United Nations Regional Centre for Peace, Disarmament and Development in Latin America and the Caribbean	w/o vote 31 Oct.	w/o vote

No.	Title	First Com. action (vote, date)	GA action, 5 Dec. (vote)
62/50	United Nations regional centres for peace and disarmament	w/o vote 1 Nov.	w/o vote
62/52	United Nations Regional Centre for Peace and Disarmament in Asia and the Pacific	w/o vote 31 Oct.	w/o vote
62/54	Report of the Disarmament Commission	w/o vote 31 Oct.	w/o vote
62/55	Report of the Conference on Disarmament	w/o vote 31 Oct.	w/o vote
62/216	United Nations Regional Centre for Peace and Disarmament in Africa	164-1-5 2 Nov.	150-0-5 21 Dec.

Resolutions

Agenda item 88 (b)

62/13 Objective information on military matters, including transparency of military expenditures

Text

The General Assembly,

Recalling its resolutions 53/72 of 4 December 1998, 54/43 of 1 December 1999, 56/14 of 29 November 2001, 58/28 of 8 December 2003 and 60/44 of 8 December 2005 on objective information on military matters, including transparency of military expenditures,

Also recalling its resolution 35/142 B of 12 December 1980, which introduced the United Nations system for the standardized reporting of military expenditures, and its resolutions 48/62 of 16 December 1993, 49/66 of 15 December 1994, 51/38 of 10 December 1996 and 52/32 of 9 December 1997, calling upon all Member States to participate in it, and its resolution 47/54 B of 9 December 1992, endorsing the guidelines and recommendations for objective information on military matters and inviting Member States to provide the Secretary-General with relevant information regarding their implementation,

Noting that since then, national reports on military expenditures and on the guidelines and recommendations for objective information on military matters have been submitted by a number of Member States belonging to different geographical regions,

Convinced that the improvement of international relations forms a sound basis for promoting further openness and transparency in all military matters,

Also convinced that transparency in military matters is an essential element for building a climate of trust and confidence between States worldwide and that a better flow of objective information on military matters can help to relieve international tension and is therefore an important contribution to conflict prevention,

Noting the role of the standardized reporting system, as instituted through its resolution 35/142 B, as an important instrument to enhance transparency in military matters,

Conscious that the value of the standardized reporting system would be enhanced by a broader participation of Member States,

Noting that the continuing operation of the standardized reporting system should be reviewed with a view to improving its further development and to broadening participation in it,

Welcoming, therefore, the report of the Secretary-General[1] on ways and means to implement the guidelines and recommendations for objective information on military matters, including, in particular, how to strengthen and broaden participation in the standardized reporting system,

Recalling that the guidelines and recommendations for objective information on military matters recommended certain areas for further consideration, such as the improvement of the standardized reporting system,

Noting the efforts of several regional organizations to promote transparency of military expenditures, including standardized annual exchanges of relevant information among their member States,

1. *Calls upon* Member States to report annually, by 30 April, to the Secretary-General their military expenditures for the latest fiscal year for which data are available, using, preferably and to the extent possible, the reporting instrument as recommended in its resolution 35/142 B or, as appropriate, any other format developed in conjunction with similar reporting on military expenditures to other international or regional organizations, and, in the same context, encourages Member States to submit nil returns, if appropriate;

2. *Recommends* the guidelines and recommendations for objective information on military matters to all Member States for implementation, fully taking into account specific political, military and other conditions prevailing in a region, on the basis of initiatives and with the agreement of the States of the region concerned;

3. *Encourages* relevant international bodies and regional organizations to promote transparency of military expenditures and to enhance complementarity among reporting systems, taking into account the particular characteristics of each region, and to consider the possibility of an exchange of information with the United Nations;

4. *Takes note* of the reports of the Secretary-General on objective information on military matters, including transparency of military expenditures;[2]

5. *Requests* the Secretary-General, within available resources:

(*a*) To continue the practice of sending an annual note verbale to Member States requesting the submission of data to the United Nations system for the standardized reporting of military expenditures, together with the

---

[1] A/54/298.
[2] A/58/202 and Add.1-3, A/59/192 and Add.1, A/60/159 and Add.1-3, A/61/133 and Add.1-3 and A/62/158 and Add.1 and 2.

reporting format and related instructions, and to publish in a timely fashion in appropriate United Nations media the due date for transmitting data on military expenditures;

(*b*) To circulate annually the reports on military expenditures as received from Member States;

(*c*) To establish a group of governmental experts, on the basis of equitable geographical representation, to review the operation and further development of the Standardized Instrument for Reporting Military Expenditures, commencing in 2010, taking into account the views expressed by Member States on the subject and the reports of the Secretary-General on objective information on military matters, including transparency of military expenditures, and to transmit the report of the group of experts to the General Assembly for consideration at its sixty-sixth session;

(*d*) To continue consultations with relevant international bodies, with a view to ascertaining requirements for adjusting the present instrument, with a view to encouraging wider participation, and to make recommendations, based on the outcome of those consultations and taking into account the views of Member States, on necessary changes to the content and structure of the standardized reporting system;

(*e*) To encourage relevant international bodies and organizations to promote transparency of military expenditures and to consult with those bodies and organizations with emphasis on examining possibilities for enhancing complementarity among international and regional reporting systems and for exchanging related information between those bodies and the United Nations;

(*f*) To encourage the United Nations regional centres for peace and disarmament in Africa, in Asia and the Pacific, and in Latin America and the Caribbean to assist Member States in their regions in enhancing their knowledge of the standardized reporting system;

(*g*) To promote international and regional/subregional symposiums and training seminars to explain the purpose of the standardized reporting system and to give relevant technical instructions;

(*h*) To report on experiences gained during such symposiums and training seminars;

6. *Encourages* Member States:

(*a*) To inform the Secretary-General about possible problems with the standardized reporting system and their reasons for not submitting the requested data;

(*b*) To continue to provide the Secretary-General, in time for deliberation by the General Assembly at its sixty-fourth session, with their views and suggestions on ways and means to strengthen and broaden participation in the standardized reporting system, including necessary changes to its content and structure;

7. *Decides* to include in the provisional agenda of its sixty-fourth session the item entitled "Objective information on military matters, including transparency of military expenditures".

Action by the General Assembly

Date: 5 December 2007   Meeting: 61st meeting
Vote: Adopted without a vote   Report: A/62/381

Sponsors

Argentina, Armenia, Austria, Belgium, Bolivia, Bosnia and Herzegovina, Brazil, Bulgaria, Burkina Faso, Canada, Chile, Croatia, Cyprus, Czech Republic, Denmark, Ecuador, Estonia, Finland, France, **Germany**, Ghana, Greece, Guatemala, Haiti, Hungary, Ireland, Italy, Latvia, Lesotho, Liechtenstein, Lithuania, Luxembourg, Malta, Netherlands, New Zealand, Norway, Peru, Poland, Portugal, Republic of Korea, Republic of Moldova, Romania, San Marino, Serbia, Slovakia, Slovenia, Spain, Sweden, Switzerland, Thailand, the former Yugoslav Republic of Macedonia, Turkey, Ukraine, United Kingdom of Great Britain and Northern Ireland, Uruguay

Co-sponsors

Albania, Azerbaijan, Benin, Costa Rica, Dominican Republic, Georgia, Iceland, India, Jamaica, Japan, Kazakhstan, Liberia, Madagascar, Mali, Monaco, Montenegro, Russian Federation, Senegal, Sierra Leone, Trinidad and Tobago

Action by the First Committee

Date: 31 October 2007   Meeting: 23rd meeting
Vote: Adopted without a vote   Draft resolution: A/C.1/62/L.33

Agenda item 89

62/14　Implementation of the Declaration of the Indian Ocean as a Zone of Peace

Text

The General Assembly,

Recalling the Declaration of the Indian Ocean as a Zone of Peace, contained in its resolution 2832 (XXVI) of 16 December 1971, and recalling also its resolutions 54/47 of 1 December 1999, 56/16 of 29 November 2001, 58/29 of 8 December 2003 and 60/48 of 8 December 2005 and other relevant resolutions,

Recalling also the report of the Meeting of the Littoral and Hinterland States of the Indian Ocean held in July 1979,[1]

Recalling further paragraph 102 of the Final Document of the Thirteenth Conference of Heads of State or Government of Non-Aligned Countries, held at Kuala Lumpur on 24 and 25 February 2003,[2] in which it was noted, inter alia, that the Chairperson of the Ad Hoc Committee on the Indian Ocean would continue his informal consultations on the future work of the Committee,

Emphasizing the need to foster consensual approaches that are conducive to the pursuit of such endeavours,

Noting the initiatives taken by countries of the region to promote cooperation, in particular economic cooperation, in the Indian Ocean area and the possible contribution of such initiatives to overall objectives of a zone of peace,

Convinced that the participation of all permanent members of the Security Council and the major maritime users of the Indian Ocean in the work of the Ad Hoc Committee is important and would assist the progress of a mutually beneficial dialogue to develop conditions of peace, security and stability in the Indian Ocean region,

Considering that greater efforts and more time are required to develop a focused discussion on practical measures to ensure conditions of peace, security and stability in the Indian Ocean region,

Having considered the report of the Ad Hoc Committee on the Indian Ocean,[3]

---

[1] *Official Records of the General Assembly, Thirty-fourth Session, Supplement No. 45 and corrigendum* (A/34/45 and Corr.1).
[2] See A/57/759-S/2003/332, annex I.
[3] *Official Records of the General Assembly, Sixty-second Session, Supplement No. 29* (A/62/29).

1. *Takes note* of the report of the Ad Hoc Committee on the Indian Ocean;[3]

2. *Reiterates its conviction* that the participation of all permanent members of the Security Council and the major maritime users of the Indian Ocean in the work of the Ad Hoc Committee is important and would greatly facilitate the development of a mutually beneficial dialogue to advance peace, security and stability in the Indian Ocean region;

3. *Requests* the Chairman of the Ad Hoc Committee to continue his informal consultations with the members of the Committee and to report through the Committee to the General Assembly at its sixty-fourth session;

4. *Requests* the Secretary-General to continue to render, within existing resources, all necessary assistance to the Ad Hoc Committee, including the provision of summary records;

5. *Decides* to include in the provisional agenda of its sixty-fourth session the item entitled "Implementation of the Declaration of the Indian Ocean as a Zone of Peace".

Action by the General Assembly

Date: 5 December 2007 Meeting: 61st meeting
Vote: 130-3-47   Report: A/62/382

Sponsors

Indonesia (on behalf of the States Members of the United Nations that are members of the Non-Aligned Movement)

Recorded vote

In favour:
Afghanistan, Algeria, Antigua and Barbuda, Argentina, Armenia, Australia, Azerbaijan, Bahamas, Bahrain, Bangladesh, Barbados, Belarus, Belize, Benin, Bhutan, Bolivia, Botswana, Brazil, Brunei Darussalam, Burkina Faso, Burundi, Cambodia, Cameroon, Cape Verde, Central African Republic, Chile, China, Colombia, Comoros, Congo, Costa Rica, Côte d'Ivoire, Cuba, Democratic People's Republic of Korea, Djibouti, Dominica, Dominican Republic, Ecuador, Egypt, El Salvador, Eritrea, Ethiopia, Fiji, Gabon, Gambia, Georgia, Ghana, Grenada, Guatemala, Guinea, Guinea-Bissau, Guyana, Haiti, Honduras, India, Indonesia, Iran (Islamic Republic of), Iraq, Jamaica, Japan, Jordan, Kazakhstan, Kenya, Kuwait, Kyrgyzstan, Lao People's Democratic Republic, Lebanon, Lesotho, Liberia, Libyan Arab Jamahiriya, Madagascar, Malawi, Malaysia, Maldives, Mali, Mauritania, Mauritius, Mexico, Mongolia, Morocco, Mozambique, Myanmar, Namibia, Nauru, Nepal, New Zealand, Nicaragua, Niger, Nigeria, Oman, Pakistan, Panama, Papua New Guinea, Paraguay, Peru, Philippines, Qatar, Republic of Korea,

Russian Federation, Saint Kitts and Nevis, Saint Lucia, Samoa, Sao Tome and Principe, Saudi Arabia, Senegal, Sierra Leone, Singapore, Solomon Islands, Somalia, South Africa, Sri Lanka, Sudan, Suriname, Swaziland, Syrian Arab Republic, Tajikistan, Thailand, Togo, Tonga, Trinidad and Tobago, Tunisia, Turkmenistan, United Arab Emirates, United Republic of Tanzania, Uruguay, Venezuela (Bolivarian Republic of), Viet Nam, Yemen, Zambia, Zimbabwe

Against:
France, United Kingdom of Great Britain and Northern Ireland, United States of America

Abstaining:
Albania, Andorra, Austria, Belgium, Bosnia and Herzegovina, Bulgaria, Canada, Croatia, Cyprus, Czech Republic, Denmark, Estonia, Finland, Germany, Greece, Hungary, Iceland, Ireland, Israel, Italy, Latvia, Liechtenstein, Lithuania, Luxembourg, Malta, Marshall Islands, Micronesia (Federated States of), Monaco, Montenegro, Netherlands, Norway, Palau, Poland, Portugal, Republic of Moldova, Romania, Rwanda, San Marino, Serbia, Slovakia, Slovenia, Spain, Sweden, Switzerland, the former Yugoslav Republic of Macedonia, Turkey, Ukraine

Action by the First Committee

Date: 1 November 2007   Meeting: 24th meeting
Vote: 120-3-45   Draft resolution: A/C.1/62/L.16

Agenda item 90

62/15 African Nuclear-Weapon-Free Zone Treaty

Text

The General Assembly,

Recalling its resolutions 51/53 of 10 December 1996 and 56/17 of 29 November 2001 and all its other relevant resolutions, as well as those of the Organization of African Unity,

Recalling also the signing of the African Nuclear-Weapon-Free Zone Treaty (Treaty of Pelindaba)[1] at Cairo on 11 April 1996,

Recalling further the Cairo Declaration adopted on that occasion,[2] which emphasized that nuclear-weapon-free zones, especially in regions of tension, such as the Middle East, enhance global and regional peace and security,

Taking note of the statement made by the President of the Security Council on behalf of the members of the Council on 12 April 1996,[3] affirming that the signature of the African Nuclear-Weapon-Free Zone Treaty constituted an important contribution by the African countries to the maintenance of international peace and security,

Considering that the establishment of nuclear-weapon-free zones, especially in the Middle East, would enhance the security of Africa and the viability of the African nuclear-weapon-free zone,

1. *Calls upon* African States that have not yet done so to sign and ratify the African Nuclear-Weapon-Free Zone Treaty (Treaty of Pelindaba)[1] as soon as possible so that it may enter into force without delay;

2. *Expresses its appreciation* to the nuclear-weapon States that have signed the Protocols that concern them, and calls upon those that have not yet ratified the Protocols concerning them to do so as soon as possible;

3. *Calls upon* the States contemplated in Protocol III to the Treaty that have not yet done so to take all necessary measures to ensure the speedy application of the Treaty to territories for which they are, de jure or de facto, internationally responsible and that lie within the limits of the geographical zone established in the Treaty;

4. *Calls upon* the African States parties to the Treaty on the Non-Proliferation of Nuclear Weapons[4] that have not yet done so to conclude comprehensive safeguards agreements with the International Atomic Energy Agency pursuant to the Treaty, thereby satisfying the requirements of

---
[1] See A/50/426, annex.
[2] A/51/113-S/1996/276, annex.
[3] S/PRST/1996/17; see *Resolutions and Decisions of the Security Council, 1996*.
[4] United Nations, *Treaty Series*, vol. 729, No. 10485.

article 9 (b) of and annex II to the Treaty of Pelindaba when it enters into force, and to conclude additional protocols to their safeguards agreements on the basis of the Model Protocol approved by the Board of Governors of the Agency on 15 May 1997;[5]

5. *Expresses its gratitude* to the Secretary-General, the Chairman of the Commission of the African Union and the Director General of the International Atomic Energy Agency for the diligence with which they have rendered effective assistance to the signatories to the Treaty;

6. *Decides* to include in the provisional agenda of its sixty-fourth session the item entitled "African Nuclear-Weapon-Free Zone Treaty".

Action by the General Assembly

Date: 5 December 2007　　　Meeting: 61st meeting
Vote: Adopted without a vote　　Report: A/62/383

Sponsors

Nigeria (on behalf of the States Members of the United Nations that are members of the Group of African States)

Action by the First Committee

Date: 30 October 2007　　　Meeting:　　22nd meeting
Vote: Adopted without a vote　　Draft resolution: A/C.1/62/L.26

---

[5] International Atomic Energy Agency, INFCIRC/540 (Corrected).

Agenda item 91

62/16 Consolidation of the regime established by the Treaty for the Prohibition of Nuclear Weapons in Latin America and the Caribbean (Treaty of Tlatelolco)

Text

The General Assembly,

Recalling that the Treaty for the Prohibition of Nuclear Weapons in Latin America and the Caribbean (Treaty of Tlatelolco)[1] was opened for signature at Mexico City on 14 February 1967,

Recalling also that, in its preamble, the Treaty of Tlatelolco states that military denuclearized zones are not an end in themselves but rather a means for achieving general and complete disarmament at a later stage,

Recalling further that, in its resolution 2286 (XXII) of 5 December 1967, it welcomed with special satisfaction the Treaty of Tlatelolco as an event of historic significance in the efforts to prevent the proliferation of nuclear weapons and to promote international peace and security,

Recalling that in 1990, 1991 and 1992 the General Conference of the Agency for the Prohibition of Nuclear Weapons in Latin America and the Caribbean approved and opened for signature a set of amendments[2] to the Treaty of Tlatelolco, with the aim of enabling the full entry into force of that instrument,

Noting with satisfaction the commemoration of the fortieth anniversary of the adoption and opening for signature of the Treaty of Tlatelolco, which was observed in Mexico City on 14 February 2007,

Highlighting that the Treaty of Tlatelolco is now in force for thirty-three sovereign States of the region, thereby consolidating the first nuclear-weapon-free zone established in a densely populated region,

Noting with satisfaction the leadership of the Agency for the Prohibition of Nuclear Weapons in Latin America and the Caribbean in the convening of the first Conference of States Parties and Signatories to Treaties that Establish Nuclear-Weapon-Free Zones, held in Tlatelolco, Mexico, from 26 to 28 April 2005,

Reaffirming the importance of strengthening the Agency as the appropriate legal and political forum for ensuring full compliance with and implementation of the Treaty of Tlatelolco, as well as cooperation with the agencies of other nuclear-weapon-free zones,

---

[1] United Nations, *Treaty Series*, vol. 634, No. 9068.
[2] A/47/467, annex.

1. *Welcomes* the fact that the Treaty for the Prohibition of Nuclear Weapons in Latin America and the Caribbean (Treaty of Tlatelolco)[1] is now in force for the sovereign States of the region;

2. *Urges* the countries of the region that have not yet done so to sign or deposit their instruments of ratification of the amendments to the Treaty of Tlatelolco approved by the General Conference of the Agency for the Prohibition of Nuclear Weapons in Latin America and the Caribbean in its resolutions 267 (E-V), 268 (XII) and 290 (E-VII);

3. *Encourages* States members of the Agency to continue activities and efforts with a view to implementing the Declaration adopted at the first Conference of States Parties and Signatories to Treaties that Establish Nuclear-Weapon-Free Zones;[3]

4. *Decides* to include in the provisional agenda of its sixty-fifth session the item entitled "Consolidation of the regime established by the Treaty for the Prohibition of Nuclear Weapons in Latin America and the Caribbean (Treaty of Tlatelolco)".

Action by the General Assembly

Date: 5 December 2007　　Meeting: 61st meeting
Vote: Adopted without a vote　　Report: A/62/384

Sponsors

Antigua and Barbuda, Argentina, Bolivia, Brazil, Chile, Colombia, Costa Rica, Cuba, Dominican Republic, Ecuador, El Salvador, Guatemala, Guyana, Haiti, Honduras, Jamaica, **Mexico**, Nicaragua, Panama, Paraguay, Peru, Saint Lucia, Saint Vincent and the Grenadines, Suriname, Uruguay, Venezuela (Bolivarian Republic of)

Co-sponsors

Bahamas, Barbados, Belize, Cambodia, Dominica, Grenada, Indonesia, Trinidad and Tobago

Action by the First Committee

Date: 30 October 2007　　Meeting: 21st meeting
Vote: Adopted without a vote　　Draft resolution: A/C.1/62/L.10

---

[3] A/60/121, annexes.

Agenda item 93

62/17   Developments in the field of information and telecommunications in the context of international security

Text

The General Assembly,

Recalling its resolutions 53/70 of 4 December 1998, 54/49 of 1 December 1999, 55/28 of 20 November 2000, 56/19 of 29 November 2001, 57/53 of 22 November 2002, 58/32 of 8 December 2003, 59/61 of 3 December 2004, 60/45 of 8 December 2005 and 61/54 of 6 December 2006,

Recalling also its resolutions on the role of science and technology in the context of international security, in which, inter alia, it recognized that scientific and technological developments could have both civilian and military applications and that progress in science and technology for civilian applications needed to be maintained and encouraged,

Noting that considerable progress has been achieved in developing and applying the latest information technologies and means of telecommunication,

Affirming that it sees in this process the broadest positive opportunities for the further development of civilization, the expansion of opportunities for cooperation for the common good of all States, the enhancement of the creative potential of humankind and additional improvements in the circulation of information in the global community,

Recalling, in this connection, the approaches and principles outlined at the Information Society and Development Conference, held in Midrand, South Africa, from 13 to 15 May 1996,

Bearing in mind the results of the Ministerial Conference on Terrorism, held in Paris on 30 July 1996, and the recommendations that it made,[1]

Bearing in mind also the results of the World Summit on the Information Society, held in Geneva from 10 to 12 December 2003 (first phase) and in Tunis from 16 to 18 November 2005 (second phase),[2]

Noting that the dissemination and use of information technologies and means affect the interests of the entire international community and that optimum effectiveness is enhanced by broad international cooperation,

Expressing its concern that these technologies and means can potentially be used for purposes that are inconsistent with the objectives of maintaining international stability and security and may adversely affect the integrity of

---

[1] See A/51/261, annex.
[2] See A/C.2/59/3 and A/60/687.

the infrastructure of States to the detriment of their security in both civil and military fields,

Considering that it is necessary to prevent the use of information resources or technologies for criminal or terrorist purposes,

Noting the contribution of those Member States that have submitted their assessments on issues of information security to the Secretary-General pursuant to paragraphs 1 to 3 of resolutions 53/70, 54/49, 55/28, 56/19, 57/53, 58/32, 59/61, 60/45 and 61/54,

Taking note of the reports of the Secretary-General containing those assessments,[3]

Welcoming the initiative taken by the Secretariat and the United Nations Institute for Disarmament Research in convening an international meeting of experts in Geneva in August 1999 on developments in the field of information and telecommunications in the context of international security, as well as its results,

Considering that the assessments of the Member States contained in the reports of the Secretary-General and the international meeting of experts have contributed to a better understanding of the substance of issues of international information security and related notions,

Bearing in mind that the Secretary-General, in fulfilment of resolution 58/32, established in 2004 a group of governmental experts, which, in accordance with its mandate, considered existing and potential threats in the sphere of information security and possible cooperative measures to address them and conducted a study on relevant international concepts aimed at strengthening the security of global information and telecommunications systems,

Taking note of the report of the Secretary-General on the Group of Governmental Experts on Developments in the Field of Information and Telecommunications in the Context of International Security, prepared on the basis of the results of the Group's work,[4]

1. *Calls upon* Member States to promote further at multilateral levels the consideration of existing and potential threats in the field of information security, as well as possible measures to limit the threats emerging in this field, consistent with the need to preserve the free flow of information;

2. *Considers* that the purpose of such measures could be served through the examination of relevant international concepts aimed at strengthening the security of global information and telecommunications systems;

---

[3] A/54/213, A/55/140 and Corr.1 and Add.1, A/56/164 and Add.1, A/57/166 and Add.1, A/58/373, A/59/116 and Add.1, A/60/95 and Add.1, and A/61/161 and Add.1.
[4] A/60/202.

3. *Invites* all Member States to continue to inform the Secretary-General of their views and assessments on the following questions:

(*a*) General appreciation of the issues of information security;

(*b*) Efforts taken at the national level to strengthen information security and promote international cooperation in this field;

(*c*) The content of the concepts mentioned in paragraph 2 above;

(*d*) Possible measures that could be taken by the international community to strengthen information security at the global level;

4. *Requests* the Secretary-General, with the assistance of a group of governmental experts, to be established in 2009 on the basis of equitable geographical distribution, to continue to study existing and potential threats in the sphere of information security and possible cooperative measures to address them, as well as the concepts referred to in paragraph 2 above, and to submit a report on the results of this study to the General Assembly at its sixty-fifth session;

5. *Decides* to include in the provisional agenda of its sixty-third session the item entitled "Developments in the field of information and telecommunications in the context of international security".

Action by the General Assembly

Date: 5 December 2007 Meeting: 61st meeting
Vote: 179-1-0 Report: A/62/386

Sponsors

Armenia, Belarus, Chile, China, Ethiopia, Kazakhstan, Kyrgyzstan, Madagascar, Mali, Myanmar, **Russian Federation**, Tajikistan, Uzbekistan

Co-sponsors

Cuba, Japan, Nicaragua, Turkmenistan

In favour:

Afghanistan, Albania, Algeria, Andorra, Antigua and Barbuda, Argentina, Armenia, Australia, Austria, Azerbaijan, Bahamas, Bahrain, Bangladesh, Barbados, Belarus, Belgium, Belize, Benin, Bhutan, Bolivia, Bosnia and Herzegovina, Botswana, Brazil, Brunei Darussalam, Bulgaria, Burkina Faso, Burundi, Cambodia, Cameroon, Canada, Cape Verde, Central African Republic, Chile, China, Colombia, Comoros, Congo, Costa Rica, Côte d'Ivoire, Croatia, Cuba, Cyprus, Czech Republic, Democratic People's Republic of Korea, Denmark, Djibouti, Dominica, Dominican Republic, Ecuador, Egypt, El Salvador, Eritrea, Estonia, Ethiopia, Fiji, Finland, France, Gabon, Gambia, Georgia, Germany, Ghana, Greece,

Grenada, Guatemala, Guinea, Guinea-Bissau, Guyana, Haiti, Honduras, Hungary, Iceland, India, Indonesia, Iran (Islamic Republic of), Iraq, Ireland, Israel, Italy, Jamaica, Japan, Jordan, Kazakhstan, Kenya, Kuwait, Kyrgyzstan, Lao People's Democratic Republic, Latvia, Lebanon, Lesotho, Liberia, Libyan Arab Jamahiriya, Liechtenstein, Lithuania, Luxembourg, Madagascar, Malawi, Malaysia, Maldives, Mali, Malta, Marshall Islands, Mauritania, Mauritius, Mexico, Micronesia (Federated States of), Monaco, Mongolia, Montenegro, Morocco, Mozambique, Myanmar, Namibia, Nauru, Nepal, Netherlands, New Zealand, Nicaragua, Niger, Nigeria, Norway, Oman, Pakistan, Palau, Panama, Papua New Guinea, Paraguay, Peru, Philippines, Poland, Portugal, Qatar, Republic of Korea, Republic of Moldova, Romania, Russian Federation, Rwanda, Saint Kitts and Nevis, Saint Lucia, Samoa, San Marino, Sao Tome and Principe, Saudi Arabia, Senegal, Serbia, Sierra Leone, Singapore, Slovakia, Slovenia, Solomon Islands, Somalia, South Africa, Spain, Sri Lanka, Sudan, Suriname, Swaziland, Sweden, Switzerland, Syrian Arab Republic, Tajikistan, Thailand, the former Yugoslav Republic of Macedonia, Togo, Tonga, Trinidad and Tobago, Tunisia, Turkey, Turkmenistan, Ukraine, United Arab Emirates, United Kingdom of Great Britain and Northern Ireland, United Republic of Tanzania, Uruguay, Venezuela (Bolivarian Republic of), Viet Nam, Yemen, Zambia, Zimbabwe

Against:
United States of America

Abstaining:
None

Action by the First Committee

Date: 1 November 2007   Meeting: 24th meeting
Vote: 168-1-0   Draft resolution: A/C.1/62/L.45

Agenda item 94

62/18   Establishment of a nuclear-weapon-free zone in the region of the Middle East

Text

The General Assembly,

Recalling its resolutions 3263 (XXIX) of 9 December 1974, 3474 (XXX) of 11 December 1975, 31/71 of 10 December 1976, 32/82 of 12 December 1977, 33/64 of 14 December 1978, 34/77 of 11 December 1979, 35/147 of 12 December 1980, 36/87 A and B of 9 December 1981, 37/75 of 9 December 1982, 38/64 of 15 December 1983, 39/54 of 12 December 1984, 40/82 of 12 December 1985, 41/48 of 3 December 1986, 42/28 of 30 November 1987, 43/65 of 7 December 1988, 44/108 of 15 December 1989, 45/52 of 4 December 1990, 46/30 of 6 December 1991, 47/48 of 9 December 1992, 48/71 of 16 December 1993, 49/71 of 15 December 1994, 50/66 of 12 December 1995, 51/41 of 10 December 1996, 52/34 of 9 December 1997, 53/74 of 4 December 1998, 54/51 of 1 December 1999, 55/30 of 20 November 2000, 56/21 of 29 November 2001, 57/55 of 22 November 2002, 58/34 of 8 December 2003, 59/63 of 3 December 2004, 60/52 of 8 December 2005 and 61/56 of 6 December 2006 on the establishment of a nuclear-weapon-free zone in the region of the Middle East,

Recalling also the recommendations for the establishment of such a zone in the Middle East consistent with paragraphs 60 to 63, and in particular paragraph 63 (*d*), of the Final Document of the Tenth Special Session of the General Assembly,[1]

Emphasizing the basic provisions of the above-mentioned resolutions, which call upon all parties directly concerned to consider taking the practical and urgent steps required for the implementation of the proposal to establish a nuclear-weapon-free zone in the region of the Middle East and, pending and during the establishment of such a zone, to declare solemnly that they will refrain, on a reciprocal basis, from producing, acquiring or in any other way possessing nuclear weapons and nuclear explosive devices and from permitting the stationing of nuclear weapons on their territory by any third party, to agree to place their nuclear facilities under International Atomic Energy Agency safeguards and to declare their support for the establishment of the zone and to deposit such declarations with the Security Council for consideration, as appropriate,

Reaffirming the inalienable right of all States to acquire and develop nuclear energy for peaceful purposes,

---

[1] Resolution S-10/2.

Emphasizing the need for appropriate measures on the question of the prohibition of military attacks on nuclear facilities,

Bearing in mind the consensus reached by the General Assembly since its thirty-fifth session that the establishment of a nuclear-weapon-free zone in the Middle East would greatly enhance international peace and security,

Desirous of building on that consensus so that substantial progress can be made towards establishing a nuclear-weapon-free zone in the Middle East,

Welcoming all initiatives leading to general and complete disarmament, including in the region of the Middle East, and in particular on the establishment therein of a zone free of weapons of mass destruction, including nuclear weapons,

Noting the peace negotiations in the Middle East, which should be of a comprehensive nature and represent an appropriate framework for the peaceful settlement of contentious issues in the region,

Recognizing the importance of credible regional security, including the establishment of a mutually verifiable nuclear-weapon-free zone,

Emphasizing the essential role of the United Nations in the establishment of a mutually verifiable nuclear-weapon-free zone,

Having examined the report of the Secretary-General on the implementation of resolution 61/56,[2]

1. *Urges* all parties directly concerned to consider seriously taking the practical and urgent steps required for the implementation of the proposal to establish a nuclear-weapon-free zone in the region of the Middle East in accordance with the relevant resolutions of the General Assembly, and, as a means of promoting this objective, invites the countries concerned to adhere to the Treaty on the Non-Proliferation of Nuclear Weapons;[3]

2. *Calls upon* all countries of the region that have not done so, pending the establishment of the zone, to agree to place all their nuclear activities under International Atomic Energy Agency safeguards;

3. *Takes note* of resolution GC(51)/RES/17, adopted on 20 September 2007 by the General Conference of the International Atomic Energy Agency at its fifty-first regular session, concerning the application of Agency safeguards in the Middle East;[4]

4. *Notes* the importance of the ongoing bilateral Middle East peace negotiations and the activities of the multilateral Working Group on Arms

---

[2] A/62/95 (Part I) and Add.1.
[3] United Nations, *Treaty Series*, vol. 729, No. 10485.
[4] See International Atomic Energy Agency, *Resolutions and Other Decisions of the General Conference, Fifty-first Regular Session, 17-21 September 2007* (GC(51)/RES/DEC(2007)).

Control and Regional Security in promoting mutual confidence and security in the Middle East, including the establishment of a nuclear-weapon-free zone;

5. *Invites* all countries of the region, pending the establishment of a nuclear-weapon-free zone in the region of the Middle East, to declare their support for establishing such a zone, consistent with paragraph 63 (*d*) of the Final Document of the Tenth Special Session of the General Assembly,[1] and to deposit those declarations with the Security Council;

6. *Also invites* those countries, pending the establishment of the zone, not to develop, produce, test or otherwise acquire nuclear weapons or permit the stationing on their territories, or territories under their control, of nuclear weapons or nuclear explosive devices;

7. *Invites* the nuclear-weapon States and all other States to render their assistance in the establishment of the zone and at the same time to refrain from any action that runs counter to both the letter and the spirit of the present resolution;

8. *Takes note* of the report of the Secretary-General;[2]

9. *Invites* all parties to consider the appropriate means that may contribute towards the goal of general and complete disarmament and the establishment of a zone free of weapons of mass destruction in the region of the Middle East;

10. *Requests* the Secretary-General to continue to pursue consultations with the States of the region and other concerned States, in accordance with paragraph 7 of resolution 46/30 and taking into account the evolving situation in the region, and to seek from those States their views on the measures outlined in chapters III and IV of the study annexed to the report of the Secretary-General of 10 October 1990[5] or other relevant measures, in order to move towards the establishment of a nuclear-weapon-free zone in the Middle East;

11. *Also requests* the Secretary-General to submit to the General Assembly at its sixty-third session a report on the implementation of the present resolution;

12. *Decides* to include in the provisional agenda of its sixty-third session the item entitled "Establishment of a nuclear-weapon-free zone in the region of the Middle East".

Action by the General Assembly

Date: 5 December 2007   Meeting: 61st meeting
Vote: Adopted without a vote   Report: A/62/387

---

[5] A/45/435.

Resolutions and decisions of the 62nd session of the General Assembly

Sponsors
> **Egypt**

Action by the First Committee
> Date: 30 October 2007   Meeting: 21st meeting
> Vote: Adopted without a vote   Draft resolution: A/C.1/62/L.1

Agenda item 95

62/19 Conclusion of effective international arrangements to assure non-nuclear-weapon States against the use or threat of use of nuclear weapons

Text

The General Assembly,

Bearing in mind the need to allay the legitimate concern of the States of the world with regard to ensuring lasting security for their peoples,

Convinced that nuclear weapons pose the greatest threat to mankind and to the survival of civilization,

Welcoming the progress achieved in recent years in both nuclear and conventional disarmament,

Noting that, despite recent progress in the field of nuclear disarmament, further efforts are necessary towards the achievement of general and complete disarmament under effective international control,

Convinced that nuclear disarmament and the complete elimination of nuclear weapons are essential to remove the danger of nuclear war,

Determined to abide strictly by the relevant provisions of the Charter of the United Nations on the non-use of force or threat of force,

Recognizing that the independence, territorial integrity and sovereignty of non-nuclear-weapon States need to be safeguarded against the use or threat of use of force, including the use or threat of use of nuclear weapons,

Considering that, until nuclear disarmament is achieved on a universal basis, it is imperative for the international community to develop effective measures and arrangements to ensure the security of non-nuclear-weapon States against the use or threat of use of nuclear weapons from any quarter,

Recognizing that effective measures and arrangements to assure non-nuclear-weapon States against the use or threat of use of nuclear weapons can contribute positively to the prevention of the spread of nuclear weapons,

Bearing in mind paragraph 59 of the Final Document of the Tenth Special Session of the General Assembly,[1] the first special session devoted to disarmament, in which it urged the nuclear-weapon States to pursue efforts to conclude, as appropriate, effective arrangements to assure non-nuclear-weapon States against the use or threat of use of nuclear weapons, and desirous of promoting the implementation of the relevant provisions of the Final Document,

---

[1] Resolution S-10/2.

Recalling the relevant parts of the special report of the Committee on Disarmament[2] submitted to the General Assembly at its twelfth special session,[3] the second special session devoted to disarmament, and of the special report of the Conference on Disarmament submitted to the Assembly at its fifteenth special session,[4] the third special session devoted to disarmament, as well as the report of the Conference on its 1992 session,[5]

Recalling also paragraph 12 of the Declaration of the 1980s as the Second Disarmament Decade, contained in the annex to its resolution 35/46 of 3 December 1980, which states, inter alia, that all efforts should be exerted by the Committee on Disarmament urgently to negotiate with a view to reaching agreement on effective international arrangements to assure non-nuclear-weapon States against the use or threat of use of nuclear weapons,

Noting the in-depth negotiations undertaken in the Conference on Disarmament and its Ad Hoc Committee on Effective International Arrangements to Assure Non-Nuclear-Weapon States against the Use or Threat of Use of Nuclear Weapons,[6] with a view to reaching agreement on this question,

Taking note of the proposals submitted under the item in the Conference on Disarmament, including the drafts of an international convention,

Taking note also of the relevant decision of the Thirteenth Conference of Heads of State or Government of Non-Aligned Countries, held at Kuala Lumpur on 24 and 25 February 2003,[7] which was reiterated at the Fourteenth Conference of Heads of State or Government of Non-Aligned Countries, held at Havana on 15 and 16 September 2006,[8] as well as the relevant recommendations of the Organization of the Islamic Conference,

Taking note further of the unilateral declarations made by all the nuclear-weapon States on their policies of non-use or non-threat of use of nuclear weapons against the non-nuclear-weapon States,

Noting the support expressed in the Conference on Disarmament and in the General Assembly for the elaboration of an international convention to assure non-nuclear-weapon States against the use or threat of use of nuclear weapons, as well as the difficulties pointed out in evolving a common approach acceptable to all,

---

[2] The Committee on Disarmament was redesignated the Conference on Disarmament as from 7 February 1984.
[3] *Official Records of the General Assembly, Twelfth Special Session, Supplement No. 2* (A/S-12/2), sect. III.C.
[4] Ibid., *Fifteenth Special Session, Supplement No. 2* (A/S-15/2), sect. III.F.
[5] Ibid., *Forty-seventh Session, Supplement No. 27* (A/47/27), sect. III.F.
[6] Ibid., *Forty-eighth Session, Supplement No. 27* (A/48/27), para. 39.
[7] See A/57/759-S/2003/332, annex I.
[8] See A/61/472-S/2006/780, annex I.

Taking note of Security Council resolution 984 (1995) of 11 April 1995 and the views expressed on it,

Recalling its relevant resolutions adopted in previous years, in particular resolutions 45/54 of 4 December 1990, 46/32 of 6 December 1991, 47/50 of 9 December 1992, 48/73 of 16 December 1993, 49/73 of 15 December 1994, 50/68 of 12 December 1995, 51/43 of 10 December 1996, 52/36 of 9 December 1997, 53/75 of 4 December 1998, 54/52 of 1 December 1999, 55/31 of 20 November 2000, 56/22 of 29 November 2001, 57/56 of 22 November 2002, 58/35 of 8 December 2003, 59/64 of 3 December 2004, 60/53 of 8 December 2005 and 61/57 of 6 December 2006,

1. *Reaffirms* the urgent need to reach an early agreement on effective international arrangements to assure non-nuclear-weapon States against the use or threat of use of nuclear weapons;

2. *Notes with satisfaction* that in the Conference on Disarmament there is no objection, in principle, to the idea of an international convention to assure non-nuclear-weapon States against the use or threat of use of nuclear weapons, although the difficulties with regard to evolving a common approach acceptable to all have also been pointed out;

3. *Appeals* to all States, especially the nuclear-weapon States, to work actively towards an early agreement on a common approach and, in particular, on a common formula that could be included in an international instrument of a legally binding character;

4. *Recommends* that further intensive efforts be devoted to the search for such a common approach or common formula and that the various alternative approaches, including, in particular, those considered in the Conference on Disarmament, be explored further in order to overcome the difficulties;

5. *Also recommends* that the Conference on Disarmament actively continue intensive negotiations with a view to reaching early agreement and concluding effective international agreements to assure the non-nuclear-weapon States against the use or threat of use of nuclear weapons, taking into account the widespread support for the conclusion of an international convention and giving consideration to any other proposals designed to secure the same objective;

6. *Decides* to include in the provisional agenda of its sixty-third session the item entitled "Conclusion of effective international arrangements to assure non-nuclear-weapon States against the use or threat of use of nuclear weapons".

Action by the General Assembly

Date: 5 December 2007 Meeting: 61st meeting
Vote: 121-1-56 Report: A/62/388

Sponsors

Bangladesh, Brunei Darussalam, Colombia, Cuba, Egypt, El Salvador, Ghana, Guinea, Haiti, Honduras, Indonesia, Iran (Islamic Republic of), Iraq, Jordan, Kuwait, Lebanon, Libyan Arab Jamahiriya, Malawi, Malaysia, Mali, **Pakistan**, Peru, Saudi Arabia, Sri Lanka, Syrian Arab Republic, Viet Nam, Zambia

Co-sponsors

Benin, Liberia, Myanmar, Philippines, Qatar, Uzbekistan

Recorded vote

In favour:

Afghanistan, Algeria, Antigua and Barbuda, Azerbaijan, Bahamas, Bahrain, Bangladesh, Barbados, Belarus, Belize, Benin, Bhutan, Bolivia, Botswana, Brazil, Brunei Darussalam, Burkina Faso, Burundi, Cambodia, Cameroon, Cape Verde, Central African Republic, Chile, China, Colombia, Comoros, Congo, Costa Rica, Côte d'Ivoire, Cuba, Democratic People's Republic of Korea, Djibouti, Dominica, Dominican Republic, Ecuador, Egypt, El Salvador, Eritrea, Ethiopia, Fiji, Gabon, Gambia, Georgia, Ghana, Grenada, Guatemala, Guinea, Guinea-Bissau, Guyana, Haiti, Honduras, India, Indonesia, Iran (Islamic Republic of), Iraq, Jamaica, Japan, Jordan, Kazakhstan, Kenya, Kuwait, Kyrgyzstan, Lao People's Democratic Republic, Lesotho, Liberia, Libyan Arab Jamahiriya, Madagascar, Malawi, Malaysia, Maldives, Mali, Mauritania, Mauritius, Mexico, Mongolia, Morocco, Mozambique, Myanmar, Namibia, Nepal, Nicaragua, Niger, Nigeria, Oman, Pakistan, Panama, Papua New Guinea, Paraguay, Peru, Philippines, Qatar, Rwanda, Saint Kitts and Nevis, Saint Lucia, Samoa, Sao Tome and Principe, Saudi Arabia, Senegal, Sierra Leone, Singapore, Solomon Islands, Somalia, Sri Lanka, Sudan, Suriname, Swaziland, Syrian Arab Republic, Tajikistan, Thailand, Togo, Trinidad and Tobago, Tunisia, Turkmenistan, United Arab Emirates, United Republic of Tanzania, Uruguay, Venezuela (Bolivarian Republic of), Viet Nam, Yemen, Zambia, Zimbabwe

Against:

United States of America

Abstaining:

Albania, Andorra, Argentina, Armenia, Australia, Austria, Belgium, Bosnia and Herzegovina, Bulgaria, Canada, Croatia, Cyprus, Czech Republic, Denmark, Estonia, Finland, France, Germany, Greece, Hungary, Iceland, Ireland, Israel, Italy, Latvia, Liechtenstein, Lithuania, Luxembourg, Malta, Marshall Islands, Micronesia (Federated States of), Monaco, Montenegro, Netherlands, New Zealand, Norway, Palau, Poland, Portugal, Republic of Korea, Republic of Moldova, Romania, Russian

Federation, San Marino, Serbia, Slovakia, Slovenia, South Africa, Spain, Sweden, Switzerland, the former Yugoslav Republic of Macedonia, Tonga, Turkey, Ukraine, United Kingdom of Great Britain and Northern Ireland

Action by the First Committee

Date: 30 October 2007   Meeting: 22nd meeting
Vote: 120-1-54   Draft resolution: A/C.1/62/L.44

Agenda item 96

62/20   Prevention of an arms race in outer space

Text

The General Assembly,

Recognizing the common interest of all mankind in the exploration and use of outer space for peaceful purposes,

Reaffirming the will of all States that the exploration and use of outer space, including the Moon and other celestial bodies, shall be for peaceful purposes and shall be carried out for the benefit and in the interest of all countries, irrespective of their degree of economic or scientific development,

Reaffirming also the provisions of articles III and IV of the Treaty on Principles Governing the Activities of States in the Exploration and Use of Outer Space, including the Moon and Other Celestial Bodies,[1]

Recalling the obligation of all States to observe the provisions of the Charter of the United Nations regarding the use or threat of use of force in their international relations, including in their space activities,

Reaffirming paragraph 80 of the Final Document of the Tenth Special Session of the General Assembly,[2] in which it is stated that in order to prevent an arms race in outer space, further measures should be taken and appropriate international negotiations held in accordance with the spirit of the Treaty,

Recalling its previous resolutions on this issue, and taking note of the proposals submitted to the General Assembly at its tenth special session and at its regular sessions, and of the recommendations made to the competent organs of the United Nations and to the Conference on Disarmament,

Recognizing that prevention of an arms race in outer space would avert a grave danger for international peace and security,

Emphasizing the paramount importance of strict compliance with existing arms limitation and disarmament agreements relevant to outer space, including bilateral agreements, and with the existing legal regime concerning the use of outer space,

Considering that wide participation in the legal regime applicable to outer space could contribute to enhancing its effectiveness,

Noting that the Ad Hoc Committee on the Prevention of an Arms Race in Outer Space, taking into account its previous efforts since its establishment in 1985 and seeking to enhance its functioning in qualitative terms, continued the examination and identification of various issues, existing agreements and

---

[1] United Nations, *Treaty Series*, vol. 610, No. 8843.
[2] Resolution S-10/2.

existing proposals, as well as future initiatives relevant to the prevention of an arms race in outer space,[3] and that this contributed to a better understanding of a number of problems and to a clearer perception of the various positions,

Noting also that there were no objections in principle in the Conference on Disarmament to the re-establishment of the Ad Hoc Committee, subject to re-examination of the mandate contained in the decision of the Conference on Disarmament of 13 February 1992,[4]

Emphasizing the mutually complementary nature of bilateral and multilateral efforts in the field of preventing an arms race in outer space, and hoping that concrete results will emerge from those efforts as soon as possible,

Convinced that further measures should be examined in the search for effective and verifiable bilateral and multilateral agreements in order to prevent an arms race in outer space, including the weaponization of outer space,

Stressing that the growing use of outer space increases the need for greater transparency and better information on the part of the international community,

Recalling, in this context, its previous resolutions, in particular resolutions 45/55 B of 4 December 1990, 47/51 of 9 December 1992 and 48/74 A of 16 December 1993, in which, inter alia, it reaffirmed the importance of confidence-building measures as a means conducive to ensuring the attainment of the objective of the prevention of an arms race in outer space,

Conscious of the benefits of confidence- and security-building measures in the military field,

Recognizing that negotiations for the conclusion of an international agreement or agreements to prevent an arms race in outer space remain a priority task of the Ad Hoc Committee and that the concrete proposals on confidence-building measures could form an integral part of such agreements,

Noting with satisfaction the constructive, structured and focused debate on the prevention of an arms race in outer space at the Conference on Disarmament in 2007,

1. *Reaffirms* the importance and urgency of preventing an arms race in outer space and the readiness of all States to contribute to that common objective, in conformity with the provisions of the Treaty on Principles Governing the Activities of States in the Exploration and Use of Outer Space, including the Moon and Other Celestial Bodies;[1]

---

[3] *Official Records of the General Assembly, Forty-ninth Session, Supplement No. 27* (A/49/27), sect. III.D (para. 5 of the quoted text).
[4] CD/1125.

2. *Reaffirms its recognition*, as stated in the report of the Ad Hoc Committee on the Prevention of an Arms Race in Outer Space, that the legal regime applicable to outer space does not in and of itself guarantee the prevention of an arms race in outer space, that the regime plays a significant role in the prevention of an arms race in that environment, that there is a need to consolidate and reinforce that regime and enhance its effectiveness and that it is important to comply strictly with existing agreements, both bilateral and multilateral;

3. *Emphasizes* the necessity of further measures with appropriate and effective provisions for verification to prevent an arms race in outer space;

4. *Calls upon* all States, in particular those with major space capabilities, to contribute actively to the objective of the peaceful use of outer space and of the prevention of an arms race in outer space and to refrain from actions contrary to that objective and to the relevant existing treaties in the interest of maintaining international peace and security and promoting international cooperation;

5. *Reiterates* that the Conference on Disarmament, as the sole multilateral disarmament negotiating forum, has the primary role in the negotiation of a multilateral agreement or agreements, as appropriate, on the prevention of an arms race in outer space in all its aspects;

6. *Invites* the Conference on Disarmament to complete the examination and updating of the mandate contained in its decision of 13 February 1992[4] and to establish an ad hoc committee as early as possible during its 2008 session;

7. *Recognizes*, in this respect, the growing convergence of views on the elaboration of measures designed to strengthen transparency, confidence and security in the peaceful uses of outer space;

8. *Urges* States conducting activities in outer space, as well as States interested in conducting such activities, to keep the Conference on Disarmament informed of the progress of bilateral and multilateral negotiations on the matter, if any, so as to facilitate its work;

9. *Decides* to include in the provisional agenda of its sixty-third session the item entitled "Prevention of an arms race in outer space".

Action by the General Assembly

Date: 5 December 2007   Meeting: 61st meeting
Vote: 178-1-1   Report: A/62/389

Sponsors

Algeria, Armenia, Bangladesh, Belarus, Bhutan, China, Cuba, Democratic People's Republic of Korea, Dominican Republic, Egypt, El Salvador, Ghana, Haiti, Honduras, India, Indonesia, Iran (Islamic Republic of), Jamaica, Jordan, Kuwait, Libyan Arab Jamahiriya, Malaysia, Mongolia,

Myanmar, Nepal, Nigeria, Pakistan, Qatar, Russian Federation, Saudi Arabia, **Sri Lanka**, Syrian Arab Republic, Uganda, Uruguay, Venezuela (Bolivarian Republic of), Zimbabwe

Co-sponsors

Benin, Ecuador, Kazakhstan, Sierra Leone, Togo, Uzbekistan

Recorded vote

In favour:

Afghanistan, Albania, Algeria, Andorra, Antigua and Barbuda, Argentina, Armenia, Australia, Austria, Azerbaijan, Bahamas, Bahrain, Bangladesh, Barbados, Belarus, Belgium, Belize, Benin, Bhutan, Bolivia, Bosnia and Herzegovina, Botswana, Brazil, Brunei Darussalam, Bulgaria, Burkina Faso, Burundi, Cambodia, Cameroon, Canada, Cape Verde, Central African Republic, Chile, China, Colombia, Comoros, Congo, Costa Rica, Côte d'Ivoire, Croatia, Cuba, Cyprus, Czech Republic, Democratic People's Republic of Korea, Denmark, Djibouti, Dominica, Dominican Republic, Ecuador, Egypt, El Salvador, Eritrea, Estonia, Ethiopia, Fiji, Finland, France, Gabon, Gambia, Georgia, Germany, Ghana, Greece, Grenada, Guatemala, Guinea, Guinea-Bissau, Guyana, Haiti, Honduras, Hungary, Iceland, India, Indonesia, Iran (Islamic Republic of), Iraq, Ireland, Italy, Jamaica, Japan, Jordan, Kazakhstan, Kenya, Kuwait, Kyrgyzstan, Lao People's Democratic Republic, Latvia, Lebanon, Lesotho, Liberia, Libyan Arab Jamahiriya, Liechtenstein, Lithuania, Luxembourg, Madagascar, Malawi, Malaysia, Maldives, Mali, Malta, Marshall Islands, Mauritania, Mauritius, Mexico, Micronesia (Federated States of), Monaco, Mongolia, Montenegro, Morocco, Mozambique, Myanmar, Namibia, Nauru, Nepal, Netherlands, New Zealand, Nicaragua, Niger, Nigeria, Norway, Oman, Pakistan, Palau, Panama, Papua New Guinea, Paraguay, Peru, Philippines, Poland, Portugal, Qatar, Republic of Korea, Republic of Moldova, Romania, Russian Federation, Rwanda, Saint Kitts and Nevis, Saint Lucia, Samoa, San Marino, Sao Tome and Principe, Saudi Arabia, Senegal, Serbia, Sierra Leone, Singapore, Slovakia, Slovenia, Solomon Islands, Somalia, South Africa, Spain, Sri Lanka, Sudan, Suriname, Swaziland, Sweden, Switzerland, Syrian Arab Republic, the former Yugoslav Republic of Macedonia, Tajikistan, Thailand, Togo, Tonga, Trinidad and Tobago, Tunisia, Turkey, Turkmenistan, Ukraine, United Arab Emirates, United Kingdom of Great Britain and Northern Ireland, United Republic of Tanzania, Uruguay, Venezuela (Bolivarian Republic of), Viet Nam, Yemen, Zambia, Zimbabwe

Against:

United States of America

Abstaining:
  Israel

Action by the First Committee

Date: 30 October 2007   Meeting: 22nd meeting
Vote: 170-1-1   Draft resolution: A/C.1/62/L.34

Agenda item 97

62/21 Verification in all its aspects, including the role of the United Nations in the field of verification

Text

The General Assembly,

Recalling its resolution 59/60 of 3 December 2004, in which it requested the Secretary-General, with the assistance of a panel of government experts, to explore the question of verification in all its aspects, including the role of the United Nations in the field of verification,

Noting two previous reports of the Secretary-General on the subject submitted in 1990 and 1995,[1]

Recalling its request to the Secretary-General, in resolution 59/60, to transmit to it the report of the Panel of Government Experts on verification in all its aspects, including the role of the United Nations in the field of verification, and the intent of the Panel to produce a report that is forward-looking and discerning of new trends and requirements,

1. *Takes note* of the report of the Panel of Government Experts on verification in all its aspects, including the role of the United Nations in the field of verification,[2] transmitted by the Secretary-General on 15 August 2007, acknowledges that the report was unanimously approved by the Panel of Government Experts, and commends the report to the attention of Member States;

2. *Requests* the Secretary-General to give the report the widest possible circulation;

3. *Encourages* Member States to consider the report, and invites Member States to offer additional views to the Secretary-General on the report;

4. *Requests* the Secretary-General to submit to the General Assembly at its sixty-third session a compilation of views received from Member States, relevant United Nations organs and international treaty organizations with respect to the report;

5. *Decides* to include in the provisional agenda of its sixty-fourth session the item entitled "Verification in all its aspects, including the role of the United Nations in the field of verification".

---

[1] A/45/372 and Corr.1 and A/50/377 and Corr.1.
[2] A/61/1028.

Action by the General Assembly

    Date: 5 December 2007   Meeting: 61st meeting
    Vote: Adopted without a vote   Report: A/62/390

Sponsors

    Canada*

Co-sponsors

    Argentina, Austria, Belgium, Benin, Bulgaria, China, Croatia, Cyprus, Czech Republic, Denmark, Estonia, Finland, France, Germany, Hungary, Ireland, Italy, Japan, Kazakhstan, Kyrgyzstan, Latvia, Liechtenstein, Luxembourg, Malta, Mexico, Netherlands, New Zealand, Nigeria, Poland, Portugal, Republic of Korea, Romania, Russian Federation, Serbia, Singapore, Slovakia, Slovenia, South Africa, Spain, Sri Lanka, Sweden, Switzerland, Ukraine, United Kingdom of Great Britain and Northern Ireland, United States of America

Action by the First Committee

    Date: 31 October 2007   Meeting: 23rd meeting
    Vote: Adopted without a vote   Draft resolution: A/C.1/62/L.47

---

    * The draft resolution was submitted by Canada.

Agenda item 98 (o)

62/22 Assistance to States for curbing the illicit traffic in small arms and light weapons and collecting them

Text

The General Assembly,

Recalling its resolution 61/71 of 6 December 2006 on assistance to States for curbing the illicit traffic in small arms and light weapons and collecting them,

Deeply concerned by the magnitude of human casualty and suffering, especially among children, caused by the illicit proliferation and use of small arms and light weapons,

Concerned by the negative impact that the illicit proliferation and use of those weapons continue to have on the efforts of States in the Sahelo-Saharan subregion in the areas of poverty eradication, sustainable development and the maintenance of peace, security and stability,

Bearing in mind the Bamako Declaration on an African Common Position on the Illicit Proliferation, Circulation and Trafficking of Small Arms and Light Weapons, adopted at Bamako on 1 December 2000,[1]

Recalling the report of the Secretary-General entitled "In larger freedom: towards development, security and human rights for all",[2] in which he emphasized that States must strive just as hard to eliminate the threat of illicit small arms and light weapons as they do to eliminate the threat of weapons of mass destruction,

Taking note of the International Instrument to Enable States to Identify and Trace, in a Timely and Reliable Manner, Illicit Small Arms and Light Weapons, adopted on 8 December 2005,[3]

Welcoming the expression of support in the 2005 World Summit Outcome for the implementation of the Programme of Action to Prevent, Combat and Eradicate the Illicit Trade in Small Arms and Light Weapons in All Its Aspects,[4]

Welcoming also the adoption, at the thirtieth ordinary summit of the Economic Community of West African States, held in Abuja in June 2006, of the Convention on Small Arms and Light Weapons, Their Ammunition and Other Related Materials, in replacement of the moratorium on the importation, exportation and manufacture of small arms and light weapons in West Africa,

---

[1] A/CONF.192/PC/23, annex.
[2] A/59/2005.
[3] A/60/88 and Corr.2, annex; see also decision 60/519.
[4] See resolution 60/1, para. 94.

Welcoming further the decision taken by the Economic Community to establish a Small Arms Unit responsible for advocating appropriate policies and developing and implementing programmes, as well as the establishment of the Economic Community's Small Arms Control Programme, launched on 6 June 2006 in Bamako, in replacement of the Programme for Coordination and Assistance for Security and Development,

Taking note of the latest report of the Secretary-General on assistance to States for curbing the illicit traffic in small arms and light weapons and collecting them and the illicit trade in small arms and light weapons in all its aspects,[5]

Welcoming, in that regard, the decision of the European Union to significantly support the Economic Community in its efforts to combat the illicit proliferation of small arms and light weapons,

Recognizing the important role that civil society organizations play, by raising public awareness, in efforts to curb the illicit traffic in small arms and light weapons,

Taking note of the report of the United Nations Conference to Review Progress Made in the Implementation of the Programme of Action to Prevent, Combat and Eradicate the Illicit Trade in Small Arms and Light Weapons in All Its Aspects, held in New York from 26 June to 7 July 2006,[6]

1. *Commends* the United Nations and international, regional and other organizations for their assistance to States for curbing the illicit traffic in small arms and light weapons and collecting them;

2. *Encourages* the Secretary-General to pursue his efforts in the context of the implementation of General Assembly resolution 49/75 G of 15 December 1994 and the recommendations of the United Nations advisory missions aimed at curbing the illicit circulation of small arms and light weapons and collecting them in the affected States that so request, with the support of the United Nations Regional Centre for Peace and Disarmament in Africa and in close cooperation with the African Union;

3. *Encourages* the international community to support the implementation of the Economic Community of West African States Convention on Small Arms and Light Weapons, Their Ammunition and Other Related Materials;

4. *Encourages* the countries of the Sahelo-Saharan subregion to facilitate the effective functioning of national commissions to combat the illicit proliferation of small arms and light weapons, and, in that regard, invites the international community to lend its support wherever possible;

5. *Encourages* the collaboration of civil society organizations and associations in the efforts of the national commissions to combat the illicit traffic in small arms and light weapons and in the implementation of the Programme

---

[5] A/62/162.
[6] A/CONF.192/2006/RC/9.

of Action to Prevent, Combat and Eradicate the Illicit Trade in Small Arms and Light Weapons in All Its Aspects;[7]

6. *Also encourages* cooperation among State organs, international organizations and civil society in supporting programmes and projects aimed at combating the illicit traffic in small arms and light weapons and collecting them;

7. *Calls upon* the international community to provide technical and financial support to strengthen the capacity of civil society organizations to take action to help to combat the illicit trade in small arms and light weapons;

8. *Invites* the Secretary-General and those States and organizations that are in a position to do so to continue to provide assistance to States for curbing the illicit traffic in small arms and light weapons and collecting them;

9. *Requests* the Secretary-General to continue to consider the matter and to report to the General Assembly at its sixty-third session on the implementation of the present resolution;

10. *Decides* to include in the provisional agenda of its sixty-third session the item entitled "Assistance to States for curbing the illicit traffic in small arms and light weapons and collecting them".

Action by the General Assembly

Date: 5 December 2007 Meeting: 61st meeting
Vote: Adopted without a vote Report: A/62/391

Sponsors

Mali (on behalf of the States Members of the United Nations which are members of the Economic Community of West African States)

Co-sponsors

Albania, Andorra, Austria, Belgium, Bulgaria, Cameroon, Canada, Chile, Congo, Croatia, Cyprus, Czech Republic, Denmark, Dominican Republic, Eritrea, Estonia, Ethiopia, Finland, France, Germany, Greece, Haiti, Ireland, Italy, Jamaica, Latvia, Lithuania, Luxembourg, Malta, Netherlands, Norway, Poland, Portugal, Romania, San Marino, Serbia, Slovakia, Slovenia, Spain, Sweden, Switzerland, the former Yugoslav Republic of Macedonia, Turkey, United Kingdom of Great Britain and Northern Ireland

Action by the First Committee

Date: 30 October 2007 Meeting: 22nd meeting
Vote: Adopted without a vote Draft resolution: A/C.1/62/L.5

---

[7] See *Report of the United Nations Conference on the Illicit Trade in Small Arms and Light Weapons in All Its Aspects, New York, 9-20 July 2001* (A/CONF.192/15), chap. IV, para. 24.

Resolutions and decisions of the 62nd session of the General Assembly

Agenda item 98 (m)

62/23 Implementation of the Convention on the Prohibition of the Development, Production, Stockpiling and Use of Chemical Weapons and on Their Destruction

Text

The General Assembly,

Recalling its previous resolutions on the subject of chemical weapons, in particular resolution 61/68 of 6 December 2006, adopted without a vote, in which it noted with appreciation the ongoing work to achieve the objective and purpose of the Convention on the Prohibition of the Development, Production, Stockpiling and Use of Chemical Weapons and on Their Destruction,[1]

Determined to achieve the effective prohibition of the development, production, acquisition, transfer, stockpiling and use of chemical weapons and their destruction,

Noting with satisfaction that, since the adoption of resolution 61/68, one additional State has acceded to the Convention, bringing the total number of States parties to the Convention to one hundred and eighty-two,

Reaffirming the importance of the outcome of the First Special Session of the Conference of the States Parties to Review the Operation of the Chemical Weapons Convention, including the Political Declaration,[2] in which the States parties reaffirmed their commitment to achieving the objective and purpose of the Convention, and the final report,[3] which addressed all aspects of the Convention and made important recommendations on its continued implementation,

1. *Emphasizes* that the universality of the Convention on the Prohibition of the Development, Production, Stockpiling and Use of Chemical Weapons and on Their Destruction[1] is fundamental to the achievement of its objective and purpose, acknowledges progress made in the implementation of the action plan for the universality of the Convention, and calls upon all States that have not yet done so to become parties to the Convention without delay;

2. *Underlines* the fact that the Convention and its implementation contribute to enhancing international peace and security, and emphasizes that its full, universal and effective implementation will contribute further to that purpose by excluding completely, for the sake of all humankind, the possibility of the use of chemical weapons;

3. *Stresses* the importance to the Convention that all possessors of chemical weapons, chemical weapons production facilities or chemical weapons

---

[1] United Nations, *Treaty Series*, vol. 1974, No. 33757.
[2] See Organization for the Prohibition of Chemical Weapons, document RC-1/3.
[3] Ibid., document RC-1/5.

development facilities, including previously declared possessor States, should be among the States parties to the Convention, and welcomes progress to that end;

4. *Reaffirms* the obligation of the States parties to the Convention to destroy chemical weapons and to destroy or convert chemical weapons production facilities within the time limits provided for by the Convention;

5. *Stresses* that the full and effective implementation of all provisions of the Convention, including those on national implementation (article VII) and assistance and protection (article X), constitutes an important contribution to the efforts of the United Nations in the global fight against terrorism in all its forms and manifestations;

6. *Notes* that the effective application of the verification system builds confidence in compliance with the Convention by States parties;

7. *Stresses* the importance of the Organization for the Prohibition of Chemical Weapons in verifying compliance with the provisions of the Convention as well as in promoting the timely and efficient accomplishment of all its objectives;

8. *Urges* all States parties to the Convention to meet in full and on time their obligations under the Convention and to support the Organization for the Prohibition of Chemical Weapons in its implementation activities;

9. *Welcomes* progress made in the national implementation of article VII obligations, commends the States parties and the Technical Secretariat for assisting other States parties, on request, with the implementation of the follow-up to the plan of action regarding article VII obligations, and urges States parties that have not fulfilled their obligations under article VII to do so without further delay, in accordance with their constitutional processes;

10. *Reaffirms* the importance of article XI provisions relating to the economic and technological development of States parties, recalls that the full, effective and non-discriminatory implementation of those provisions contributes to universality, and also reaffirms the undertaking of the States parties to foster international cooperation for peaceful purposes in the field of chemical activities of the States parties and the importance of that cooperation and its contribution to the promotion of the Convention as a whole;

11. *Notes with appreciation* the ongoing work of the Organization for the Prohibition of Chemical Weapons to achieve the objective and purpose of the Convention, to ensure the full implementation of its provisions, including those for international verification of compliance with it, and to provide a forum for consultation and cooperation among States parties, and also notes with appreciation the substantial contribution of the Technical Secretariat and the Director-General to the continued development and success of the Organization;

12. *Welcomes* the ongoing preparatory work by the States parties on the substance of the Second Special Session of the Conference of the States Parties to Review the Operation of the Chemical Weapons Convention;

13. *Also welcomes* all the national and international events conducted throughout 2007 devoted to the tenth anniversary of the entry into force of the Convention, in particular the unveiling in The Hague, on 9 May 2007, of the Permanent Memorial to All Victims of Chemical Weapons as testimony to the international community's commitment to peace and hope for the future;

14. *Notes with satisfaction* that the High-level Meeting on the Tenth Anniversary of the Entry into Force of the Convention, convened by Poland and the Netherlands at the United Nations in New York on 27 September 2007, provided a special occasion for the international community to remember all victims of chemical weapons and to reaffirm the commitment to multilateralism and to the object and purpose of the Convention;

15. *Welcomes* the cooperation between the United Nations and the Organization for the Prohibition of Chemical Weapons within the framework of the Relationship Agreement between the United Nations and the Organization, in accordance with the provisions of the Convention;

16. *Decides* to include in the provisional agenda of its sixty-third session the item entitled "Implementation of the Convention on the Prohibition of the Development, Production, Stockpiling and Use of Chemical Weapons and on Their Destruction".

Action by the General Assembly

Date: 5 December 2007   Meeting: 61st meeting
Vote: Adopted without a vote   Report: A/62/391

Sponsors

Poland

Action by the First Committee

Date: 30 October 2007   Meeting: 21st meeting
Vote: Adopted without a vote   Draft resolution: A/C.1/62/L.7

Agenda item 98 (d)

62/24   Follow-up to nuclear disarmament obligations agreed to at the 1995 and 2000 Review Conferences of the Parties to the Treaty on the Non-Proliferation of Nuclear Weapons

Text

The General Assembly,

Recalling its various resolutions in the field of nuclear disarmament, including its most recent, resolutions 60/72 of 8 December 2005, and 61/78, 61/83 and 61/97 of 6 December 2006,

Bearing in mind its resolution 2373 (XXII) of 12 June 1968, the annex to which contains the Treaty on the Non-Proliferation of Nuclear Weapons,[1]

Noting the provisions of article VIII, paragraph 3, of the Treaty regarding the convening of review conferences at five-year intervals,

Recalling its resolution 50/70 Q of 12 December 1995, in which the General Assembly noted that the States parties to the Treaty affirmed the need to continue to move with determination towards the full realization and effective implementation of the provisions of the Treaty, and accordingly adopted a set of principles and objectives,

Recalling also that, on 11 May 1995, the 1995 Review and Extension Conference of the Parties to the Treaty on the Non-Proliferation of Nuclear Weapons adopted three decisions on strengthening the review process for the Treaty, principles and objectives for nuclear non-proliferation and disarmament, and extension of the Treaty,[2]

Reaffirming the resolution on the Middle East adopted on 11 May 1995 by the 1995 Review and Extension Conference of the Parties to the Treaty,[2] in which the Conference reaffirmed the importance of the early realization of universal adherence to the Treaty and placement of nuclear facilities under full-scope International Atomic Energy Agency safeguards,

Reaffirming also its resolution 55/33 D of 20 November 2000, in which the General Assembly welcomed the adoption by consensus on 19 May 2000 of the Final Document of the 2000 Review Conference of the Parties to the Treaty on the Non-Proliferation of Nuclear Weapons,[3] including, in particular, the

---

[1] See also United Nations, *Treaty Series*, vol. 729, No. 10485.

[2] See *1995 Review and Extension Conference of the Parties to the Treaty on the Non-Proliferation of Nuclear Weapons, Final Document, Part I* (NPT/CONF.1995/32 (Part I) and Corr.2), annex.

[3] *2000 Review Conference of the Parties to the Treaty on the Non-Proliferation of Nuclear Weapons, Final Document*, vols. I-III (NPT/CONF.2000/28 (Parts I-IV)).

documents entitled "Review of the operation of the Treaty, taking into account the decisions and the resolution adopted by the 1995 Review and Extension Conference" and "Improving the effectiveness of the strengthened review process for the Treaty",[4]

Taking into consideration the unequivocal undertaking by the nuclear-weapon States, in the Final Document of the 2000 Review Conference of the Parties to the Treaty, to accomplish the total elimination of their nuclear arsenals leading to nuclear disarmament, to which all States parties to the Treaty are committed under article VI of the Treaty,

Gravely concerned over the failure of the 2005 Review Conference of the Parties to the Treaty to reach any substantive agreement on the follow-up to the nuclear disarmament obligations,

Noting that the Preparatory Committee for the 2010 Review Conference of the Parties to the Treaty held a successful first meeting in Vienna in April/May 2007,

1. *Determines* to pursue practical steps for systematic and progressive efforts to implement article VI of the Treaty on the Non-Proliferation of Nuclear Weapons[1] and paragraphs 3 and 4 (c) of the decision on principles and objectives for nuclear non-proliferation and disarmament of the 1995 Review and Extension Conference of the Parties to the Treaty on the Non-Proliferation of Nuclear Weapons;[2]

2. *Calls for* practical steps, as agreed to at the 2000 Review Conference of the Parties to the Treaty on the Non-Proliferation of Nuclear Weapons, to be taken by all nuclear-weapon States that would lead to nuclear disarmament in a way that promotes international stability and, based upon the principle of undiminished security for all, for:

(*a*) Further efforts to be made by the nuclear-weapon States to reduce their nuclear arsenals unilaterally;

(*b*) Increased transparency by the nuclear-weapon States with regard to nuclear weapons capabilities and the implementation of agreements pursuant to article VI of the Treaty and as a voluntary confidence-building measure to support further progress in nuclear disarmament;

(*c*) The further reduction of non-strategic nuclear weapons, based on unilateral initiatives and as an integral part of the nuclear arms reduction and disarmament process;

(*d*) Concrete agreed measures to reduce further the operational status of nuclear weapons systems;

---

[4] Ibid., vol. I (NPT/CONF.2000/28 (Parts I and II)), part I.

(e) A diminishing role for nuclear weapons in security policies so as to minimize the risk that these weapons will ever be used and to facilitate the process of their total elimination;

(f) The engagement, as soon as appropriate, of all the nuclear-weapon States in the process leading to the total elimination of their nuclear weapons;

3. *Notes* that the 2000 Review Conference of the Parties to the Treaty agreed that legally binding security assurances by the five nuclear-weapon States to the non-nuclear-weapon States parties to the Treaty strengthen the nuclear non-proliferation regime;

4. *Urges* the States parties to the Treaty to follow up on the implementation of the nuclear disarmament obligations under the Treaty agreed to at the 1995 and 2000 Review Conferences of the Parties to the Treaty within the framework of the 2010 Review Conference of the Parties to the Treaty and its Preparatory Committee;

5. *Decides* to include in the provisional agenda of its sixty-fourth session an item entitled "Follow-up to nuclear disarmament obligations agreed to at the 1995 and 2000 Review Conferences of the Parties to the Treaty on the Non-Proliferation of Nuclear Weapons".

Action by the General Assembly

Date: 5 December 2007　　Meeting: 61st meeting
Vote: 109-55-15, as a whole　Report: A/62/391
114-50-10, p. para. 6

Sponsors

Iran (Islamic Republic of)

Recorded vote

As a whole*

In favour:

Algeria, Antigua and Barbuda, Argentina, Bahamas, Bahrain, Bangladesh, Barbados, Belarus, Belize, Benin, Bhutan, Bolivia, Botswana, Brazil, Brunei Darussalam, Burkina Faso, Burundi, Cambodia, Cameroon, Cape Verde, Central African Republic, Chile, Comoros, Congo, Cuba, Democratic People's Republic of Korea, Djibouti, Dominica, Dominican Republic, Ecuador, Egypt, El Salvador, Eritrea, Ethiopia, Fiji, Gabon, Gambia, Ghana, Grenada, Guinea, Guinea-Bissau, Guyana, Haiti, Indonesia, Iran (Islamic Republic of), Iraq, Jamaica, Jordan, Kazakhstan, Kenya, Kuwait, Kyrgyzstan, Lao People's Democratic Republic, Lebanon,

---

* Subsequent to the voting, the delegation of France advised the Secretariat that it had intended to vote against. The voting tally above does not reflect this information.

Lesotho, Liberia, Libyan Arab Jamahiriya, Malawi, Malaysia, Maldives, Mali, Mauritania, Mauritius, Mexico, Mongolia, Morocco, Mozambique, Myanmar, Namibia, Nauru, Nepal, Nicaragua, Niger, Nigeria, Oman, Philippines, Qatar, Rwanda, Saint Kitts and Nevis, Saint Lucia, Saint Vincent and the Grenadines, Sao Tome and Principe, Saudi Arabia, Senegal, Sierra Leone, Singapore, Solomon Islands, Somalia, South Africa, Sri Lanka, Sudan, Suriname, Swaziland, Syrian Arab Republic, Tajikistan, Thailand, Togo, Tonga, Trinidad and Tobago, Tunisia, Turkmenistan, United Arab Emirates, United Republic of Tanzania, Uruguay, Venezuela (Bolivarian Republic of), Viet Nam, Yemen, Zambia, Zimbabwe

Against:
Albania, Andorra, Australia, Austria, Belgium, Bosnia and Herzegovina, Bulgaria, Canada, Croatia, Cyprus, Czech Republic, Denmark, Estonia, Finland, France, Georgia, Germany, Greece, Hungary, Iceland, Ireland, Israel, Italy, Japan, Latvia, Liechtenstein, Lithuania, Luxembourg, Malta, Marshall Islands, Micronesia (Federated States of), Monaco, Montenegro, Netherlands, New Zealand, Norway, Palau, Poland, Portugal, Republic of Korea, Republic of Moldova, Romania, Russian Federation, San Marino, Serbia, Slovakia, Slovenia, Spain, Sweden, Switzerland, the former Yugoslav Republic of Macedonia, Turkey, Ukraine, United Kingdom of Great Britain and Northern Ireland, United States of America

Abstaining:
Armenia, Azerbaijan, China, Colombia, Costa Rica, Côte d'Ivoire, Guatemala, Honduras, India, Pakistan, Panama, Papua New Guinea, Paraguay, Peru, Samoa

Preambular paragraph 6

In favour:
Algeria, Antigua and Barbuda, Argentina, Bahamas, Bahrain, Bangladesh, Barbados, Belarus, Belize, Benin, Bolivia, Botswana, Brazil, Brunei Darussalam, Burkina Faso, Cambodia, Cameroon, Cape Verde, Central African Republic, Chile, Colombia, Comoros, Congo, Costa Rica, Côte d'Ivoire, Cuba, Djibouti, Dominica, Dominican Republic, Ecuador, Egypt, El Salvador, Eritrea, Ethiopia, Fiji, Gabon, Gambia, Ghana, Grenada, Guatemala, Guinea, Guinea-Bissau, Guyana, Haiti, Honduras, Indonesia, Iran (Islamic Republic of), Iraq, Jamaica, Jordan, Kazakhstan, Kenya, Kuwait, Kyrgyzstan, Lao People's Democratic Republic, Lebanon, Lesotho, Liberia, Libyan Arab Jamahiriya, Liechtenstein, Malawi, Malaysia, Maldives, Mali, Mauritania, Mexico, Mongolia, Morocco, Mozambique, Myanmar, Namibia, Nauru, Nepal, New Zealand, Nicaragua, Niger, Nigeria, Oman, Panama, Philippines, Qatar, Rwanda, Saint Kitts and Nevis, Saint Lucia, Saint Vincent and the Grenadines, Sao Tome and Principe, Saudi Arabia, Senegal, Sierra Leone, Singapore,

Solomon Islands, Somalia, South Africa, Sri Lanka, Sudan, Suriname, Swaziland, Switzerland, Syrian Arab Republic, Tajikistan, Thailand, Togo, Tonga, Trinidad and Tobago, Tunisia, Turkmenistan, United Arab Emirates, United Republic of Tanzania, Uruguay, Venezuela (Bolivarian Republic of), Viet Nam, Yemen, Zambia, Zimbabwe

Against:
Albania, Andorra, Australia, Austria, Belgium, Bosnia and Herzegovina, Bulgaria, Canada, Croatia, Cyprus, Czech Republic, Denmark, Estonia, Finland, Georgia, Germany, Greece, Hungary, Iceland, India, Ireland, Israel, Italy, Japan, Latvia, Lithuania, Luxembourg, Malta, Marshall Islands, Micronesia (Federated States of), Monaco, Montenegro, Netherlands, Norway, Poland, Portugal, Republic of Korea, Republic of Moldova, Romania, San Marino, Serbia, Slovakia, Slovenia, Spain, Sweden, the former Yugoslav Republic of Macedonia, Turkey, Ukraine, United Kingdom of Great Britain and Northern Ireland, United States of America

Abstaining:
Armenia, Azerbaijan, Bhutan, Burundi, Pakistan, Papua New Guinea, Paraguay, Peru, Russian Federation, Samoa

Action by the First Committee

Date: 30 October 2007 Meeting: 22nd meeting
Vote: 103-53-15, as a whole Draft resolution: A/C.1/62/L.8
102-48-11, p. para. 6

Agenda item 98 (k)

62/25 Towards a nuclear-weapon-free world: accelerating the implementation of nuclear disarmament commitments

Text

The General Assembly,

Recalling its resolution 61/65 of 6 December 2006,

Expressing its grave concern at the danger to humanity posed by the possibility that nuclear weapons could be used,

Reaffirming that nuclear disarmament and nuclear non-proliferation are mutually reinforcing processes requiring urgent irreversible progress on both fronts,

Recalling the decisions and the resolution on the Middle East of the 1995 Review and Extension Conference of the Parties to the Treaty on the Non-Proliferation of Nuclear Weapons[1] and the Final Document of the 2000 Review Conference of the Parties to the Treaty on the Non-Proliferation of Nuclear Weapons,[2]

Recalling also the unequivocal undertaking by the nuclear-weapon States to accomplish the total elimination of their nuclear arsenals, leading to nuclear disarmament, in accordance with commitments made under article VI of the Treaty on the Non-Proliferation of Nuclear Weapons,[3]

Urging States parties to exert all possible efforts to ensure a successful and productive preparatory process for the 2010 Review Conference of the Parties to the Treaty,

1. *Welcomes* the first session of the Preparatory Committee for the 2010 Review Conference of the Parties to the Treaty on the Non-Proliferation of Nuclear Weapons, held in Vienna from 30 April to 11 May 2007, and looks forward to a constructive and successful preparatory process leading to the 2010 Review Conference which should contribute to strengthening the Treaty and achieving its full implementation and universality;

2. *Continues to emphasize* the central role of the Treaty on the Non-Proliferation of Nuclear Weapons[3] and its universality in achieving nuclear disarmament and nuclear non-proliferation, and calls upon all States parties to respect their obligations;

---

[1] See *1995 Review and Extension Conference of the Parties to the Treaty on the Non-Proliferation of Nuclear Weapons, Final Document, Part I* (NPT/CONF.1995/32 (Part I) and Corr.2), annex.
[2] *2000 Review Conference of the Parties to the Treaty on the Non-Proliferation of Nuclear Weapons, Final Document*, vols. I-III (NPT/CONF.2000/28 (Parts I-IV)).
[3] United Nations, *Treaty Series*, vol. 729, No. 10485.

3. *Reaffirms* that the outcome of the 2000 Review Conference of the Parties to the Treaty sets out the agreed process for systematic and progressive efforts towards nuclear disarmament;[2]

4. *Reiterates its call upon* the nuclear-weapon States to accelerate the implementation of the practical steps towards nuclear disarmament that were agreed upon at the 2000 Review Conference of the Parties to the Treaty, thereby contributing to a safer world for all;

5. *Calls upon* all States to comply fully with all commitments made regarding nuclear disarmament and nuclear non-proliferation and not to act in any way that may compromise either cause or that may lead to a new nuclear arms race;

6. *Again calls upon* all States parties to spare no effort to achieve the universality of the Treaty on the Non-Proliferation of Nuclear Weapons, and urges India, Israel and Pakistan, which are not yet parties to the Treaty, to accede to it as non-nuclear-weapon States promptly and without conditions;

7. *Urges* the Democratic People's Republic of Korea to rescind its announced withdrawal from the Treaty on the Non-Proliferation of Nuclear Weapons;

8. *Recognizes* the vital importance of the early entry into force of the Comprehensive Nuclear-Test-Ban Treaty[4] to the achievement of nuclear disarmament and nuclear non-proliferation, and takes note of the Final Declaration and Measures to promote its entry into force, adopted by consensus at the Fifth Conference on Facilitating the Entry into Force of the Comprehensive Nuclear-Test-Ban Treaty, held in Vienna on 17 and 18 September 2007;

9. *Decides* to include in the provisional agenda of its sixty-third session the item entitled "Towards a nuclear-weapon-free world: accelerating the implementation of nuclear disarmament commitments" and to review the implementation of the present resolution at that session.

Action by the General Assembly

Date: 5 December 2007　　　Meeting: 61st meeting
Vote: 156-5-14, as a whole　　Report: A/62/391
　　　165-4-2, op. para. 6

Sponsors

Brazil, Egypt, Ireland, **Mexico**, New Zealand, South Africa, Sweden

Co-sponsors

Austria, Costa Rica, Guyana, Malta

---

[4] See resolution 50/245.

Resolutions and decisions of the 62nd session of the General Assembly

Recorded vote

As a whole

In favour:
Afghanistan, Algeria, Andorra, Antigua and Barbuda, Argentina, Armenia, Austria, Azerbaijan, Bahamas, Bahrain, Bangladesh, Barbados, Belarus, Belgium, Belize, Benin, Bolivia, Bosnia and Herzegovina, Botswana, Brazil, Brunei Darussalam, Bulgaria, Burkina Faso, Burundi, Cambodia, Cameroon, Canada, Cape Verde, Central African Republic, Chile, China, Colombia, Comoros, Congo, Costa Rica, Côte d'Ivoire, Croatia, Cuba, Cyprus, Czech Republic, Denmark, Djibouti, Dominican Republic, Ecuador, Egypt, El Salvador, Eritrea, Estonia, Ethiopia, Fiji, Finland, Gabon, Gambia, Georgia, Germany, Ghana, Grenada, Guatemala, Guinea, Guinea-Bissau, Guyana, Haiti, Honduras, Iceland, Indonesia, Iran (Islamic Republic of), Iraq, Ireland, Italy, Jamaica, Japan, Jordan, Kazakhstan, Kenya, Kuwait, Kyrgyzstan, Lao People's Democratic Republic, Lebanon, Liberia, Libyan Arab Jamahiriya, Liechtenstein, Lithuania, Luxembourg, Malawi, Malaysia, Maldives, Mali, Malta, Marshall Islands, Mauritania, Mauritius, Mexico, Mongolia, Montenegro, Morocco, Mozambique, Myanmar, Namibia, Nauru, Nepal, Netherlands, New Zealand, Nicaragua, Niger, Nigeria, Norway, Oman, Panama, Papua New Guinea, Paraguay, Peru, Philippines, Portugal, Qatar, Republic of Moldova, Rwanda, Saint Kitts and Nevis, Saint Lucia, Saint Vincent and the Grenadines, Samoa, San Marino, Sao Tome and Principe, Saudi Arabia, Senegal, Serbia, Sierra Leone, Singapore, Slovakia, Solomon Islands, Somalia, South Africa, Spain, Sri Lanka, Sudan, Suriname, Swaziland, Sweden, Switzerland, Syrian Arab Republic, Tajikistan, Thailand, the former Yugoslav Republic of Macedonia, Togo, Tonga, Trinidad and Tobago, Tunisia, Turkey, Ukraine, United Arab Emirates, United Republic of Tanzania, Uruguay, Venezuela (Bolivarian Republic of), Viet Nam, Yemen, Zambia, Zimbabwe

Against:
Democratic People's Republic of Korea, France, India, Israel, United States of America

Abstaining:
Albania, Australia, Bhutan, Greece, Hungary, Latvia, Micronesia (Federated States of), Pakistan, Palau, Poland, Romania, Russian Federation, Slovenia, United Kingdom of Great Britain and Northern Ireland

Operative paragraph 6*

In favour:
Afghanistan, Albania, Algeria, Andorra, Antigua and Barbuda, Argentina, Armenia, Australia, Austria, Azerbaijan, Bahamas, Bahrain, Bangladesh, Barbados, Belarus, Belgium, Belize, Benin, Bolivia, Bosnia and Herzegovina, Botswana, Brazil, Brunei Darussalam, Bulgaria, Burkina Faso, Burundi, Cambodia, Cameroon, Canada, Cape Verde, Central African Republic, Chile, China, Colombia, Comoros, Congo, Costa Rica, Côte d'Ivoire, Croatia, Cuba, Cyprus, Czech Republic, Denmark, Djibouti, Dominican Republic, Ecuador, Egypt, El Salvador, Eritrea, Estonia, Ethiopia, Fiji, Finland, Gabon, Gambia, Georgia, Germany, Ghana, Grenada, Guatemala, Guinea, Guinea-Bissau, Guyana, Haiti, Honduras, Hungary, Iceland, Indonesia, Iran (Islamic Republic of), Iraq, Ireland, Italy, Jamaica, Japan, Jordan, Kazakhstan, Kenya, Kuwait, Kyrgyzstan, Lao People's Democratic Republic, Latvia, Lebanon, Lesotho, Liberia, Libyan Arab Jamahiriya, Liechtenstein, Lithuania, Luxembourg, Malawi, Malaysia, Maldives, Mali, Malta, Mauritania, Mexico, Mongolia, Montenegro, Morocco, Mozambique, Myanmar, Namibia, Nauru, Nepal, Netherlands, New Zealand, Nicaragua, Niger, Nigeria, Norway, Oman, Panama, Papua New Guinea, Paraguay, Peru, Philippines, Poland, Portugal, Qatar, Republic of Korea, Republic of Moldova, Romania, Russian Federation, Rwanda, Saint Kitts and Nevis, Saint Lucia, Saint Vincent and the Grenadines, Samoa, San Marino, Sao Tome and Principe, Saudi Arabia, Senegal, Serbia, Sierra Leone, Singapore, Slovakia, Slovenia, Solomon Islands, Somalia, South Africa, Spain, Sri Lanka, Sudan, Suriname, Swaziland, Sweden, Switzerland, Syrian Arab Republic, Tajikistan, Thailand, the former Yugoslav Republic of Macedonia, Togo, Tonga, Trinidad and Tobago, Tunisia, Turkey, Ukraine, United Arab Emirates, United Kingdom of Great Britain and Northern Ireland, United Republic of Tanzania, Uruguay, Venezuela (Bolivarian Republic of), Viet Nam, Yemen, Zambia, Zimbabwe

Against:
India, Israel, Pakistan, United States of America

Abstaining:
Bhutan, Greece

Action by the First Committee

Date: 31 October 2007   Meeting: 23rd meeting
Vote: 151-5-13, as a whole   Draft resolution: A/C.1/62/L.9
155-4-2, op. para. 6

---

* Subsequent to the voting on op. para. 6, the delegation of France advised the Secretariat that it had intended to abstain. The voting tally above does not reflect this information.

Agenda item 98

62/26　National legislation on transfer of arms, military equipment and dual-use goods and technology

Text

The General Assembly,

Recognizing that disarmament, arms control and non-proliferation are essential for the maintenance of international peace and security,

Recalling that effective national control of the transfer of arms, military equipment and dual-use goods and technology, including those transfers that could contribute to proliferation activities, is an important tool for achieving those objectives,

Recalling also that the States parties to the international disarmament and non-proliferation treaties have undertaken to facilitate the fullest possible exchange of materials, equipment and technological information for peaceful purposes, in accordance with the provisions of those treaties,

Considering that the exchange of national legislation, regulations and procedures on the transfer of arms, military equipment and dual-use goods and technology contributes to mutual understanding and confidence among Member States,

Convinced that such an exchange would be beneficial to Member States that are in the process of developing such legislation,

Welcoming the electronic database established by the Office for Disarmament Affairs,[1] in which all information exchanged pursuant to General Assembly resolutions 57/66 of 22 November 2002, 58/42 of 8 December 2003, 59/66 of 3 December 2004 and 60/69 of 3 December 2005, entitled "National legislation on transfer of arms, military equipment and dual-use goods and technology", can be consulted,

Reaffirming the inherent right of individual or collective self-defence in accordance with Article 51 of the Charter of the United Nations,

1.　*Invites* Member States that are in a position to do so, without prejudice to the provisions contained in Security Council resolutions 1540 (2004) of 28 April 2004 and 1673 (2006) of 27 April 2006, to enact or improve national legislation, regulations and procedures to exercise effective control over the transfer of arms, military equipment and dual-use goods and technology, while ensuring that such legislation, regulations and procedures are consistent with the obligations of States parties under international treaties;

---

[1] Available at http://disarmament.un.org/cab/NLDU%202007/nlduindex.html.

2. *Encourages* Member States to provide, on a voluntary basis, information to the Secretary-General on their national legislation, regulations and procedures on the transfer of arms, military equipment and dual-use goods and technology, as well as the changes therein, and requests the Secretary-General to make that information accessible to Member States;

3. *Decides* to remain attentive to the matter.

Action by the General Assembly

Date: 5 December 2007 Meeting: 61st meeting
Vote: Adopted without a vote Report: A/62/391

Sponsors

Netherlands

Action by the First Committee

Date: 31 October 2007 Meeting: 23rd meeting
Vote: Adopted without a vote Draft resolution: A/C.1/62/L.12

Agenda item 98 (h)

62/27 Promotion of multilateralism in the area of disarmament and non-proliferation

Text

The General Assembly,

Determined to foster strict respect for the purposes and principles enshrined in the Charter of the United Nations,

Recalling its resolution 56/24 T of 29 November 2001 on multilateral cooperation in the area of disarmament and non-proliferation and global efforts against terrorism and other relevant resolutions, as well as its resolutions 57/63 of 22 November 2002, 58/44 of 8 December 2003, 59/69 of 3 December 2004, 60/59 of 8 December 2005 and 61/62 of 6 December 2006 on the promotion of multilateralism in the area of disarmament and non-proliferation,

Recalling also the purpose of the United Nations to maintain international peace and security and, to that end, to take effective collective measures for the prevention and removal of threats to the peace and for the suppression of acts of aggression or other breaches of the peace, and to bring about by peaceful means, and in conformity with the principles of justice and international law, adjustment or settlement of international disputes or situations which might lead to a breach of the peace, as enshrined in the Charter,

Recalling further the United Nations Millennium Declaration,[1] which states, inter alia, that the responsibility for managing worldwide economic and social development, as well as threats to international peace and security, must be shared among the nations of the world and should be exercised multilaterally and that, as the most universal and most representative organization in the world, the United Nations must play the central role,

Convinced that, in the globalization era and with the information revolution, arms regulation, non-proliferation and disarmament problems are more than ever the concern of all countries in the world, which are affected in one way or another by these problems and, therefore, should have the possibility to participate in the negotiations that arise to tackle them,

Bearing in mind the existence of a broad structure of disarmament and arms regulation agreements resulting from non-discriminatory and transparent multilateral negotiations with the participation of a large number of countries, regardless of their size and power,

Aware of the need to advance further in the field of arms regulation, non-proliferation and disarmament on the basis of universal, multilateral,

---

[1] See resolution 55/2.

non-discriminatory and transparent negotiations with the goal of reaching general and complete disarmament under strict international control,

Recognizing the complementarity of bilateral, plurilateral and multilateral negotiations on disarmament,

Recognizing also that the proliferation and development of weapons of mass destruction, including nuclear weapons, are among the most immediate threats to international peace and security which need to be dealt with, with the highest priority,

Considering that the multilateral disarmament agreements provide the mechanism for States parties to consult one another and to cooperate in solving any problems which may arise in relation to the objective of, or in the application of, the provisions of the agreements and that such consultations and cooperation may also be undertaken through appropriate international procedures within the framework of the United Nations and in accordance with the Charter,

Stressing that international cooperation, the peaceful settlement of disputes, dialogue and confidence-building measures would contribute essentially to the creation of multilateral and bilateral friendly relations among peoples and nations,

Being concerned at the continuous erosion of multilateralism in the field of arms regulation, non-proliferation and disarmament, and recognizing that a resort to unilateral actions by Member States in resolving their security concerns would jeopardize international peace and security and undermine confidence in the international security system as well as the foundations of the United Nations itself,

Noting that the Fourteenth Conference of Heads of State or Government of Non-Aligned Countries, held at Havana on 15 and 16 September 2006, welcomed the adoption of General Assembly resolution 60/59, and underlined the fact that multilateralism and multilaterally agreed solutions, in accordance with the Charter, provide the only sustainable method of addressing disarmament and international security issues,

Reaffirming the absolute validity of multilateral diplomacy in the field of disarmament and non-proliferation, and determined to promote multilateralism as an essential way to develop arms regulation and disarmament negotiations,

1. *Reaffirms* multilateralism as the core principle in negotiations in the area of disarmament and non-proliferation with a view to maintaining and strengthening universal norms and enlarging their scope;

2. *Also reaffirms* multilateralism as the core principle in resolving disarmament and non-proliferation concerns;

3. *Urges* the participation of all interested States in multilateral negotiations on arms regulation, non-proliferation and disarmament in a non-discriminatory and transparent manner;

4. *Underlines* the importance of preserving the existing agreements on arms regulation and disarmament, which constitute an expression of the results of international cooperation and multilateral negotiations in response to the challenges facing mankind;

5. *Calls once again upon* all Member States to renew and fulfil their individual and collective commitments to multilateral cooperation as an important means of pursuing and achieving their common objectives in the area of disarmament and non-proliferation;

6. *Requests* the States parties to the relevant instruments on weapons of mass destruction to consult and cooperate among themselves in resolving their concerns with regard to cases of non-compliance as well as on implementation, in accordance with the procedures defined in those instruments, and to refrain from resorting or threatening to resort to unilateral actions or directing unverified non-compliance accusations against one another to resolve their concerns;

7. *Takes note* of the report of the Secretary-General containing the replies of Member States on the promotion of multilateralism in the area of disarmament and non-proliferation, submitted pursuant to resolution 61/62;[2]

8. *Requests* the Secretary-General to seek the views of Member States on the issue of the promotion of multilateralism in the area of disarmament and non-proliferation and to submit a report thereon to the General Assembly at its sixty-third session;

9. *Decides* to include in the provisional agenda of its sixty-third session the item entitled "Promotion of multilateralism in the area of disarmament and non-proliferation".

Action by the General Assembly

Date: 5 December 2007   Meeting: 61st meeting
Vote: 123-6-51   Report: A/62/391

Sponsors

Indonesia (on behalf of the States Members of the United Nations that are members of the Movement of Non-Aligned Countries)

Recorded vote

In favour:
Afghanistan, Algeria, Antigua and Barbuda, Argentina, Bahamas, Bahrain, Bangladesh, Barbados, Belarus, Belize, Benin, Bhutan, Bolivia,

---

[2] A/62/133.

Botswana, Brazil, Brunei Darussalam, Burkina Faso, Burundi, Cambodia, Cameroon, Cape Verde, Central African Republic, Chile, China, Colombia, Comoros, Congo, Costa Rica, Côte d'Ivoire, Cuba, Democratic People's Republic of Korea, Djibouti, Dominican Republic, Ecuador, Egypt, El Salvador, Eritrea, Ethiopia, Fiji, Gabon, Gambia, Ghana, Grenada, Guatemala, Guinea, Guinea-Bissau, Guyana, Haiti, Honduras, India, Indonesia, Iran (Islamic Republic of), Iraq, Jamaica, Jordan, Kazakhstan, Kenya, Kuwait, Kyrgyzstan, Lao People's Democratic Republic, Lebanon, Lesotho, Liberia, Libyan Arab Jamahiriya, Madagascar, Malawi, Malaysia, Maldives, Mali, Mauritania, Mauritius, Mexico, Mongolia, Morocco, Mozambique, Myanmar, Namibia, Nauru, Nepal, Nicaragua, Niger, Nigeria, Oman, Pakistan, Panama, Papua New Guinea, Paraguay, Peru, Philippines, Qatar, Russian Federation, Rwanda, Saint Kitts and Nevis, Saint Lucia, Saint Vincent and the Grenadines, Sao Tome and Principe, Saudi Arabia, Senegal, Sierra Leone, Singapore, Solomon Islands, Somalia, South Africa, Sri Lanka, Sudan, Suriname, Swaziland, Syrian Arab Republic, Tajikistan, Thailand, Togo, Tonga, Trinidad and Tobago, Tunisia, Turkmenistan, United Arab Emirates, United Republic of Tanzania, Uruguay, Venezuela (Bolivarian Republic of), Viet Nam, Yemen, Zambia, Zimbabwe

Against:
Israel, Marshall Islands, Micronesia (Federated States of), Palau, United Kingdom of Great Britain and Northern Ireland, United States of America

Abstaining:
Albania, Andorra, Armenia, Australia, Austria, Azerbaijan, Belgium, Bosnia and Herzegovina, Bulgaria, Canada, Croatia, Cyprus, Czech Republic, Denmark, Estonia, Finland, France, Georgia, Germany, Greece, Hungary, Iceland, Ireland, Italy, Japan, Latvia, Liechtenstein, Lithuania, Luxembourg, Malta, Monaco, Montenegro, Netherlands, New Zealand, Norway, Poland, Portugal, Republic of Korea, Republic of Moldova, Romania, Samoa, San Marino, Serbia, Slovakia, Slovenia, Spain, Sweden, Switzerland, the former Yugoslav Republic of Macedonia, Turkey, Ukraine

Action by the First Committee

Date: 1 November 2007   Meeting: 24th meeting
Vote: 112-4-51   Draft resolution: A/C.1/62/L.13

Agenda item 98 (i)

62/28 Observance of environmental norms in the drafting and implementation of agreements on disarmament and arms control

Text

The General Assembly,

Recalling its resolutions 50/70 M of 12 December 1995, 51/45 E of 10 December 1996, 52/38 E of 9 December 1997, 53/77 J of 4 December 1998, 54/54 S of 1 December 1999, 55/33 K of 20 November 2000, 56/24 F of 29 November 2001, 57/64 of 22 November 2002, 58/45 of 8 December 2003, 59/68 of 3 December 2004, 60/60 of 8 December 2005 and 61/63 of 6 December 2006,

Emphasizing the importance of the observance of environmental norms in the preparation and implementation of disarmament and arms limitation agreements,

Recognizing that it is necessary to take duly into account the agreements adopted at the United Nations Conference on Environment and Development, as well as prior relevant agreements, in the drafting and implementation of agreements on disarmament and arms limitation,

Taking note of the report of the Secretary-General submitted pursuant to resolution 61/63,[1]

Mindful of the detrimental environmental effects of the use of nuclear weapons,

1. *Reaffirms* that international disarmament forums should take fully into account the relevant environmental norms in negotiating treaties and agreements on disarmament and arms limitation and that all States, through their actions, should contribute fully to ensuring compliance with the aforementioned norms in the implementation of treaties and conventions to which they are parties;

2. *Calls upon* States to adopt unilateral, bilateral, regional and multilateral measures so as to contribute to ensuring the application of scientific and technological progress within the framework of international security, disarmament and other related spheres, without detriment to the environment or to its effective contribution to attaining sustainable development;

3. *Welcomes* the information provided by Member States on the implementation of the measures they have adopted to promote the objectives envisaged in the present resolution;[1]

---

[1] A/62/134.

4. *Invites* all Member States to communicate to the Secretary-General information on the measures they have adopted to promote the objectives envisaged in the present resolution, and requests the Secretary-General to submit a report containing that information to the General Assembly at its sixty-third session;

5. *Decides* to include in the provisional agenda of its sixty-third session the item entitled "Observance of environmental norms in the drafting and implementation of agreements on disarmament and arms control".

Action by the General Assembly

Date: 5 December 2007   Meeting: 61st session
Vote: 175-1-3   Report: A/62/391

Sponsors

Indonesia (on behalf of the States Members of the United Nations that are members of the Movement of Non-Aligned Countries)

*Recorded vote**

In favour:
Afghanistan, Albania, Algeria, Andorra, Antigua and Barbuda, Argentina, Armenia, Australia, Austria, Azerbaijan, Bahamas, Bahrain, Bangladesh, Barbados, Belarus, Belgium, Belize, Benin, Bhutan, Bolivia, Bosnia and Herzegovina, Botswana, Brazil, Brunei Darussalam, Bulgaria, Burkina Faso, Burundi, Cambodia, Cameroon, Canada, Cape Verde, Central African Republic, Chile, China, Colombia, Comoros, Congo, Costa Rica, Côte d'Ivoire, Croatia, Cuba, Cyprus, Czech Republic, Democratic People's Republic of Korea, Denmark, Djibouti, Dominican Republic, Ecuador, Egypt, El Salvador, Eritrea, Estonia, Ethiopia, Fiji, Finland, France, Gabon, Gambia, Georgia, Germany, Ghana, Greece, Grenada, Guatemala, Guinea, Guinea-Bissau, Guyana, Haiti, Honduras, Hungary, Iceland, India, Indonesia, Iran (Islamic Republic of), Iraq, Ireland, Italy, Jamaica, Japan, Jordan, Kazakhstan, Kenya, Kuwait, Kyrgyzstan, Lao People's Democratic Republic, Latvia, Lebanon, Lesotho, Liberia, Libyan Arab Jamahiriya, Liechtenstein, Lithuania, Luxembourg, Madagascar, Malawi, Malaysia, Maldives, Mali, Malta, Marshall Islands, Mauritania, Mauritius, Mexico, Micronesia (Federated States of), Monaco, Mongolia, Montenegro, Morocco, Mozambique, Myanmar, Namibia, Nepal, Netherlands, New Zealand, Nicaragua, Niger, Nigeria, Norway, Oman, Pakistan, Panama, Papua New Guinea, Paraguay, Peru, Philippines, Poland, Portugal, Qatar, Republic of Korea, Republic of Moldova, Romania, Russian Federation, Rwanda, Saint Kitts and Nevis, Saint Lucia, Saint

---

* Subsequent to the voting, France advised the Secretariat that it had intended to abstain. The voting tally above does not reflect this information.

Vincent and the Grenadines, Samoa, San Marino, Sao Tome and Principe, Saudi Arabia, Senegal, Serbia, Sierra Leone, Singapore, Slovakia, Slovenia, Solomon Islands, Somalia, South Africa, Spain, Sri Lanka, Sudan, Suriname, Swaziland, Sweden, Switzerland, Syrian Arab Republic, the former Yugoslav Republic of Macedonia, Tajikistan, Thailand, Togo, Tonga, Trinidad and Tobago, Tunisia, Turkey, Turkmenistan, Ukraine, United Arab Emirates, United Republic of Tanzania, Uruguay, Venezuela (Bolivarian Republic of), Viet Nam, Yemen, Zambia, Zimbabwe

Against:
United States of America

Abstaining:
Israel, Palau, United Kingdom of Great Britain and Northern Ireland

Action by the First Committee

Date: 1 November 2007   Meeting: 24th meeting
Vote: 162-1-3   Draft resolution: A/C.1/62/L.14

Agenda item 98 (g)

62/29 Convening of the fourth special session of the General Assembly devoted to disarmament

Text

The General Assembly,

Recalling its resolutions 49/75 I of 15 December 1994, 50/70 F of 12 December 1995, 51/45 C of 10 December 1996, 52/38 F of 9 December 1997, 53/77 AA of 4 December 1998, 54/54 U of 1 December 1999, 55/33 M of 20 November 2000, 56/24 D of 29 November 2001, 57/61 of 22 November 2002, 59/71 of 3 December 2004 and 61/60 of 6 December 2006, as well as its decisions 58/521 of 8 December 2003, 60/518 of 8 December 2005 and 60/559 of 6 June 2006,

Recalling also that, there being a consensus to do so in each case, three special sessions of the General Assembly devoted to disarmament were held in 1978, 1982 and 1988, respectively,

Bearing in mind the Final Document of the Tenth Special Session of the General Assembly, adopted by consensus at the first special session devoted to disarmament,[1]

Bearing in mind also the ultimate objective of general and complete disarmament under effective international control,

Taking note of paragraph 80 of the Final Document of the Fourteenth Conference of Heads of State or Government of Non-Aligned Countries, held at Havana on 15 and 16 September 2006,[2] which supported the convening of the fourth special session of the General Assembly devoted to disarmament, which would offer an opportunity to review, from a perspective more in tune with the current international situation, the most critical aspects of the process of disarmament and to mobilize the international community and public opinion in favour of the elimination of nuclear and other weapons of mass destruction and of the control and reduction of conventional weapons,

Recalling the United Nations Millennium Declaration, adopted by the Heads of State and Government during the Millennium Summit of the United Nations, held in New York from 6 to 8 September 2000,[3] in which the Heads of State and Government resolved "to strive for the elimination of weapons of mass destruction, particularly nuclear weapons, and to keep all options open for achieving this aim, including the possibility of convening an international conference to identify ways of eliminating nuclear dangers",

---

[1] Resolution S-10/2.
[2] A/61/472-S/2006/780, annex I.
[3] See resolution 55/2.

Reiterating its conviction that a special session of the General Assembly devoted to disarmament can set the future course of action in the fields of disarmament, arms control, non-proliferation and related international security matters,

Emphasizing the importance of multilateralism in the process of disarmament, arms control, non-proliferation and related international security matters,

Taking note of the paper presented by the Chairman of Working Group II during the 1999 substantive session of the Disarmament Commission,[4] and the written proposals and views submitted by Member States as contained in the working papers presented during the three substantive sessions of the Open-ended Working Group in 2003[5] as well as the reports of the Secretary-General regarding the views of Member States on the objectives, agenda and timing of the fourth special session of the General Assembly devoted to disarmament,[6]

Taking note also of the reports of the Open-ended Working Group to consider the objectives and agenda, including the possible establishment of the preparatory committee, for the fourth special session of the General Assembly devoted to disarmament,[7]

1. *Decides* to convene the Open-ended Working Group, working on the basis of consensus, to consider the objectives and agenda, including the possible establishment of the preparatory committee, for the fourth special session of the General Assembly devoted to disarmament;

2. *Also decides* that the Open-ended Working Group shall hold its organizational session as soon as possible for the purpose of setting a date for its substantive sessions in 2008, and submit a report on its work, including possible substantive recommendations, before the end of the sixty-second session of the General Assembly;

3. *Requests* the Secretary-General, within existing resources, to provide the Open-ended Working Group with the necessary assistance and services as may be required to discharge its tasks;

4. *Decides* to include in the provisional agenda of its sixty-third session the item entitled "Convening of the fourth special session of the General Assembly devoted to disarmament".

---

[4] *Official Records of the General Assembly, Fifty-fourth Session, Supplement No. 42* (A/54/42), annex II.
[5] See A/AC.268/2003/WP.2.
[6] A/55/130 and Add.1, A/56/166 and A/57/120.
[7] A/57/848 and A/AC.268/2007/2.

United Nations Disarmament YEARBOOK 2007: Part I

Action by the General Assembly

Date: 5 December 2007 Meeting: 61st meeting
Vote: 179-1-1 Report: A/62/391

Sponsors

Indonesia (on behalf of the States Members of the United Nations that are members of the Movement of Non-Aligned Countries)

*Recorded vote**

In favour:

Afghanistan, Albania, Algeria, Andorra, Antigua and Barbuda, Argentina, Armenia, Australia, Austria, Azerbaijan, Bahamas, Bahrain, Bangladesh, Barbados, Belarus, Belgium, Belize, Benin, Bhutan, Bolivia, Bosnia and Herzegovina, Botswana, Brazil, Brunei Darussalam, Bulgaria, Burkina Faso, Burundi, Cambodia, Cameroon, Canada, Cape Verde, Central African Republic, Chile, China, Colombia, Comoros, Congo, Costa Rica, Côte d'Ivoire, Croatia, Cuba, Cyprus, Czech Republic, Democratic People's Republic of Korea, Denmark, Djibouti, Dominican Republic, Ecuador, Egypt, El Salvador, Eritrea, Estonia, Ethiopia, Fiji, Finland, France, Gabon, Gambia, Georgia, Germany, Ghana, Greece, Grenada, Guatemala, Guinea, Guinea-Bissau, Guyana, Haiti, Honduras, Hungary, Iceland, India, Indonesia, Iran (Islamic Republic of), Iraq, Ireland, Israel, Italy, Jamaica, Japan, Jordan, Kazakhstan, Kenya, Kuwait, Kyrgyzstan, Lao People's Democratic Republic, Latvia, Lebanon, Lesotho, Liberia, Libyan Arab Jamahiriya, Liechtenstein, Lithuania, Luxembourg, Madagascar, Malawi, Malaysia, Maldives, Mali, Malta, Marshall Islands, Mauritania, Mauritius, Mexico, Micronesia (Federated States of), Monaco, Mongolia, Montenegro, Morocco, Mozambique, Myanmar, Namibia, Nepal, Netherlands, New Zealand, Nicaragua, Niger, Nigeria, Norway, Oman, Pakistan, Palau, Panama, Papua New Guinea, Paraguay, Peru, Philippines, Poland, Portugal, Qatar, Republic of Korea, Republic of Moldova, Romania, Russian Federation, Rwanda, Saint Kitts and Nevis, Saint Lucia, Saint Vincent and the Grenadines, Samoa, San Marino, Sao Tome and Principe, Saudi Arabia, Senegal, Serbia, Sierra Leone, Singapore, Slovakia, Slovenia, Solomon Islands, Somalia, South Africa, Spain, Sri Lanka, Sudan, Suriname, Swaziland, Sweden, Switzerland, Syrian Arab Republic, Tajikistan, Thailand, the former Yugoslav Republic of Macedonia, Togo, Tonga, Trinidad and Tobago, Tunisia, Turkey, Turkmenistan, Ukraine, United Arab Emirates, United Kingdom of Great Britain and Northern Ireland, United Republic

---

* Subsequent to the voting, the delegation of Nauru advised the Secretariat that it had intended to vote in favour. The voting tally above does not reflect this information.

of Tanzania, Uruguay, Uzbekistan, Venezuela (Bolivarian Republic of), Viet Nam, Yemen, Zambia, Zimbabwe

Against:
United States of America

Abstaining:
Nauru

Action by the First Committee

Date: 1 November 2007 Meeting: 24th meeting
Vote: 166-1-0 Draft resolution: A/C.1/62/L.17/Rev.1

Agenda item 98

62/30 Effects of the use of armaments and ammunitions containing depleted uranium

Text

The General Assembly,

Guided by the purposes and principles enshrined in the Charter of the United Nations and the rules of humanitarian international law,

Determined to promote multilateralism as an essential means to carry forward negotiations on arms regulation and disarmament,

Convinced that as humankind is more aware of the need to take immediate measures to protect the environment, any event that could jeopardize such efforts requires urgent attention to implement the required measures,

Taking into consideration the potential harmful effects of the use of armaments and ammunitions containing depleted uranium on human health and the environment,

1. *Requests* the Secretary-General to seek the views of Member States and relevant international organizations on the effects of the use of armaments and ammunitions containing depleted uranium, and to submit a report on this subject to the General Assembly at its sixty-third session;

2. *Decides* to include in the provisional agenda of its sixty-third session an item entitled "Effects of the use of armaments and ammunitions containing depleted uranium".

Action by the General Assembly

Date: 5 December 2007   Meeting: 61st meeting
Vote: 136-5-36   Report: A/62/391

Sponsors

Indonesia (on behalf of the States Members of the United Nations that are members of the Movement of Non-Aligned Countries)

*Recorded vote**

In favour:

Afghanistan, Algeria, Antigua and Barbuda, Argentina, Armenia, Austria, Azerbaijan, Bahamas, Bahrain, Bangladesh, Barbados, Belarus, Belize, Benin, Bhutan, Bolivia, Bosnia and Herzegovina, Botswana, Brazil, Brunei Darussalam, Burkina Faso, Burundi, Cambodia, Cameroon, Cape

---

* Subsequent to the voting, the delegation of France advised the Secretariat that it had intended to vote against. The voting tally above does not reflect this information.

Verde, Central African Republic, Chile, Colombia, Comoros, Congo, Costa Rica, Côte d'Ivoire, Cuba, Cyprus, Democratic People's Republic of Korea, Djibouti, Dominican Republic, Ecuador, Egypt, El Salvador, Eritrea, Ethiopia, Fiji, Gabon, Gambia, Germany, Ghana, Grenada, Guatemala, Guinea, Guinea-Bissau, Guyana, Haiti, Honduras, India, Indonesia, Iran (Islamic Republic of), Iraq, Ireland, Italy, Jamaica, Japan, Jordan, Kenya, Kuwait, Lao People's Democratic Republic, Lebanon, Lesotho, Liberia, Libyan Arab Jamahiriya, Liechtenstein, Madagascar, Malawi, Malaysia, Maldives, Mali, Marshall Islands, Mauritania, Mauritius, Mexico, Mongolia, Montenegro, Morocco, Mozambique, Myanmar, Namibia, Nauru, Nepal, New Zealand, Nicaragua, Niger, Nigeria, Oman, Pakistan, Panama, Papua New Guinea, Paraguay, Peru, Philippines, Qatar, Rwanda, Saint Kitts and Nevis, Saint Lucia, Saint Vincent and the Grenadines, Samoa, San Marino, Sao Tome and Principe, Saudi Arabia, Senegal, Serbia, Sierra Leone, Singapore, Solomon Islands, Somalia, South Africa, Sri Lanka, Sudan, Suriname, Swaziland, Switzerland, Syrian Arab Republic, Thailand, Togo, Tonga, Trinidad and Tobago, Tunisia, Turkmenistan, United Arab Emirates, United Republic of Tanzania, Uruguay, Uzbekistan, Venezuela (Bolivarian Republic of), Viet Nam, Yemen, Zambia, Zimbabwe

Against:
Czech Republic, Israel, Netherlands, United Kingdom of Great Britain and Northern Ireland, United States of America

Abstaining:
Albania, Andorra, Australia, Belgium, Bulgaria, Canada, Croatia, Denmark, Estonia, Finland, Georgia, Greece, Hungary, Iceland, Kazakhstan, Latvia, Lithuania, Luxembourg, Malta, Micronesia (Federated States of), Norway, Palau, Poland, Portugal, Republic of Korea, Republic of Moldova, Romania, Russian Federation, Slovakia, Slovenia, Spain, Sweden, Tajikistan, the former Yugoslav Republic of Macedonia, Turkey, Ukraine

Action by the First Committee

Date: 1 November 2007　　　Meeting:　　24th meeting
Vote: 122-6-35　　　　　　　Draft resolution:　A/C.1/62/L.18/Rev.1

Agenda item 98

62/31 Treaty on the South-East Asia Nuclear-Weapon-Free Zone (Bangkok Treaty)

Text

The General Assembly,

Recalling its resolution 60/56 of 8 December 2005, entitled "Towards a nuclear-weapon-free world: accelerating the implementation of nuclear disarmament commitments", and its resolution 61/69 of 6 December 2006, entitled "Nuclear-weapon-free southern hemisphere and adjacent areas",

Welcoming the desire of the South-East Asian States to maintain peace and stability in the region in the spirit of peaceful coexistence and mutual understanding and cooperation,

Reaffirming its conviction of the important role of nuclear-weapon-free zones in strengthening the nuclear non-proliferation regime and in extending the areas of the world that are nuclear-weapon-free, and, with particular reference to the responsibilities of the nuclear-weapon States, calling upon all States to support the process of nuclear disarmament and to work for the total elimination of all nuclear weapons,

Convinced that the establishment of a South-East Asia Nuclear-Weapon-Free Zone, as an essential component of the Declaration on the Zone of Peace, Freedom and Neutrality, signed in Kuala Lumpur on 27 November 1971, will contribute towards strengthening the security of States within the Zone and towards enhancing international peace and security as a whole,

Noting the entry into force of the Treaty on the South-East Asia Nuclear-Weapon-Free Zone on 27 March 1997[1] and the tenth anniversary of its entry into force in 2007,

Welcoming the reaffirmation of South-East Asian States that the South-East Asia Nuclear-Weapon-Free Zone shall continue to play a pivotal role in the area of confidence-building measures, preventive diplomacy and the approaches to conflict resolution as enshrined in the Declaration of the Association of Southeast Asian Nations Concord II (Bali Concord II),[2]

Reaffirming the inalienable right of all the parties to the Treaty on the South-East Asia Nuclear-Weapon-Free Zone to develop research, production and use of nuclear energy for peaceful purposes without discrimination and in conformity with the Treaty on the Non-Proliferation of Nuclear Weapons,[3]

---

[1] United Nations, *Treaty Series*, vol. 1981, No. 33873.
[2] A/58/548, annex I.
[3] United Nations, *Treaty Series*, vol. 729, No. 10485.

Recognizing that by signing and ratifying the relevant protocols to the treaties establishing nuclear-weapon-free zones, nuclear-weapon States undertake legally binding commitments to respect the status of such zones and not to use or threaten to use nuclear weapons against States parties to such treaties,

Recalling the applicable principles and rules of international law relating to the freedom of the high seas and the rights of innocent passage, archipelagic sea lanes passage or transit passage of ships and aircraft, particularly those of the United Nations Convention on the Law of the Sea,[4]

1. *Welcomes* the commitment of the Commission for the Treaty on the South-East Asia Nuclear-Weapon-Free Zone to further enhance and strengthen the implementation of the Bangkok Treaty[1] by adopting a Plan of Action for the period 2007-2012 in Manila on 29 July 2007;

2. *Encourages* States parties to the Treaty to work towards resuming direct consultations with the five nuclear-weapon States to resolve comprehensively, in accordance with the objectives and principles of the Treaty, existing outstanding issues on a number of provisions of the Treaty and the Protocol thereto;

3. *Encourages* nuclear-weapon States and States parties to the Treaty to continue to work constructively with a view to ensuring the early accession of the nuclear-weapon States to the Protocol to the Treaty;

4. *Underlines* the value of enhancing and implementing further ways and means of cooperation among nuclear-weapon-free zones;

5. *Decides* to include in the provisional agenda of its sixty-fourth session an item entitled "Treaty on the South-East Asia Nuclear-Weapon-Free Zone (Bangkok Treaty)".

Action by the General Assembly

Date: 5 December 2007 Meeting: 61st meeting
Vote: 174-1-5 Report: A/62/391

Sponsors

Brunei Darussalam, Cambodia, **Indonesia**, Lao People's Democratic Republic, Malaysia, Myanmar, Philippines, Singapore, Thailand, Viet Nam

Co-sponsors

Brazil, Chile, Egypt, Jamaica, Jordan, Mexico, Mongolia, Uzbekistan

---

[4] Ibid., vol. 1833, No. 31363.

Recorded vote

In favour:
Afghanistan, Albania, Algeria, Andorra, Antigua and Barbuda, Argentina, Armenia, Australia, Austria, Azerbaijan, Bahamas, Bahrain, Bangladesh, Barbados, Belarus, Belgium, Belize, Benin, Bhutan, Bolivia, Bosnia and Herzegovina, Botswana, Brazil, Brunei Darussalam, Bulgaria, Burkina Faso, Burundi, Cambodia, Cameroon, Canada, Cape Verde, Central African Republic, Chile, China, Colombia, Comoros, Congo, Costa Rica, Côte d'Ivoire, Croatia, Cuba, Cyprus, Czech Republic, Democratic People's Republic of Korea, Denmark, Djibouti, Dominican Republic, Ecuador, Egypt, El Salvador, Eritrea, Estonia, Ethiopia, Fiji, Finland, Gabon, Gambia, Georgia, Germany, Ghana, Greece, Grenada, Guatemala, Guinea, Guinea-Bissau, Guyana, Haiti, Honduras, Hungary, Iceland, India, Indonesia, Iran (Islamic Republic of), Iraq, Ireland, Italy, Jamaica, Japan, Jordan, Kazakhstan, Kenya, Kuwait, Kyrgyzstan, Lao People's Democratic Republic, Latvia, Lebanon, Lesotho, Liberia, Libyan Arab Jamahiriya, Liechtenstein, Lithuania, Luxembourg, Madagascar, Malawi, Malaysia, Maldives, Mali, Malta, Marshall Islands, Mauritania, Mauritius, Mexico, Mongolia, Montenegro, Morocco, Mozambique, Myanmar, Namibia, Nauru, Nepal, Netherlands, New Zealand, Nicaragua, Niger, Nigeria, Norway, Oman, Pakistan, Panama, Papua New Guinea, Paraguay, Peru, Philippines, Poland, Portugal, Qatar, Republic of Korea, Republic of Moldova, Romania, Russian Federation, Rwanda, Saint Kitts and Nevis, Saint Lucia, Saint Vincent and the Grenadines, Samoa, San Marino, Sao Tome and Principe, Saudi Arabia, Senegal, Serbia, Sierra Leone, Singapore, Slovakia, Slovenia, Solomon Islands, Somalia, South Africa, Spain, Sri Lanka, Sudan, Suriname, Swaziland, Sweden, Switzerland, Syrian Arab Republic, Tajikistan, Thailand, the former Yugoslav Republic of Macedonia, Togo, Tonga, Trinidad and Tobago, Tunisia, Turkey, Turkmenistan, Ukraine, United Arab Emirates, United Republic of Tanzania, Uruguay, Uzbekistan, Venezuela (Bolivarian Republic of), Viet Nam, Yemen, Zambia, Zimbabwe

Against:
United States of America

Abstaining:
France, Israel, Micronesia (Federated States of), Palau, United Kingdom of Great Britain and Northern Ireland

Action by the First Committee

Date: 1 November 2007   Meeting: 24th meeting
Vote: 161-1-4   Draft resolution: A/C.1/62/L.19/Rev.1

Agenda item 98 (y)

62/32   Reducing nuclear danger

Text

The General Assembly,

Bearing in mind that the use of nuclear weapons poses the most serious threat to mankind and to the survival of civilization,

Reaffirming that any use or threat of use of nuclear weapons would constitute a violation of the Charter of the United Nations,

Convinced that the proliferation of nuclear weapons in all its aspects would seriously enhance the danger of nuclear war,

Convinced also that nuclear disarmament and the complete elimination of nuclear weapons are essential to remove the danger of nuclear war,

Considering that, until nuclear weapons cease to exist, it is imperative on the part of the nuclear-weapon States to adopt measures that assure non-nuclear-weapon States against the use or threat of use of nuclear weapons,

Considering also that the hair-trigger alert of nuclear weapons carries unacceptable risks of unintentional or accidental use of nuclear weapons, which would have catastrophic consequences for all mankind,

Emphasizing the need to adopt measures to avoid accidental, unauthorized or unexplained incidents arising from computer anomaly or other technical malfunctions,

Conscious that limited steps relating to de-alerting and de-targeting have been taken by the nuclear-weapon States and that further practical, realistic and mutually reinforcing steps are necessary to contribute to the improvement in the international climate for negotiations leading to the elimination of nuclear weapons,

Mindful that a diminishing role for nuclear weapons in the security policies of nuclear-weapon States would positively impact on international peace and security and improve the conditions for the further reduction and the elimination of nuclear weapons,

Reiterating the highest priority accorded to nuclear disarmament in the Final Document of the Tenth Special Session of the General Assembly[1] and by the international community,

Recalling the advisory opinion of the International Court of Justice on the *Legality of the Threat or Use of Nuclear Weapons*[2] that there exists an

---

[1] Resolution S-10/2.
[2] A/51/218, annex; see also *Legality of the Threat or Use of Nuclear Weapons, Advisory Opinion, I.C.J. Reports 1996*, p. 226.

obligation for all States to pursue in good faith and bring to a conclusion negotiations leading to nuclear disarmament in all its aspects under strict and effective international control,

Recalling also the call in the United Nations Millennium Declaration[3] to seek to eliminate the dangers posed by weapons of mass destruction and the resolve to strive for the elimination of weapons of mass destruction, particularly nuclear weapons, including the possibility of convening an international conference to identify ways of eliminating nuclear dangers,

1. *Calls for* a review of nuclear doctrines and, in this context, immediate and urgent steps to reduce the risks of unintentional and accidental use of nuclear weapons, including through de-alerting and de-targeting of nuclear weapons;

2. *Requests* the five nuclear-weapon States to take measures towards the implementation of paragraph 1 above;

3. *Calls upon* Member States to take the necessary measures to prevent the proliferation of nuclear weapons in all its aspects and to promote nuclear disarmament, with the objective of eliminating nuclear weapons;

4. *Takes note* of the report of the Secretary-General submitted pursuant to paragraph 5 of General Assembly resolution 61/85 of 6 December 2006;[4]

5. *Requests* the Secretary-General to intensify efforts and support initiatives that would contribute towards the full implementation of the seven recommendations identified in the report of the Advisory Board on Disarmament Matters that would significantly reduce the risk of nuclear war,[5] and also to continue to encourage Member States to consider the convening of an international conference as proposed in the United Nations Millennium Declaration,[3] to identify ways of eliminating nuclear dangers, and to report thereon to the General Assembly at its sixty-third session;

6. *Decides* to include in the provisional agenda of its sixty-third session the item entitled "Reducing nuclear danger".

Action by the General Assembly

Date: 5 December 2007   Meeting: 61st meeting
Vote: 117-52-12   Report: A/62/391

Sponsors

Afghanistan, Bangladesh, Chile, **India**, Madagascar, Malaysia, Mauritius, Viet Nam

Co-sponsors

Bhutan, Botswana, Cambodia, Colombia, Cuba, El Salvador, Haiti, Jamaica, Jordan, Libyan Arab Jamahiriya, Nicaragua, Samoa, Zambia

---

[3] See resolution 55/2.
[4] A/62/165 and Add.1.
[5] See A/56/400, para. 3.

Recorded vote

In favour:
Afghanistan, Algeria, Antigua and Barbuda, Bahamas, Bahrain, Bangladesh, Barbados, Belize, Benin, Bhutan, Bolivia, Botswana, Brazil, Brunei Darussalam, Burkina Faso, Burundi, Cambodia, Cameroon, Cape Verde, Central African Republic, Chile, Colombia, Comoros, Congo, Costa Rica, Côte d'Ivoire, Cuba, Democratic People's Republic of Korea, Djibouti, Dominica, Dominican Republic, Ecuador, Egypt, El Salvador, Eritrea, Ethiopia, Fiji, Gabon, Gambia, Ghana, Grenada, Guatemala, Guinea, Guinea-Bissau, Guyana, Haiti, Honduras, India, Indonesia, Iran (Islamic Republic of), Iraq, Jamaica, Jordan, Kenya, Kuwait, Lao People's Democratic Republic, Lebanon, Lesotho, Liberia, Libyan Arab Jamahiriya, Madagascar, Malawi, Malaysia, Maldives, Mali, Mauritania, Mauritius, Mexico, Mongolia, Morocco, Mozambique, Myanmar, Namibia, Nepal, Nicaragua, Niger, Nigeria, Oman, Pakistan, Panama, Papua New Guinea, Paraguay, Peru, Philippines, Qatar, Rwanda, Saint Kitts and Nevis, Saint Lucia, Saint Vincent and the Grenadines, Samoa, Sao Tome and Principe, Saudi Arabia, Senegal, Sierra Leone, Singapore, Solomon Islands, Somalia, South Africa, Sri Lanka, Sudan, Suriname, Swaziland, Syrian Arab Republic, Thailand, Togo, Tonga, Trinidad and Tobago, Tunisia, Turkmenistan, United Arab Emirates, United Republic of Tanzania, Uruguay, Venezuela (Bolivarian Republic of), Viet Nam, Yemen, Zambia, Zimbabwe

Against:
Albania, Andorra, Australia, Austria, Belgium, Bosnia and Herzegovina, Bulgaria, Canada, Croatia, Cyprus, Czech Republic, Denmark, Estonia, Finland, France, Georgia, Germany, Greece, Hungary, Iceland, Ireland, Israel, Italy, Latvia, Liechtenstein, Lithuania, Luxembourg, Malta, Marshall Islands, Micronesia (Federated States of), Monaco, Montenegro, Netherlands, New Zealand, Norway, Palau, Poland, Portugal, Republic of Moldova, Romania, San Marino, Serbia, Slovakia, Slovenia, Spain, Sweden, Switzerland, the former Yugoslav Republic of Macedonia, Turkey, Ukraine, United Kingdom of Great Britain and Northern Ireland, United States of America

Abstaining:
Argentina, Armenia, Azerbaijan, Belarus, China, Japan, Kazakhstan, Kyrgyzstan, Republic of Korea, Russian Federation, Tajikistan, Uzbekistan

Action by the First Committee

Date: 30 October 2007   Meeting: 22nd meeting
Vote: 113-50-13   Draft resolution: A/C.1/62/L.21

Agenda item 98 (z)

62/33   Measures to prevent terrorists from acquiring weapons of mass destruction

Text

The General Assembly,

Recalling its resolution 61/86 of 6 December 2006,

Recognizing the determination of the international community to combat terrorism, as evidenced in relevant General Assembly and Security Council resolutions,

Deeply concerned by the growing risk of linkages between terrorism and weapons of mass destruction, and in particular by the fact that terrorists may seek to acquire weapons of mass destruction,

Cognizant of the steps taken by States to implement Security Council resolution 1540 (2004) on the non-proliferation of weapons of mass destruction, adopted on 28 April 2004,

Welcoming the entry into force on 7 July 2007 of the International Convention for the Suppression of Acts of Nuclear Terrorism,[1]

Welcoming also the adoption, by consensus, of amendments to strengthen the Convention on the Physical Protection of Nuclear Material[2] by the International Atomic Energy Agency on 8 July 2005,

Noting the support expressed in the Final Document of the Fourteenth Conference of Heads of State or Government of Non-Aligned Countries, held in Havana on 15 and 16 September 2006,[3] for measures to prevent terrorists from acquiring weapons of mass destruction,

Noting also that the Group of Eight, the European Union, the Regional Forum of the Association of Southeast Asian Nations and others have taken into account in their deliberations the dangers posed by the likely acquisition by terrorists of weapons of mass destruction, and the need for international cooperation in combating it,

Acknowledging the consideration of issues relating to terrorism and weapons of mass destruction by the Advisory Board on Disarmament Matters,[4]

---

[1] Resolution 59/290, annex.
[2] United Nations, *Treaty Series*, vol. 1456, No. 24631.
[3] A/61/472-S/2006/780, annex I.
[4] See A/59/361.

Taking note of the relevant resolutions adopted by the General Conference of the International Atomic Energy Agency at its fifty-first regular session,[5]

Taking note also of the 2005 World Summit Outcome adopted on 16 September 2005 at the High-level Plenary Meeting of the sixtieth session of the General Assembly[6] and the adoption on 8 September 2006 of the United Nations Global Counter-Terrorism Strategy,[7]

Taking note further of the report of the Secretary-General submitted pursuant to paragraphs 3 and 5 of resolution 61/86,[8]

Mindful of the urgent need for addressing, within the United Nations framework and through international cooperation, this threat to humanity,

Emphasizing that progress is urgently needed in the area of disarmament and non-proliferation in order to maintain international peace and security and to contribute to global efforts against terrorism,

1. *Calls upon* all Member States to support international efforts to prevent terrorists from acquiring weapons of mass destruction and their means of delivery;

2. *Appeals* to Member States to consider early accession to and ratification of the International Convention for the Suppression of Acts of Nuclear Terrorism;[1]

3. *Urges* all Member States to take and strengthen national measures, as appropriate, to prevent terrorists from acquiring weapons of mass destruction, their means of delivery and materials and technologies related to their manufacture, and invites them to inform the Secretary-General, on a voluntary basis, of the measures taken in this regard;

4. *Encourages* cooperation among and between Member States and relevant regional and international organizations for strengthening national capacities in this regard;

5. *Requests* the Secretary-General to compile a report on measures already taken by international organizations on issues relating to the linkage between the fight against terrorism and the proliferation of weapons of mass destruction and seek the views of Member States on additional relevant measures for tackling the global threat posed by the acquisition by terrorists of weapons of mass destruction and to report to the General Assembly at its sixty-third session;

---

[5] See International Atomic Energy Agency, *Resolutions and Other Decisions of the General Conference, Fifty-first Regular Session, 17-21 September 2007* (GC(51)/RES/DEC(2007)).
[6] See resolution 60/1.
[7] Resolution 60/288.
[8] A/62/156.

6. *Decides* to include in the provisional agenda of its sixty-third session the item entitled "Measures to prevent terrorists from acquiring weapons of mass destruction".

Action by the General Assembly

Date: 5 December 2007   Meeting: 61st meeting
Vote: Adopted without a vote   Report: A/62/391

Sponsors

Afghanistan, Bangladesh, Bhutan, Chile, Finland, Germany, **India**, Ireland, Kuwait, Latvia, Luxembourg, Malaysia, Mauritius, Nepal, Poland, Portugal, Spain, Sri Lanka, Thailand, the former Yugoslav Republic of Macedonia, Turkey

Co-sponsors

Albania, Argentina, Armenia, Azerbaijan, Belgium, Botswana, Bulgaria, Cambodia, Colombia, Croatia, Cyprus, Czech Republic, El Salvador, Estonia, France, Greece, Guatemala, Haiti, Honduras, Hungary, Italy, Kyrgyzstan, Lithuania, Monaco, Myanmar, Netherlands, Nicaragua, Norway, Philippines, Romania, Samoa, Serbia, Singapore, Slovakia, Slovenia, Togo, United States of America, Zambia

Action by the First Committee

Date: 30 October 2007   Meeting: 22nd meeting
Vote: Adopted without a vote   Draft resolution: A/C.1/62/L.22

Agenda item 98 (c)

62/34 Prohibition of the dumping of radioactive wastes

Text

The General Assembly,

Bearing in mind resolutions CM/Res.1153 (XLVIII) of 1988[1] and CM/Res.1225 (L) of 1989,[2] adopted by the Council of Ministers of the Organization of African Unity, concerning the dumping of nuclear and industrial wastes in Africa,

Welcoming resolution GC(XXXIV)/RES/530 establishing a Code of Practice on the International Transboundary Movement of Radioactive Waste, adopted on 21 September 1990 by the General Conference of the International Atomic Energy Agency at its thirty-fourth regular session,[3]

Taking note of the commitment by the participants in the Summit on Nuclear Safety and Security, held in Moscow on 19 and 20 April 1996, to ban the dumping at sea of radioactive wastes,[4]

Considering its resolution 2602 C (XXIV) of 16 December 1969, in which it requested the Conference of the Committee on Disarmament,[5] inter alia, to consider effective methods of control against the use of radiological methods of warfare,

Aware of the potential hazards underlying any use of radioactive wastes that would constitute radiological warfare and its implications for regional and international security, in particular for the security of developing countries,

Recalling all its resolutions on the matter since its forty-third session in 1988, including its resolution 51/45 J of 10 December 1996,

Also recalling resolution GC(45)/RES/10 adopted by consensus on 21 September 2001 by the General Conference of the International Atomic Energy Agency at its forty-fifth regular session,[6] in which States shipping radioactive materials are invited to provide, as appropriate, assurances to concerned States, upon their request, that the national regulations of the shipping

---

[1] See A/43/398, annex I.
[2] See A/44/603, annex I.
[3] See International Atomic Energy Agency, *Resolutions and Other Decisions of the General Conference, Thirty-fourth Regular Session, 17-21 September 1990* (GC(XXXIV)/RESOLUTIONS (1990)).
[4] A/51/131, annex I, para. 20.
[5] The Conference of the Committee on Disarmament became the Committee on Disarmament as from the tenth special session of the General Assembly. The Committee on Disarmament was redesignated the Conference on Disarmament as from 7 February 1984.
[6] See International Atomic Energy Agency, *Resolutions and Other Decisions of the General Conference, Forty-fifth Regular Session, 17-21 September 2001* (GC(45)/RES/DEC(2001)).

State take into account the Agency's transport regulations and to provide them with relevant information relating to the shipment of such materials; the information provided should in no case be contradictory to the measures of physical security and safety,

Welcoming the adoption at Vienna, on 5 September 1997, of the Joint Convention on the Safety of Spent Fuel Management and on the Safety of Radioactive Waste Management,[7] as recommended by the participants in the Summit on Nuclear Safety and Security,

Noting with satisfaction that the Joint Convention entered into force on 18 June 2001,

Noting that the first Review Meeting of the Contracting Parties to the Joint Convention on the Safety of Spent Fuel Management and on the Safety of Radioactive Waste Management was convened in Vienna from 3 to 14 November 2003,

Desirous of promoting the implementation of paragraph 76 of the Final Document of the Tenth Special Session of the General Assembly,[8] the first special session devoted to disarmament,

1. *Takes note* of the part of the report of the Conference on Disarmament relating to a future convention on the prohibition of radiological weapons;[9]

2. *Expresses grave concern* regarding any use of nuclear wastes that would constitute radiological warfare and have grave implications for the national security of all States;

3. *Calls upon* all States to take appropriate measures with a view to preventing any dumping of nuclear or radioactive wastes that would infringe upon the sovereignty of States;

4. *Requests* the Conference on Disarmament to take into account, in the negotiations for a convention on the prohibition of radiological weapons, radioactive wastes as part of the scope of such a convention;

5. *Also requests* the Conference on Disarmament to intensify efforts towards an early conclusion of such a convention and to include in its report to the General Assembly at its sixty-fourth session the progress recorded in the negotiations on this subject;

6. *Takes note* of resolution CM/Res.1356 (LIV) of 1991, adopted by the Council of Ministers of the Organization of African Unity,[10] on the Bamako Convention on the Ban on the Import of Hazardous Wastes into Africa and on the Control of Their Transboundary Movements within Africa;

---

[7] United Nations, *Treaty Series*, vol. 2153, No. 37605.
[8] Resolution S-10/2.
[9] See *Official Records of the General Assembly, Fifty-fourth Session, Supplement No. 27* (A/54/27), chap. III, sect. E.
[10] See A/46/390, annex I.

7. *Expresses the hope* that the effective implementation of the International Atomic Energy Agency Code of Practice on the International Transboundary Movement of Radioactive Waste will enhance the protection of all States from the dumping of radioactive wastes on their territories;

8. *Appeals* to all Member States that have not yet taken the necessary steps to become party to the Joint Convention on the Safety of Spent Fuel Management and on the Safety of Radioactive Waste Management[7] to do so as soon as possible;

9. *Decides* to include in the provisional agenda of its sixty-fourth session the item entitled "Prohibition of the dumping of radioactive wastes".

Action by the General Assembly

Date: 5 December 2007　　Meeting: 61st meeting
Vote: Adopted without a vote　　Report: A/62/391

Sponsors

Nigeria (on behalf of the States Members of the United Nations that are members of the Group of African States)

Co-sponsors

Dominican Republic

Action by the First Committee

Date: 30 October 2007　　Meeting:　　22nd meeting
Vote: Adopted without a vote　　Draft resolution: A/C.1/62/L.25

Agenda item 98 (n)

62/35 Nuclear-weapon-free southern hemisphere and adjacent areas

Text

The General Assembly,

Recalling its resolutions 51/45 B of 10 December 1996, 52/38 N of 9 December 1997, 53/77 Q of 4 December 1998, 54/54 L of 1 December 1999, 55/33 I of 20 November 2000, 56/24 G of 29 November 2001, 57/73 of 22 November 2002, 58/49 of 8 December 2003, 59/85 of 3 December 2004, 60/58 of 8 December 2005 and 61/69 of 6 December 2006,

Recalling also the adoption by the Disarmament Commission at its 1999 substantive session of a text entitled "Establishment of nuclear-weapon-free zones on the basis of arrangements freely arrived at among the States of the region concerned",[1]

Determined to pursue the total elimination of nuclear weapons,

Determined also to continue to contribute to the prevention of the proliferation of nuclear weapons in all its aspects and to the process of general and complete disarmament under strict and effective international control, in particular in the field of nuclear weapons and other weapons of mass destruction, with a view to strengthening international peace and security, in accordance with the purposes and principles of the Charter of the United Nations,

Recalling the provisions on nuclear-weapon-free zones of the Final Document of the Tenth Special Session of the General Assembly,[2] the first special session devoted to disarmament,

Stressing the importance of the treaties of Tlatelolco,[3] Rarotonga,[4] Bangkok[5] and Pelindaba[6] establishing nuclear-weapon-free zones, as well as the Antarctic Treaty,[7] to, inter alia, achieve a world entirely free of nuclear weapons,

Underlining the value of enhancing cooperation among the nuclear-weapon-free-zone treaty members by means of mechanisms such as joint meetings of States parties, signatories and observers to those treaties,

---

[1] *Official Records of the General Assembly, Fifty-fourth Session, Supplement No. 42* (A/54/42), annex I.
[2] Resolution S-10/2.
[3] United Nations, *Treaty Series*, vol. 634, No. 9068.
[4] See *The United Nations Disarmament Yearbook*, vol. 10: 1985 (United Nations publication, Sales No. E.86.IX.7), appendix VII.
[5] United Nations, *Treaty Series*, vol. 1981, No. 33873.
[6] A/50/426, annex.
[7] United Nations, *Treaty Series*, vol. 402, No. 5778.

Noting the adoption of the Declaration of Santiago de Chile by the Governments of the States members of the Agency for the Prohibition of Nuclear Weapons in Latin America and the Caribbean and the States parties to the Treaty of Tlatelolco, during the nineteenth regular session of the General Conference of the Agency, held in Santiago on 7 and 8 November 2005,[8]

Recalling the applicable principles and rules of international law relating to the freedom of the high seas and the rights of passage through maritime space, including those of the United Nations Convention on the Law of the Sea,[9]

1. *Welcomes* the continued contribution that the Antarctic Treaty[7] and the treaties of Tlatelolco,[3] Rarotonga,[4] Bangkok[5] and Pelindaba[6] are making towards freeing the southern hemisphere and adjacent areas covered by those treaties from nuclear weapons;

2. *Also welcomes* the ratification by all original parties of the Treaty of Rarotonga, and calls upon eligible States to adhere to the Treaty and the protocols thereto;

3. *Further welcomes* the efforts towards the completion of the ratification process of the Treaty of Pelindaba, and calls upon the States of the region that have not yet done so to sign and ratify the Treaty, with the aim of its early entry into force;

4. *Welcomes* the signing of the Semipalatinsk Treaty on 8 September 2006,[10] and urges all relevant States to cooperate in resolving outstanding issues with a view to the full implementation of the Treaty;

5. *Calls upon* all concerned States to continue to work together in order to facilitate adherence to the protocols to nuclear-weapon-free-zone treaties by all relevant States that have not yet adhered to them;

6. *Welcomes* the steps taken to conclude further nuclear-weapon-free-zone treaties on the basis of arrangements freely arrived at among the States of the region concerned, and calls upon all States to consider all relevant proposals, including those reflected in its resolutions on the establishment of nuclear-weapon-free zones in the Middle East and South Asia;

7. *Affirms its conviction* of the important role of nuclear-weapon-free zones in strengthening the nuclear non-proliferation regime and in extending the areas of the world that are nuclear-weapon-free, and, with particular reference to the responsibilities of the nuclear-weapon States, calls upon all States to support the process of nuclear disarmament and to work for the total elimination of all nuclear weapons;

---

[8] See A/60/678.
[9] United Nations, *Treaty Series*, vol. 1833, No. 31363.
[10] Treaty on a Nuclear-Weapon-Free Zone in Central Asia.

8. *Welcomes* the progress made on increased collaboration within and between zones at the first Conference of States Parties and Signatories to Treaties that Establish Nuclear-Weapon-Free Zones, held in Tlatelolco, Mexico, from 26 to 28 April 2005, at which States reaffirmed their need to cooperate in order to achieve their common objectives;

9. *Congratulates* the States parties and signatories to the treaties of Tlatelolco, Rarotonga, Bangkok and Pelindaba, as well as Mongolia, for their efforts to pursue the common goals envisaged in those treaties and to promote the nuclear-weapon-free status of the southern hemisphere and adjacent areas, and calls upon them to explore and implement further ways and means of cooperation among themselves and their treaty agencies;

10. *Encourages* the competent authorities of the nuclear-weapon-free-zone treaties to provide assistance to the States parties and signatories to those treaties so as to facilitate the accomplishment of the goals;

11. *Decides* to include in the provisional agenda of its sixty-third session the item entitled "Nuclear-weapon-free southern hemisphere and adjacent areas".

Action by the General Assembly

Date: 5 December 2007　　Meeting: 61st meeting
Vote: 169-3-8, as a whole　　Report: A/62/391
163-1-8, op. para. 6
163-1-9, "and South Asia" in op. para. 6

Sponsors

Brazil, New Zealand

Co-sponsors

Angola, Antigua and Barbuda, Argentina, Barbados, Belize, Bolivia, Brunei Darussalam, Cambodia, Chile, Colombia, Costa Rica, Cuba, Dominica, Dominican Republic, Ecuador, El Salvador, Guatemala, Guyana, Haiti, Honduras, Indonesia, Jamaica, Liberia, Mexico, Mongolia, Panama, Papua New Guinea, Paraguay, Peru, Samoa, Sierra Leone, Singapore, South Africa, Thailand, Timor-Leste, Uruguay, Uzbekistan, Venezuela (Bolivarian Republic of)

Recorded vote

As a whole

In favour:

Afghanistan, Albania, Algeria, Andorra, Antigua and Barbuda, Argentina, Armenia, Australia, Austria, Azerbaijan, Bahamas, Bahrain, Bangladesh, Barbados, Belarus, Belgium, Belize, Benin, Bolivia, Bosnia and

Herzegovina, Botswana, Brazil, Brunei Darussalam, Bulgaria, Burkina Faso, Burundi, Cambodia, Cameroon, Canada, Cape Verde, Central African Republic, Chile, China, Colombia, Comoros, Congo, Costa Rica, Côte d'Ivoire, Croatia, Cuba, Cyprus, Czech Republic, Democratic People's Republic of Korea, Denmark, Djibouti, Dominican Republic, Ecuador, Egypt, El Salvador, Eritrea, Estonia, Ethiopia, Fiji, Finland, Gabon, Gambia, Georgia, Germany, Ghana, Greece, Grenada, Guatemala, Guinea, Guinea-Bissau, Guyana, Haiti, Honduras, Hungary, Iceland, Indonesia, Iran (Islamic Republic of), Iraq, Ireland, Italy, Jamaica, Japan, Jordan, Kazakhstan, Kenya, Kuwait, Kyrgyzstan, Lao People's Democratic Republic, Latvia, Lebanon, Lesotho, Liberia, Libyan Arab Jamahiriya, Liechtenstein, Lithuania, Luxembourg, Madagascar, Malawi, Malaysia, Maldives, Mali, Malta, Mauritania, Mauritius, Mexico, Mongolia, Montenegro, Morocco, Mozambique, Myanmar, Namibia, Nauru, Nepal, Netherlands, New Zealand, Nicaragua, Niger, Nigeria, Norway, Oman, Panama, Papua New Guinea, Paraguay, Peru, Philippines, Poland, Portugal, Qatar, Republic of Korea, Republic of Moldova, Romania, Rwanda, Saint Kitts and Nevis, Saint Lucia, Saint Vincent and the Grenadines, Samoa, San Marino, Sao Tome and Principe, Saudi Arabia, Senegal, Serbia, Sierra Leone, Singapore, Slovakia, Slovenia, Solomon Islands, Somalia, South Africa, Spain, Sri Lanka, Sudan, Suriname, Swaziland, Sweden, Switzerland, Syrian Arab Republic, Tajikistan, Thailand, the former Yugoslav Republic of Macedonia, Togo, Tonga, Trinidad and Tobago, Tunisia, Turkey, Turkmenistan, Ukraine, United Arab Emirates, United Republic of Tanzania, Uruguay, Uzbekistan, Venezuela (Bolivarian Republic of), Viet Nam, Yemen, Zambia, Zimbabwe

Against:
France, United Kingdom of Great Britain and Northern Ireland, United States of America

Abstaining:
Bhutan, India, Israel, Marshall Islands, Micronesia (Federated States of), Pakistan, Palau, Russian Federation

Operative paragraph 6

In favour:
Afghanistan, Albania, Algeria, Andorra, Antigua and Barbuda, Argentina, Armenia, Australia, Austria, Azerbaijan, Bahamas, Bahrain, Bangladesh, Barbados, Belarus, Belgium, Belize, Benin, Bolivia, Bosnia and Herzegovina, Botswana, Brazil, Brunei Darussalam, Bulgaria, Burkina Faso, Burundi, Cambodia, Cameroon, Canada, Cape Verde, Central African Republic, Chile, China, Colombia, Comoros, Congo, Costa Rica, Côte d'Ivoire, Croatia, Cuba, Cyprus, Czech Republic, Denmark, Djibouti, Dominican Republic, Ecuador, Egypt, El Salvador, Eritrea,

Estonia, Ethiopia, Fiji, Finland, Gabon, Georgia, Germany, Ghana, Greece, Grenada, Guatemala, Guinea, Guinea-Bissau, Guyana, Haiti, Honduras, Hungary, Iceland, Indonesia, Iran (Islamic Republic of), Iraq, Ireland, Italy, Jamaica, Japan, Jordan, Kazakhstan, Kenya, Kuwait, Kyrgyzstan, Latvia, Lebanon, Lesotho, Liberia, Libyan Arab Jamahiriya, Liechtenstein, Lithuania, Luxembourg, Madagascar, Malawi, Malaysia, Maldives, Mali, Malta, Mauritania, Mexico, Mongolia, Montenegro, Morocco, Mozambique, Myanmar, Namibia, Nauru, Nepal, Netherlands, New Zealand, Nicaragua, Niger, Nigeria, Norway, Oman, Panama, Papua New Guinea, Paraguay, Peru, Poland, Portugal, Qatar, Republic of Korea, Republic of Moldova, Romania, Rwanda, Saint Kitts and Nevis, Saint Lucia, Saint Vincent and the Grenadines, Samoa, San Marino, Sao Tome and Principe, Saudi Arabia, Senegal, Serbia, Sierra Leone, Singapore, Slovakia, Slovenia, Solomon Islands, Somalia, South Africa, Spain, Sri Lanka, Sudan, Suriname, Swaziland, Sweden, Switzerland, Syrian Arab Republic, Tajikistan, Thailand, the former Yugoslav Republic of Macedonia, Togo, Tonga, Trinidad and Tobago, Tunisia, Turkey, Ukraine, United Arab Emirates, United Republic of Tanzania, Uruguay, Uzbekistan, Venezuela (Bolivarian Republic of), Viet Nam, Yemen, Zambia, Zimbabwe

Against:
India

Abstaining:
Bhutan, France, Israel, Marshall Islands, Pakistan, Russian Federation, United Kingdom of Great Britain and Northern Ireland, United States of America

"and South Asia" in op. para. 6*

In favour:
Afghanistan, Albania, Algeria, Andorra, Antigua and Barbuda, Argentina, Armenia, Australia, Austria, Azerbaijan, Bahamas, Bahrain, Bangladesh, Barbados, Belarus, Belgium, Belize, Benin, Bolivia, Bosnia and Herzegovina, Botswana, Brazil, Brunei Darussalam, Bulgaria, Burkina Faso, Burundi, Cambodia, Cameroon, Canada, Cape Verde, Central African Republic, Chile, China, Colombia, Comoros, Congo, Costa Rica, Côte d'Ivoire, Croatia, Cuba, Cyprus, Czech Republic, Denmark, Djibouti, Dominican Republic, Ecuador, Egypt, El Salvador, Eritrea, Estonia, Ethiopia, Fiji, Finland, Gabon, Georgia, Germany, Ghana, Greece, Grenada, Guatemala, Guinea, Guinea-Bissau, Guyana, Haiti, Honduras, Hungary, Iceland, Indonesia, Iran (Islamic Republic of), Iraq, Ireland, Italy, Jamaica, Japan, Jordan, Kazakhstan, Kenya, Kuwait,

---

* Subsequent to the voting, the delegation of Pakistan advised the Secretariat that it had intended to vote against. The voting tally above does not reflect this information.

Kyrgyzstan, Latvia, Lebanon, Lesotho, Liberia, Libyan Arab Jamahiriya, Liechtenstein, Lithuania, Luxembourg, Madagascar, Malawi, Malaysia, Maldives, Mali, Malta, Mauritania, Mexico, Mongolia, Montenegro, Morocco, Mozambique, Namibia, Nauru, Nepal, Netherlands, New Zealand, Nicaragua, Niger, Nigeria, Norway, Oman, Panama, Papua New Guinea, Paraguay, Peru, Philippines, Poland, Portugal, Qatar, Republic of Korea, Republic of Moldova, Romania, Rwanda, Saint Kitts and Nevis, Saint Lucia, Saint Vincent and the Grenadines, Samoa, San Marino, Sao Tome and Principe, Saudi Arabia, Senegal, Serbia, Sierra Leone, Singapore, Slovakia, Slovenia, Solomon Islands, Somalia, South Africa, Spain, Sri Lanka, Sudan, Suriname, Swaziland, Sweden, Switzerland, Syrian Arab Republic, Tajikistan, Thailand, the former Yugoslav Republic of Macedonia, Togo, Tonga, Trinidad and Tobago, Tunisia, Turkey, Ukraine, United Arab Emirates, United Republic of Tanzania, Uruguay, Uzbekistan, Venezuela (Bolivarian Republic of), Viet Nam, Yemen, Zambia, Zimbabwe

Against:
India

Abstaining:
Bhutan, France, Israel, Marshall Islands, Myanmar, Pakistan, Russian Federation, United Kingdom of Great Britain and Northern Ireland, United States of America

Action by the First Committee

Date: 31 October 2007 Meeting: 23rd meeting
Vote: 162-3-7, as a whole Draft resolution: A/C.1/62/L.27
156-1-8, op. para. 6
154-2-9, "and South Asia" in op. para. 6

Agenda item 98

62/36   Decreasing the operational readiness of nuclear weapons systems

Text

The General Assembly,

Recalling that the maintenance of nuclear weapons on high alert was a feature of cold war nuclear postures, and welcoming the increased confidence and transparency since the cessation of the cold war,

Concerned that, notwithstanding the end of the cold war, several thousand nuclear weapons remain on high alert, ready to be launched within minutes,

Noting the increased engagement in multilateral disarmament forums in support of further reductions to the operational status of nuclear weapons systems,

Recognizing that the maintenance of nuclear weapons systems at a high level of readiness increases the risk of the use of such weapons, including the unintentional or accidental use, which would have catastrophic consequences,

Also recognizing that reductions in deployments and the lowering of operational status contribute to the maintenance of international peace and security, as well as to the process of nuclear disarmament, through the enhancement of confidence-building and transparency measures and a diminishing role for nuclear weapons in security policies,

Welcoming bilateral initiatives, such as the proposed United States/Russian Federation Joint Centre for the Exchange of Data from Early Warning Systems and Notification of Missile Launches, which can play a central role in operational status reduction processes,

Also welcoming the steps taken by some States to reduce the operational status of their nuclear weapons systems, including de-targeting initiatives and increasing the amount of preparation time required for deployment,

1. *Calls for* further practical steps to be taken to decrease the operational readiness of nuclear weapons systems, with a view to ensuring that all nuclear weapons are removed from high alert status;

2. *Urges* States to update the General Assembly on progress made in the implementation of the present resolution;

3. *Decides* to remain seized of the matter.

Action by the General Assembly

Date:	5 December 2007	Meeting:	61st meeting
Vote:	139-3-36	Report:	A/62/391

Sponsors

Chile, **New Zealand**, Nigeria, Sweden, Switzerland

Co-sponsors

Argentina, Austria, Benin, Brazil, Dominican Republic, Ecuador, Ireland, Liechtenstein, Malaysia, Malta, Mexico, Peru, Samoa, Sierra Leone, Timor-Leste, Uruguay

Recorded vote

In favour:

Afghanistan, Algeria, Antigua and Barbuda, Argentina, Armenia, Austria, Azerbaijan, Bahamas, Bahrain, Bangladesh, Barbados, Belarus, Belize, Benin, Bhutan, Botswana, Brazil, Brunei Darussalam, Burkina Faso, Burundi, Cambodia, Cameroon, Cape Verde, Central African Republic, Chile, Colombia, Comoros, Congo, Costa Rica, Côte d'Ivoire, Cuba, Cyprus, Djibouti, Dominican Republic, Ecuador, Egypt, El Salvador, Eritrea, Ethiopia, Fiji, Finland, Gabon, Gambia, Germany, Ghana, Grenada, Guatemala, Guinea, Guinea-Bissau, Guyana, Haiti, Honduras, Iceland, India, Indonesia, Iran (Islamic Republic of), Iraq, Ireland, Italy, Jamaica, Japan, Jordan, Kazakhstan, Kenya, Kuwait, Kyrgyzstan, Lao People's Democratic Republic, Lebanon, Lesotho, Liberia, Libyan Arab Jamahiriya, Liechtenstein, Madagascar, Malawi, Malaysia, Maldives, Mali, Malta, Mauritania, Mauritius, Mexico, Mongolia, Morocco, Mozambique, Myanmar, Namibia, Nauru, Nepal, New Zealand, Nicaragua, Niger, Nigeria, Norway, Oman, Pakistan, Panama, Papua New Guinea, Paraguay, Peru, Philippines, Portugal, Qatar, Rwanda, Saint Kitts and Nevis, Saint Lucia, Saint Vincent and the Grenadines, Samoa, San Marino, Sao Tome and Principe, Saudi Arabia, Senegal, Sierra Leone, Singapore, Solomon Islands, Somalia, South Africa, Spain, Sri Lanka, Sudan, Suriname, Swaziland, Sweden, Switzerland, Syrian Arab Republic, Tajikistan, Thailand, Togo, Trinidad and Tobago, Tunisia, Turkmenistan, United Arab Emirates, United Republic of Tanzania, Uruguay, Uzbekistan, Venezuela (Bolivarian Republic of), Viet Nam, Yemen, Zambia, Zimbabwe

Against:

France, United Kingdom of Great Britain and Northern Ireland, United States of America

Abstaining:

Albania, Andorra, Australia, Belgium, Bolivia, Bosnia and Herzegovina, Bulgaria, Canada, China, Croatia, Czech Republic, Denmark, Estonia, Georgia, Greece, Hungary, Israel, Latvia, Lithuania, Luxembourg, Marshall Islands, Micronesia (Federated States of), Montenegro, Netherlands, Palau, Poland, Republic of Korea, Republic of Moldova,

Romania, Serbia, Slovakia, Slovenia, the former Yugoslav Republic of Macedonia, Tonga, Turkey, Ukraine

Action by the First Committee

Date: 1 November 2007   Meeting: 24th meeting
Vote: 124-3-34   Draft resolution: A/C.1/62/L.29

Agenda item 98

62/37   Renewed determination towards the total elimination of nuclear weapons

Text

The General Assembly,

Recalling the need for all States to take further practical steps and effective measures towards the total elimination of nuclear weapons, with a view to achieving a peaceful and safe world free of nuclear weapons, and renewing the determination to do so,

Noting that the ultimate objective of the efforts of States in the disarmament process is general and complete disarmament under strict and effective international control,

Recalling its resolution 61/74 of 6 December 2006,

Convinced that every effort should be made to avoid nuclear war and nuclear terrorism,

Reaffirming the crucial importance of the Treaty on the Non-Proliferation of Nuclear Weapons[1] as the cornerstone of the international nuclear disarmament and non-proliferation regime, and expressing regret over the lack of agreement on substantive issues at the Review Conference of the Parties to the Treaty on the Non-Proliferation of Nuclear Weapons, as well as over the elimination of references to nuclear disarmament and non-proliferation in the World Summit Outcome in 2005,[2] the year of the sixtieth anniversary of the atomic bombings in Hiroshima and Nagasaki, Japan,

Recalling the decisions and the resolution of the 1995 Review and Extension Conference of the Parties to the Treaty on the Non-Proliferation of Nuclear Weapons[3] and the Final Document of the 2000 Review Conference of the Parties to the Treaty,[4]

Recognizing that the enhancement of international peace and security and the promotion of nuclear disarmament are mutually reinforcing,

Reaffirming that further advancement in nuclear disarmament will contribute to consolidating the international regime for nuclear non-proliferation and thereby ensuring international peace and security,

---

[1] United Nations, *Treaty Series*, vol. 729, No. 10485.
[2] See resolution 60/1.
[3] See *1995 Review and Extension Conference of the Parties to the Treaty on the Non-Proliferation of Nuclear Weapons, Final Document, Part I* (NPT/CONF.1995/32 (Part I) and Corr.2), annex.
[4] *2000 Review Conference of the Parties to the Treaty on the Non-Proliferation of Nuclear Weapons, Final Document*, vols. I-III (NPT/CONF.2000/28 (Parts I-IV)).

Expressing deep concern regarding the growing dangers posed by the proliferation of weapons of mass destruction, inter alia, nuclear weapons, including that caused by proliferation networks,

Recognizing the importance of implementing Security Council resolution 1718 (2006) of 14 October 2006 with regard to the nuclear test proclaimed by the Democratic People's Republic of Korea on 9 October 2006, while welcoming the recent progress achieved by the Six-Party Talks,

1. *Reaffirms* the importance of all States parties to the Treaty on the Non-Proliferation of Nuclear Weapons[1] complying with their obligations under all the articles of the Treaty;

2. *Stresses* the importance of an effective Treaty review process, welcoming a successful start of the 2010 review process with the first session of the Preparatory Committee in 2007, and calls upon all States parties to the Treaty to work together to ensure that the second session of the Preparatory Committee, in 2008, is held constructively, in order to facilitate the successful outcome of the 2010 Review Conference of the Parties to the Treaty on the Non-Proliferation of Nuclear Weapons;

3. *Reaffirms* the importance of the universality of the Treaty, and calls upon States not parties to the Treaty to accede to it as non-nuclear-weapon States without delay and without conditions, and pending their accession to refrain from acts that would defeat the objective and purpose of the Treaty as well as to take practical steps in support of the Treaty;

4. *Encourages* further steps leading to nuclear disarmament, to which all States parties to the Treaty are committed under article VI of the Treaty, including deeper reductions in all types of nuclear weapons, and emphasizes the importance of applying irreversibility and verifiability, as well as increased transparency in a way that promotes international stability and undiminished security for all, in the process of working towards the elimination of nuclear weapons;

5. *Encourages* the Russian Federation and the United States of America to implement fully the Treaty on Strategic Offensive Reductions,[5] which should serve as a step for further nuclear disarmament, and to undertake nuclear arms reductions beyond those provided for by the Treaty, while welcoming the progress made by nuclear-weapon States, including the Russian Federation and the United States of America, on nuclear arms reductions;

6. *Encourages* States to continue to pursue efforts, within the framework of international cooperation, contributing to the reduction of nuclear-weapons-related materials;

---

[5] See CD/1674.

7. *Calls for* the nuclear-weapon States to further reduce the operational status of nuclear weapons systems in ways that promote international stability and security;

8. *Stresses* the necessity of a diminishing role for nuclear weapons in security policies to minimize the risk that these weapons will ever be used and to facilitate the process of their total elimination, in a way that promotes international stability and based on the principle of undiminished security for all;

9. *Urges* all States that have not yet done so to sign and ratify the Comprehensive Nuclear-Test-Ban Treaty[6] at the earliest opportunity with a view to its early entry into force, stresses the importance of maintaining existing moratoriums on nuclear-weapon test explosions pending the entry into force of the Treaty, and reaffirms the importance of the continued development of the Treaty verification regime, including the international monitoring system, which will be required to provide assurance of compliance with the Treaty;

10. *Calls upon* the Conference on Disarmament to immediately resume its substantive work to its fullest, considering the developments of this year in the Conference;

11. *Emphasizes* the importance of the immediate commencement of negotiations on a fissile material cut-off treaty and its early conclusion, and calls upon all nuclear-weapon States and States not parties to the Treaty on the Non-Proliferation of Nuclear Weapons to declare moratoriums on the production of fissile material for any nuclear weapons or other nuclear explosive devices pending the entry into force of the Treaty;

12. *Calls upon* all States to redouble their efforts to prevent and curb the proliferation of nuclear and other weapons of mass destruction and their means of delivery;

13. *Stresses* the importance of further efforts for non-proliferation, including the universalization of the International Atomic Energy Agency comprehensive safeguards agreements and Model Protocol Additional to the Agreement(s) between State(s) and the International Atomic Energy Agency for the Application of Safeguards approved by the Board of Governors of the International Atomic Energy Agency on 15 May 1997[7] and the full implementation of relevant Security Council resolutions including resolution 1540 (2004) of 28 April 2004;

14. *Encourages* all States to undertake concrete activities to implement, as appropriate, the recommendations contained in the report of the Secretary-General on the United Nations study on disarmament and non-proliferation

---

[6] See resolution 50/245.
[7] International Atomic Energy Agency, INFCIRC/540 (Corrected).

education, submitted to the General Assembly at its fifty-seventh session,[8] and to voluntarily share information on efforts they have been undertaking to that end;

15. *Encourages* the constructive role played by civil society in promoting nuclear non-proliferation and nuclear disarmament.

Action by the General Assembly

Date: 5 December 2007   Meeting: 61st meeting
Vote: 170-3-9   Report: A/62/391

Sponsors

Australia, Austria, Chile, Dominican Republic, Eritrea, Finland, Germany, Guatemala, Japan,* Lithuania, Luxembourg, Nepal, Netherlands, Spain, Switzerland, Ukraine

Co-sponsors

Afghanistan, Andorra, Belgium, Benin, Bosnia and Herzegovina, Bulgaria, Cameroon, Canada, Costa Rica, Croatia, Cyprus, Czech Republic, El Salvador, Equatorial Guinea, Gabon, Guinea, Haiti, Iceland, Iraq, Italy, Lebanon, Liechtenstein, Madagascar, Montenegro, Norway, Palau, Papua New Guinea, Paraguay, Peru, Samoa, Serbia, Slovenia, Solomon Islands, Swaziland, Thailand, the former Yugoslav Republic of Macedonia, Togo, Trinidad and Tobago, United Republic of Tanzania, Uruguay

Recorded vote

In favour:

Afghanistan, Albania, Algeria, Andorra, Antigua and Barbuda, Argentina, Armenia, Australia, Austria, Azerbaijan, Bahamas, Bahrain, Bangladesh, Barbados, Belarus, Belgium, Belize, Benin, Bolivia, Bosnia and Herzegovina, Botswana, Brazil, Brunei Darussalam, Bulgaria, Burkina Faso, Burundi, Cambodia, Cameroon, Canada, Cape Verde, Central African Republic, Chile, Colombia, Comoros, Congo, Costa Rica, Côte d'Ivoire, Croatia, Cyprus, Czech Republic, Denmark, Djibouti, Dominica, Dominican Republic, Ecuador, Egypt, El Salvador, Eritrea, Estonia, Ethiopia, Fiji, Finland, Gabon, Gambia, Georgia, Germany, Ghana, Greece, Grenada, Guatemala, Guinea, Guinea-Bissau, Guyana, Haiti, Honduras, Hungary, Iceland, Indonesia, Iraq, Ireland, Italy, Jamaica, Japan, Jordan, Kazakhstan, Kenya, Kuwait, Kyrgyzstan, Lao People's Democratic Republic, Latvia, Lebanon, Lesotho, Liberia, Libyan Arab Jamahiriya, Liechtenstein, Lithuania, Luxembourg, Madagascar, Malawi, Malaysia, Maldives, Mali, Malta, Marshall Islands, Mauritania, Mauritius, Mexico,

---

[8] A/57/124.
* The draft resolution was submitted by Japan.

Micronesia (Federated States of), Monaco, Mongolia, Montenegro, Morocco, Mozambique, Namibia, Nauru, Nepal, Netherlands, New Zealand, Niger, Nigeria, Norway, Oman, Palau, Panama, Papua New Guinea, Paraguay, Peru, Philippines, Poland, Portugal, Qatar, Republic of Korea, Republic of Moldova, Romania, Russian Federation, Rwanda, Saint Kitts and Nevis, Saint Lucia, Saint Vincent and the Grenadines, Samoa, San Marino, Sao Tome and Principe, Saudi Arabia, Senegal, Serbia, Sierra Leone, Singapore, Slovakia, Slovenia, Solomon Islands, Somalia, South Africa, Spain, Sri Lanka, Sudan, Suriname, Swaziland, Sweden, Switzerland, Syrian Arab Republic, Tajikistan, Thailand, the former Yugoslav Republic of Macedonia, Togo, Tonga, Trinidad and Tobago, Tunisia, Turkey, Turkmenistan, Ukraine, United Arab Emirates, United Kingdom of Great Britain and Northern Ireland, United Republic of Tanzania, Uruguay, Uzbekistan, Venezuela (Bolivarian Republic of), Viet Nam, Yemen, Zambia, Zimbabwe

Against:
Democratic People's Republic of Korea, India, United States of America

Abstaining:
Bhutan, China, Cuba, France, Iran (Islamic Republic of), Israel, Myanmar, Nicaragua, Pakistan

Action by the First Committee

Date: 30 October 2007   Meeting: 22nd meeting
Vote: 165-3-10   Draft resolution: A/C.1/62/L.30

Agenda item 98 (t)

62/38   Regional disarmament

Text

The General Assembly,

Recalling its resolutions 45/58 P of 4 December 1990, 46/36 I of 6 December 1991, 47/52 J of 9 December 1992, 48/75 I of 16 December 1993, 49/75 N of 15 December 1994, 50/70 K of 12 December 1995, 51/45 K of 10 December 1996, 52/38 P of 9 December 1997, 53/77 O of 4 December 1998, 54/54 N of 1 December 1999, 55/33 O of 20 November 2000, 56/24 H of 29 November 2001, 57/76 of 22 November 2002, 58/38 of 8 December 2003, 59/89 of 3 December 2004, 60/63 of 8 December 2005 and 61/80 of 6 December 2006 on regional disarmament,

Believing that the efforts of the international community to move towards the ideal of general and complete disarmament are guided by the inherent human desire for genuine peace and security, the elimination of the danger of war and the release of economic, intellectual and other resources for peaceful pursuits,

Affirming the abiding commitment of all States to the purposes and principles enshrined in the Charter of the United Nations in the conduct of their international relations,

Noting that essential guidelines for progress towards general and complete disarmament were adopted at the tenth special session of the General Assembly,[1]

Taking note of the guidelines and recommendations for regional approaches to disarmament within the context of global security adopted by the Disarmament Commission at its 1993 substantive session,[2]

Welcoming the prospects of genuine progress in the field of disarmament engendered in recent years as a result of negotiations between the two super-Powers,

Taking note of the recent proposals for disarmament at the regional and subregional levels,

Recognizing the importance of confidence-building measures for regional and international peace and security,

Convinced that endeavours by countries to promote regional disarmament, taking into account the specific characteristics of each region and in accordance

---

[1] See resolution S-10/2.
[2] *Official Records of the General Assembly, Forty-eighth Session, Supplement No. 42* (A/48/42), annex II.

with the principle of undiminished security at the lowest level of armaments, would enhance the security of all States and would thus contribute to international peace and security by reducing the risk of regional conflicts,

1. *Stresses* that sustained efforts are needed, within the framework of the Conference on Disarmament and under the umbrella of the United Nations, to make progress on the entire range of disarmament issues;

2. *Affirms* that global and regional approaches to disarmament complement each other and should therefore be pursued simultaneously to promote regional and international peace and security;

3. *Calls upon* States to conclude agreements, wherever possible, for nuclear non-proliferation, disarmament and confidence-building measures at the regional and subregional levels;

4. *Welcomes* the initiatives towards disarmament, nuclear non-proliferation and security undertaken by some countries at the regional and subregional levels;

5. *Supports and encourages* efforts aimed at promoting confidence-building measures at the regional and subregional levels to ease regional tensions and to further disarmament and nuclear non-proliferation measures at the regional and subregional levels;

6. *Decides* to include in the provisional agenda of its sixty-third session the item entitled "Regional disarmament".

Action by the General Assembly

Date: 5 December 2007   Meeting: 61st meeting
Vote: Adopted without a vote   Report: A/62/391

Sponsors

Bangladesh, Colombia, Ecuador, Egypt, Indonesia, Jordan, Kuwait, Malaysia, Nepal, **Pakistan**, Peru, Saudi Arabia, Sri Lanka, Sudan, Turkey

Co-sponsors

Liberia

Action by the First Committee

Date: 30 October 2007   Meeting: 22nd meeting
Vote: Adopted without a vote   Draft resolution: A/C.1/62/L.31

Agenda item 98 (w)

62/39 Follow-up to the Advisory Opinion of the International Court of Justice on the *Legality of the Threat or Use of Nuclear Weapons*

Text

The General Assembly,

Recalling its resolutions 49/75 K of 15 December 1994, 51/45 M of 10 December 1996, 52/38 O of 9 December 1997, 53/77 W of 4 December 1998, 54/54 Q of 1 December 1999, 55/33 X of 20 November 2000, 56/24 S of 29 November 2001, 57/85 of 22 November 2002, 58/46 of 8 December 2003, 59/83 of 3 December 2004, 60/76 of 8 December 2005 and 61/83 of 6 December 2006,

Convinced that the continuing existence of nuclear weapons poses a threat to all humanity and that their use would have catastrophic consequences for all life on Earth, and recognizing that the only defence against a nuclear catastrophe is the total elimination of nuclear weapons and the certainty that they will never be produced again,

Reaffirming the commitment of the international community to the goal of the total elimination of nuclear weapons and the creation of a nuclear-weapon-free world,

Mindful of the solemn obligations of States parties, undertaken in article VI of the Treaty on the Non-Proliferation of Nuclear Weapons,[1] particularly to pursue negotiations in good faith on effective measures relating to cessation of the nuclear arms race at an early date and to nuclear disarmament,

Recalling the principles and objectives for nuclear non-proliferation and disarmament adopted at the 1995 Review and Extension Conference of the Parties to the Treaty on the Non-Proliferation of Nuclear Weapons,[2]

Emphasizing the unequivocal undertaking by the nuclear-weapon States to accomplish the total elimination of their nuclear arsenals leading to nuclear disarmament, adopted at the 2000 Review Conference of the Parties to the Treaty on the Non-Proliferation of Nuclear Weapons,[3]

---

[1] United Nations, *Treaty Series*, vol. 729, No. 10485.
[2] *1995 Review and Extension Conference of the Parties to the Treaty on the Non-Proliferation of Nuclear Weapons, Final Document, Part I* (NPT/CONF.1995/32 (Part I) and Corr.2), annex, decision 2.
[3] *2000 Review Conference of the Parties to the Treaty on the Non-Proliferation of Nuclear Weapons, Final Document*, vol. I (NPT/CONF.2000/28 (Parts I and II)), part I, section entitled "Article VI and eighth to twelfth preambular paragraphs", para. 15:6.

Recalling the adoption of the Comprehensive Nuclear-Test-Ban Treaty in its resolution 50/245 of 10 September 1996, and expressing its satisfaction at the increasing number of States that have signed and ratified the Treaty,

Recognizing with satisfaction that the Antarctic Treaty[4] and the treaties of Tlatelolco,[5] Rarotonga,[6] Bangkok,[7] Pelindaba[8] and Semipalatinsk,[9] as well as Mongolia's nuclear-weapon-free status, are gradually freeing the entire southern hemisphere and adjacent areas covered by those treaties from nuclear weapons,

Stressing the importance of strengthening all existing nuclear-related disarmament and arms control and reduction measures,

Recognizing the need for a multilaterally negotiated and legally binding instrument to assure non-nuclear-weapon States against the threat or use of nuclear weapons,

Reaffirming the central role of the Conference on Disarmament as the sole multilateral disarmament negotiating forum, and regretting the lack of progress in disarmament negotiations, particularly nuclear disarmament, in the Conference during its 2007 session,

Emphasizing the need for the Conference on Disarmament to commence negotiations on a phased programme for the complete elimination of nuclear weapons with a specified framework of time,

Expressing its regret over the failure of the 2005 Review Conference of the Parties to the Treaty on the Non-Proliferation of Nuclear Weapons to reach agreement on any substantive issues,

Expressing its deep concern at the lack of progress in the implementation of the thirteen steps to implement article VI of the Treaty on the Non-Proliferation of Nuclear Weapons agreed to at the 2000 Review Conference of the Parties to the Treaty,[10]

Desiring to achieve the objective of a legally binding prohibition of the development, production, testing, deployment, stockpiling, threat or use of nuclear weapons and their destruction under effective international control,

---

[4] United Nations, *Treaty Series*, vol. 402, No. 5778.
[5] Ibid., vol. 634, No. 9068.
[6] See *The United Nations Disarmament Yearbook*, vol. 10: 1985 (United Nations publication, Sales No. E.86.IX.7), appendix VII.
[7] United Nations, *Treaty Series*, vol. 1981, No. 33873.
[8] A/50/426, annex.
[9] Treaty on a Nuclear-Weapon-Free Zone in Central Asia.
[10] See *2000 Review Conference of the Parties to the Treaty on the Non-Proliferation of Nuclear Weapons, Final Document*, vol. I (NPT/CONF.2000/28 (Parts I and II)), part I, section entitled "Article VI and eighth to twelfth preambular paragraphs", para. 15.

Recalling the advisory opinion of the International Court of Justice on the *Legality of the Threat or Use of Nuclear Weapons*, issued on 8 July 1996,[11]

Taking note of the relevant portions of the report of the Secretary-General relating to the implementation of resolution 61/83,[12]

1. *Underlines once again* the unanimous conclusion of the International Court of Justice that there exists an obligation to pursue in good faith and bring to a conclusion negotiations leading to nuclear disarmament in all its aspects under strict and effective international control;

2. *Calls once again upon* all States immediately to fulfil that obligation by commencing multilateral negotiations leading to an early conclusion of a nuclear weapons convention prohibiting the development, production, testing, deployment, stockpiling, transfer, threat or use of nuclear weapons and providing for their elimination;

3. *Requests* all States to inform the Secretary-General of the efforts and measures they have taken on the implementation of the present resolution and nuclear disarmament, and requests the Secretary-General to apprise the General Assembly of that information at its sixty-third session;

4. *Decides* to include in the provisional agenda of its sixty-third session the item entitled "Follow-up to the advisory opinion of the International Court of Justice on the *Legality of the Threat or Use of Nuclear Weapons*".

Action by the General Assembly

Date: 5 December 2007　　Meeting: 61st meeting
Vote: 127-27-27　　　　　　Report: A/62/391

Sponsors

Algeria, Bolivia, Brunei Darussalam, Burkina Faso, Chile, Costa Rica, Cuba, Dominican Republic, Ecuador, Guatemala, India, Indonesia, Iran (Islamic Republic of), Kuwait, Lao People's Democratic Republic, Libyan Arab Jamahiriya, **Malaysia**, Mexico, Myanmar, Nepal, Pakistan, Peru, Philippines, Qatar, Singapore, Syrian Arab Republic, Thailand, Viet Nam

Co-sponsors

Benin, Cambodia, Egypt, Honduras, Jamaica, Jordan, Mali, Nicaragua, Samoa, Sierra Leone, Uruguay

---

[11] A/51/218, annex; see also *Legality of the Threat or Use of Nuclear Weapons, Advisory Opinion, I.C.J. Reports 1996*, p. 226.
[12] A/62/165 and Add.1.

*Recorded vote**

In favour:
Afghanistan, Algeria, Antigua and Barbuda, Argentina, Austria, Bahamas, Bahrain, Bangladesh, Barbados, Belize, Benin, Bhutan, Bolivia, Botswana, Brazil, Brunei Darussalam, Bulgaria, Burkina Faso, Burundi, Cambodia, Cameroon, Cape Verde, Central African Republic, Chile, China, Colombia, Comoros, Congo, Costa Rica, Côte d'Ivoire, Cuba, Democratic People's Republic of Korea, Djibouti, Dominica, Dominican Republic, Ecuador, Egypt, El Salvador, Equatorial Guinea, Eritrea, Ethiopia, Fiji, Gabon, Gambia, Ghana, Grenada, Guatemala, Guinea, Guinea-Bissau, Guyana, Haiti, Honduras, India, Indonesia, Iran (Islamic Republic of), Iraq, Ireland, Jamaica, Jordan, Kenya, Kuwait, Lao People's Democratic Republic, Lebanon, Lesotho, Liberia, Libyan Arab Jamahiriya, Madagascar, Malawi, Malaysia, Maldives, Mali, Malta, Mauritania, Mauritius, Mexico, Mongolia, Morocco, Mozambique, Myanmar, Namibia, Nepal, New Zealand, Nicaragua, Niger, Nigeria, Oman, Pakistan, Panama, Papua New Guinea, Paraguay, Peru, Philippines, Qatar, Rwanda, Saint Kitts and Nevis, Saint Lucia, Saint Vincent and the Grenadines, Samoa, San Marino, Sao Tome and Principe, Saudi Arabia, Senegal, Sierra Leone, Singapore, Solomon Islands, Somalia, South Africa, Sri Lanka, Sudan, Suriname, Swaziland, Sweden, Syrian Arab Republic, Thailand, Togo, Tonga, Trinidad and Tobago, Tunisia, Turkmenistan, United Arab Emirates, United Republic of Tanzania, Uruguay, Venezuela (Bolivarian Republic of), Viet Nam, Yemen, Zambia, Zimbabwe

Against:
Albania, Belgium, Czech Republic, Denmark, France, Georgia, Germany, Greece, Hungary, Iceland, Israel, Italy, Latvia, Lithuania, Luxembourg, Netherlands, Norway, Palau, Poland, Portugal, Russian Federation, Slovakia, Slovenia, Spain, Turkey, United Kingdom of Great Britain and Northern Ireland, United States of America

Abstaining:
Andorra, Armenia, Australia, Azerbaijan, Belarus, Bosnia and Herzegovina, Canada, Croatia, Cyprus, Estonia, Finland, Japan, Kazakhstan, Kyrgyzstan, Liechtenstein, Marshall Islands, Micronesia (Federated States of), Montenegro, Republic of Korea, Republic of Moldova, Romania, Serbia, Switzerland, Tajikistan, the former Yugoslav Republic of Macedonia, Ukraine, Uzbekistan

Action by the First Committee

Date: 30 October 2007   Meeting: 22nd meeting
Vote: 121-25-29   Draft resolution: A/C.1/62/L.36

---

* Subsequent to the voting, the delegation of Bulgaria advised the Secretariat that it had intended to vote against. The voting tally above does not reflect this information.

Agenda item 98

62/40 Prevention of the illicit transfer and unauthorized access to and use of man-portable air defence systems

Text

The General Assembly,

Recalling its resolutions 58/42 and 58/54 of 8 December 2003, 58/241 of 23 December 2003, 59/90 of 3 December 2004, 60/77 of 8 December 2005 and 60/288 of 8 September 2006, and its decision 60/519 of 8 December 2005,

Recognizing that disarmament, arms control and non-proliferation are essential for the maintenance of international peace and security,

Acknowledging the authorized trade in man-portable air defence systems between Governments,

Acknowledging also the legitimate right of Governments to manufacture, import, export, transfer and possess man-portable air defence systems in the interests of their national security and self-defence,

Recognizing the threat to civil aviation, peacekeeping, crisis management and security posed by the illicit transfer and unauthorized access to and use of man-portable air defence systems,

Taking into account the fact that man-portable air defence systems are easily carried, concealed, fired and, in certain circumstances, obtained,

Recognizing that effective control over man-portable air defence systems acquires special importance in the context of the intensified international fight against global terrorism,

Convinced of the importance of effective national control of transfers of man-portable air defence systems and their training and instruction materials and of the safe and effective management of stockpiles of such weapons,

Acknowledging the role of the unauthorized transfer of relevant materials and information in assisting the illicit manufacture and illicit transfer of man-portable air defence systems and related components,

Welcoming the ongoing efforts of, and noting declarations by, various international and regional forums to enhance transport security and to strengthen management of man-portable air defence systems stockpiles in order to prevent the illicit transfer and unauthorized access to and use of such weapons,

Noting the importance of information exchange and transparency in the trade in man-portable air defence systems to build confidence and security among States and to prevent the illicit trade in and unauthorized access to such weapons,

Acknowledging the considerable efforts of some Member States to collect, secure and destroy voluntarily those man-portable air defence systems declared to be surplus by the competent national authority,

1. *Emphasizes* the importance of the full implementation of the Programme of Action to Prevent, Combat and Eradicate the Illicit Trade in Small Arms and Light Weapons in All Its Aspects, adopted by the United Nations Conference on the Illicit Trade in Small Arms and Light Weapons in All Its Aspects;[1]

2. *Urges* Member States to support current international, regional and national efforts to combat and prevent the illicit transfer of man-portable air defence systems and unauthorized access to and use of such weapons;

3. *Stresses* the importance of effective and comprehensive national controls on the production, stockpiling, transfer and brokering of man-portable air defence systems to prevent the illicit trade in and unauthorized access to and use of such weapons, their components and training and instruction materials;

4. *Encourages* Member States to enact or improve legislation, regulations, procedures and stockpile management practices and to assist other States, at their request, to exercise effective control over access to and transfer of man-portable air defence systems so as to prevent the illicit brokering and transfer of and unauthorized access to and use of such weapons;

5. *Also encourages* Member States, in accordance with their legal and constitutional processes, to enact or improve legislation, regulations and procedures to ban the transfer of man-portable air defence systems to non-State end-users and to ensure that such weapons are exported only to Governments or agents authorized by a Government;

6. *Encourages* initiatives to exchange information and to mobilize resources and technical expertise to assist States, at their request, in enhancing national controls and stockpile management practices to prevent unauthorized access to and use and transfer of man-portable air defence systems and to destroy excess or obsolete stockpiles of such weapons, as appropriate;

7. *Decides* to remain seized of the matter.

Action by the General Assembly

Date: 5 December 2007 Meeting: 61st meeting
Vote: Adopted without a vote Report: A/62/391

---

[1] See *Report of the United Nations Conference on the Illicit Trade in Small Arms and Light Weapons in All Its Aspects, New York, 9-20 July 2001* (A/CONF.192/15), chap. IV, para. 24.

Sponsors

Argentina, Armenia, **Australia**, Austria, Belgium, Bosnia and Herzegovina, Bulgaria, Cambodia, Canada, Chile, Croatia, Cyprus, Czech Republic, Denmark, Estonia, Finland, Germany, Greece, Hungary, Ireland, Italy, Jamaica, Japan, Kazakhstan, Kenya, Latvia, Lithuania, Luxembourg, Malta, Monaco, Netherlands, New Zealand, Norway, Poland, Portugal, Romania, Samoa, Serbia, Sierra Leone, Slovakia, Slovenia, Spain, Sweden, Switzerland, Thailand, the former Yugoslav Republic of Macedonia, Turkey, United Kingdom of Great Britain and Northern Ireland

Co-sponsors

Albania, Andorra, Cameroon, France, Ghana, Israel, Liberia, Montenegro, Papua New Guinea, Philippines, Russian Federation, Singapore

Action by the First Committee

Date: 1 November 2007 Meeting: 24th meeting
Vote: Adopted without a vote Draft resolution: A/C.1/62/L.38/Rev.1

Resolutions and decisions of the 62nd session of the General Assembly

Agenda item 98 (x)

62/41 Implementation of the Convention on the Prohibition of the Use, Stockpiling, Production and Transfer of Anti-personnel Mines and on Their Destruction

Text

The General Assembly,

Recalling its resolutions 54/54 B of 1 December 1999, 55/33 V of 20 November 2000, 56/24 M of 29 November 2001, 57/74 of 22 November 2002, 58/53 of 8 December 2003, 59/84 of 3 December 2004, 60/80 of 8 December 2005 and 61/84 of 6 December 2006,

Reaffirming its determination to put an end to the suffering and casualties caused by anti-personnel mines, which kill or maim hundreds of people every week, mostly innocent and defenceless civilians, including children, obstruct economic development and reconstruction, inhibit the repatriation of refugees and internally displaced persons and have other severe consequences for years after emplacement,

Believing it necessary to do the utmost to contribute in an efficient and coordinated manner to facing the challenge of removing anti-personnel mines placed throughout the world and to assure their destruction,

Wishing to do the utmost in ensuring assistance for the care and rehabilitation, including the social and economic reintegration, of mine victims,

Recalling that 2007 marks the tenth anniversary of the adoption and opening for signature of the Convention on the Prohibition of the Use, Stockpiling, Production and Transfer of Anti-personnel Mines and on Their Destruction,[1] and welcoming its entry into force on 1 March 1999,

Noting with satisfaction the work undertaken to implement the Convention and the substantial progress made towards ending, for all people and for all time, the suffering caused by anti-personnel mines, as well as regular reporting of this progress,

Recalling the first to seventh meetings of the States parties to the Convention held in Maputo (1999),[2] Geneva (2000),[3] Managua (2001),[4] Geneva

---

[1] United Nations, *Treaty Series*, vol. 2056, No. 35597.
[2] See APLC/MSP.1/1999/1.
[3] See APLC/MSP.2/2000/1.
[4] See APLC/MSP.3/2001/1.

(2002),[5] Bangkok (2003),[6] Zagreb (2005)[7] and Geneva (2006),[8] and the First Review Conference of the States Parties to the Convention, held in Nairobi (2004),[9]

Noting with satisfaction that additional States have ratified or acceded to the Convention, bringing the total number of States that have formally accepted the obligations of the Convention to one hundred and fifty-five,

Emphasizing the desirability of attracting the adherence of all States to the Convention, and determined to work strenuously towards the promotion of its universalization,

Noting with regret that anti-personnel mines continue to be used in conflicts around the world, causing human suffering and impeding post-conflict development,

1. *Invites* all States that have not signed the Convention on the Prohibition of the Use, Stockpiling, Production and Transfer of Anti-personnel Mines and on Their Destruction[1] to accede to it without delay;

2. *Urges* all States that have signed but have not ratified the Convention to ratify it without delay;

3. *Stresses* the importance of the full and effective implementation of and compliance with the Convention, including through the continued implementation of the Nairobi Action Plan 2005-2009;[10]

4. *Urges* all States parties to provide the Secretary-General with complete and timely information as required under article 7 of the Convention in order to promote transparency and compliance with the Convention;

5. *Invites* all States that have not ratified the Convention or acceded to it to provide, on a voluntary basis, information to make global mine action efforts more effective;

6. *Renews its call upon* all States and other relevant parties to work together to promote, support and advance the care, rehabilitation and social and economic reintegration of mine victims, mine risk education programmes and the removal and destruction of anti-personnel mines placed or stockpiled throughout the world;

7. *Urges* all States to remain seized of the issue at the highest political level and, where in a position to do so, to promote adherence to the Convention through bilateral, subregional, regional and multilateral contacts, outreach, seminars and other means;

---

[5] See APLC/MSP.4/2002/1.
[6] See APLC/MSP.5/2003/5.
[7] See APLC/MSP.6/2005/5.
[8] See APLC/MSP.7/2006/5.
[9] See APLC/CONF/2004/5 and Corr.1.
[10] Ibid., part III.

8. *Reiterates its invitation and encouragement* to all interested States, the United Nations, other relevant international organizations or institutions, regional organizations, the International Committee of the Red Cross and relevant non-governmental organizations to participate in the eighth meeting of the States parties to the Convention, to be held in Jordan from 18 to 22 November 2007, and in the intersessional work programme established at the first meeting of the States parties and further developed at subsequent meetings of the States parties;

9. *Requests* the Secretary-General, in accordance with article 11, paragraph 2, of the Convention, to undertake the preparations necessary to convene the next meeting of the States parties and, pending a decision to be taken at the eighth meeting of States parties, and on behalf of the States parties and in accordance with article 11, paragraph 4, of the Convention, to invite States not parties to the Convention, as well as the United Nations, other relevant international organizations or institutions, regional organizations, the International Committee of the Red Cross and relevant non-governmental organizations to attend the ninth meeting of the States parties as observers;

10. *Decides* to remain seized of the matter.

Action by the General Assembly

Date: 5 December 2007 Meeting: 61st meeting
Vote: 164-0-18 Report: A/62/391

Sponsors

Australia, Croatia, Jordan

Recorded vote

In favour:
Afghanistan, Albania, Algeria, Andorra, Antigua and Barbuda, Argentina, Armenia, Australia, Austria, Azerbaijan, Bahamas, Bahrain, Bangladesh, Barbados, Belarus, Belgium, Belize, Benin, Bhutan, Bolivia, Bosnia and Herzegovina, Botswana, Brazil, Brunei Darussalam, Bulgaria, Burkina Faso, Burundi, Cambodia, Cameroon, Canada, Cape Verde, Central African Republic, Chile, China, Colombia, Comoros, Congo, Costa Rica, Côte d'Ivoire, Croatia, Cyprus, Czech Republic, Denmark, Djibouti, Dominica, Dominican Republic, Ecuador, El Salvador, Equatorial Guinea, Eritrea, Estonia, Ethiopia, Fiji, Finland, France, Gabon, Gambia, Georgia, Germany, Ghana, Greece, Grenada, Guatemala, Guinea, Guinea-Bissau, Guyana, Haiti, Honduras, Hungary, Iceland, Indonesia, Iraq, Ireland, Italy, Jamaica, Japan, Jordan, Kazakhstan, Kenya, Kuwait, Lao People's Democratic Republic, Latvia, Lesotho, Liberia, Liechtenstein, Lithuania, Luxembourg, Madagascar, Malawi, Malaysia, Maldives, Mali, Malta, Marshall Islands, Mauritania, Mauritius, Mexico, Micronesia (Federated

States of), Monaco, Mongolia, Montenegro, Morocco, Mozambique, Namibia, Nauru, Netherlands, New Zealand, Nicaragua, Niger, Nigeria, Norway, Oman, Palau, Panama, Papua New Guinea, Paraguay, Peru, Philippines, Poland, Portugal, Qatar, Republic of Moldova, Romania, Rwanda, Saint Kitts and Nevis, Saint Lucia, Saint Vincent and the Grenadines, Samoa, San Marino, Sao Tome and Principe, Senegal, Serbia, Sierra Leone, Singapore, Slovakia, Slovenia, Solomon Islands, Somalia, South Africa, Spain, Sri Lanka, Sudan, Suriname, Swaziland, Sweden, Switzerland, Tajikistan, Thailand, the former Yugoslav Republic of Macedonia, Togo, Tonga, Trinidad and Tobago, Tunisia, Turkey, Turkmenistan, Ukraine, United Arab Emirates, United Kingdom of Great Britain and Northern Ireland, United Republic of Tanzania, Uruguay, Venezuela (Bolivarian Republic of), Yemen, Zambia, Zimbabwe

Against:
None

Abstaining:
Cuba, Democratic People's Republic of Korea, Egypt, India, Iran (Islamic Republic of), Israel, Kyrgyzstan, Lebanon, Libyan Arab Jamahiriya, Myanmar, Nepal, Pakistan, Republic of Korea, Russian Federation, Syrian Arab Republic, United States of America, Uzbekistan, Viet Nam

Action by the First Committee

Date: 31 October 2007　　　Meeting:　　23rd meeting
Vote: 154-0-18　　　　　　　Draft resolution: A/C.1/62/L.39

Agenda item 98 (s)

62/42   Nuclear disarmament

Text

The General Assembly,

Recalling its resolution 49/75 E of 15 December 1994 on a step-by-step reduction of the nuclear threat, and its resolutions 50/70 P of 12 December 1995, 51/45 O of 10 December 1996, 52/38 L of 9 December 1997, 53/77 X of 4 December 1998, 54/54 P of 1 December 1999, 55/33 T of 20 November 2000, 56/24 R of 29 November 2001, 57/79 of 22 November 2002, 58/56 of 8 December 2003, 59/77 of 3 December 2004, 60/70 of 8 December 2005 and 61/78 of 6 December 2006 on nuclear disarmament,

Reaffirming the commitment of the international community to the goal of the total elimination of nuclear weapons and the establishment of a nuclear-weapon-free world,

Bearing in mind that the Convention on the Prohibition of the Development, Production and Stockpiling of Bacteriological (Biological) and Toxin Weapons and on Their Destruction of 1972[1] and the Convention on the Prohibition of the Development, Production, Stockpiling and Use of Chemical Weapons and on Their Destruction of 1993[2] have already established legal regimes on the complete prohibition of biological and chemical weapons, respectively, and determined to achieve a nuclear weapons convention on the prohibition of the development, testing, production, stockpiling, loan, transfer, use and threat of use of nuclear weapons and on their destruction, and to conclude such an international convention at an early date,

Recognizing that there now exist conditions for the establishment of a world free of nuclear weapons, and stressing the need to take concrete practical steps towards achieving this goal,

Bearing in mind paragraph 50 of the Final Document of the Tenth Special Session of the General Assembly,[3] the first special session devoted to disarmament, calling for the urgent negotiation of agreements for the cessation of the qualitative improvement and development of nuclear-weapon systems, and for a comprehensive and phased programme with agreed time frames, wherever feasible, for the progressive and balanced reduction of nuclear weapons and their means of delivery, leading to their ultimate and complete elimination at the earliest possible time,

---

[1] United Nations, *Treaty Series*, vol. 1015, No. 14860.
[2] Ibid., vol. 1974, No. 33757.
[3] Resolution S-10/2.

Reaffirming the conviction of the States parties to the Treaty on the Non-Proliferation of Nuclear Weapons[4] that the Treaty is a cornerstone of nuclear non-proliferation and nuclear disarmament and the importance of the decision on strengthening the review process for the Treaty, the decision on principles and objectives for nuclear non-proliferation and disarmament, the decision on the extension of the Treaty and the resolution on the Middle East, adopted by the 1995 Review and Extension Conference of the Parties to the Treaty on the Non-Proliferation of Nuclear Weapons,[5]

Stressing the importance of the thirteen steps for the systematic and progressive efforts to achieve the objective of nuclear disarmament leading to the total elimination of nuclear weapons, as agreed to by the States parties in the Final Document of the 2000 Review Conference of the Parties to the Treaty on the Non-Proliferation of Nuclear Weapons,[6]

Reiterating the highest priority accorded to nuclear disarmament in the Final Document of the Tenth Special Session of the General Assembly and by the international community,

Reiterating its call for an early entry into force of the Comprehensive Nuclear-Test-Ban Treaty,[7]

Noting with appreciation the entry into force of the Treaty on the Reduction and Limitation of Strategic Offensive Arms (START I),[8] to which Belarus, Kazakhstan, the Russian Federation, Ukraine and the United States of America are States parties,

Noting with appreciation also the entry into force of the Treaty on Strategic Offensive Reductions ("the Moscow Treaty") between the United States of America and the Russian Federation[9] as a significant step towards reducing their deployed strategic nuclear weapons, while calling for further irreversible deep cuts in their nuclear arsenals,

Noting with appreciation further the unilateral measures taken by the nuclear-weapon States for nuclear arms limitation, and encouraging them to take further such measures, while reiterating deep concern over the slow pace of progress towards nuclear disarmament and the lack of progress by the

---

[4] United Nations, *Treaty Series*, vol. 729, No. 10485.
[5] See *1995 Review and Extension Conference of the Parties to the Treaty on the Non-Proliferation of Nuclear Weapons, Final Document, Part I* (NPT/CONF.1995/32 (Part I) and Corr.2), annex.
[6] See *2000 Review Conference of the Parties to the Treaty on the Non-Proliferation of Nuclear Weapons, Final Document*, vol. I (NPT/CONF.2000/28 (Parts I and II)), part I, section entitled "Article VI and eighth to twelfth preambular paragraphs", para. 15.
[7] See resolution 50/245.
[8] *The United Nations Disarmament Yearbook*, vol. 16: 1991 (United Nations publication, Sales No. E.92.IX.1), appendix II.
[9] See CD/1674.

nuclear-weapon States towards accomplishing the total elimination of their nuclear arsenals,

Recognizing the complementarity of bilateral, plurilateral and multilateral negotiations on nuclear disarmament, and that bilateral negotiations can never replace multilateral negotiations in this respect,

Noting the support expressed in the Conference on Disarmament and in the General Assembly for the elaboration of an international convention to assure non-nuclear-weapon States against the use or threat of use of nuclear weapons, and the multilateral efforts in the Conference on Disarmament to reach agreement on such an international convention at an early date,

Recalling the advisory opinion of the International Court of Justice on the *Legality of the Threat or Use of Nuclear Weapons*, issued on 8 July 1996,[10] and welcoming the unanimous reaffirmation by all Judges of the Court that there exists an obligation for all States to pursue in good faith and bring to a conclusion negotiations leading to nuclear disarmament in all its aspects under strict and effective international control,

Mindful of paragraph 64 of the Final Document of the Ministerial Meeting of the Coordinating Bureau of the Movement of Non-Aligned Countries, held in Putrajaya, Malaysia, on 29 and 30 May 2006,[11]

Recalling paragraph 70 and other relevant recommendations in the Final Document of the Fourteenth Conference of Heads of State or Government of Non-Aligned Countries, held in Havana on 15 and 16 September 2006,[12] calling upon the Conference on Disarmament to establish, as soon as possible and as the highest priority, an ad hoc committee on nuclear disarmament and to commence negotiations on a phased programme for the complete elimination of nuclear weapons with a specified time framework,

Reaffirming the specific mandate conferred upon the Disarmament Commission by the General Assembly, in its decision 52/492 of 8 September 1998, to discuss the subject of nuclear disarmament as one of its main substantive agenda items,

Recalling the United Nations Millennium Declaration,[13] in which Heads of State and Government resolved to strive for the elimination of weapons of mass destruction, in particular nuclear weapons, and to keep all options open for achieving this aim, including the possibility of convening an international conference to identify ways of eliminating nuclear dangers,

---

[10] A/51/218, annex; see also *Legality of the Threat or Use of Nuclear Weapons, Advisory Opinion, I.C.J. Reports 1996*, p. 226.
[11] A/60/1002-S/2006/718, annex I.
[12] A/61/472-S/2006/780, annex I.
[13] See resolution 55/2.

Reaffirming that, in accordance with the Charter of the United Nations, States should refrain from the use or threat of use of nuclear weapons in settling their disputes in international relations,

Seized of the danger of the use of weapons of mass destruction, particularly nuclear weapons, in terrorist acts and the urgent need for concerted international efforts to control and overcome it,

1. *Recognizes* that the time is now opportune for all the nuclear-weapon States to take effective disarmament measures with a view to achieving the elimination of these weapons;

2. *Reaffirms* that nuclear disarmament and nuclear non-proliferation are substantively interrelated and mutually reinforcing, that the two processes must go hand in hand and that there is a genuine need for a systematic and progressive process of nuclear disarmament;

3. *Welcomes and encourages* the efforts to establish new nuclear-weapon-free zones in different parts of the world on the basis of agreements or arrangements freely arrived at among the States of the regions concerned, which is an effective measure for limiting the further spread of nuclear weapons geographically and contributes to the cause of nuclear disarmament;

4. *Recognizes* that there is a genuine need to diminish the role of nuclear weapons in strategic doctrines and security policies to minimize the risk that these weapons will ever be used and to facilitate the process of their total elimination;

5. *Urges* the nuclear-weapon States to stop immediately the qualitative improvement, development, production and stockpiling of nuclear warheads and their delivery systems;

6. *Also urges* the nuclear-weapon States, as an interim measure, to de-alert and deactivate immediately their nuclear weapons and to take other concrete measures to reduce further the operational status of their nuclear-weapon systems;

7. *Reiterates its call upon* the nuclear-weapon States to undertake the step-by-step reduction of the nuclear threat and to carry out effective nuclear disarmament measures with a view to achieving the total elimination of these weapons;

8. *Calls upon* the nuclear-weapon States, pending the achievement of the total elimination of nuclear weapons, to agree on an internationally and legally binding instrument on a joint undertaking not to be the first to use nuclear weapons, and calls upon all States to conclude an internationally and legally binding instrument on security assurances of non-use and non-threat of use of nuclear weapons against non-nuclear-weapon States;

9. *Urges* the nuclear-weapon States to commence plurilateral negotiations among themselves at an appropriate stage on further deep reductions of nuclear weapons as an effective measure of nuclear disarmament;

10. *Underlines* the importance of applying the principle of irreversibility to the process of nuclear disarmament, and nuclear and other related arms control and reduction measures;

11. *Underscores* the importance of the unequivocal undertaking by the nuclear-weapon States, in the Final Document of the 2000 Review Conference of the Parties to the Treaty on the Non-Proliferation of Nuclear Weapons, to accomplish the total elimination of their nuclear arsenals leading to nuclear disarmament, to which all States parties are committed under article VI of the Treaty,[14] and the reaffirmation by the States parties that the total elimination of nuclear weapons is the only absolute guarantee against the use or threat of use of nuclear weapons;[15]

12. *Calls for* the full and effective implementation of the thirteen steps for nuclear disarmament contained in the Final Document of the 2000 Review Conference;[6]

13. *Urges* the nuclear-weapon States to carry out further reductions of non-strategic nuclear weapons, based on unilateral initiatives and as an integral part of the nuclear arms reduction and disarmament process;

14. *Calls for* the immediate commencement of negotiations in the Conference on Disarmament on a non-discriminatory, multilateral and internationally and effectively verifiable treaty banning the production of fissile material for nuclear weapons or other nuclear explosive devices on the basis of the report of the Special Coordinator[16] and the mandate contained therein;

15. *Urges* the Conference on Disarmament to agree on a programme of work that includes the immediate commencement of negotiations on such a treaty with a view to their conclusion within five years;

16. *Calls for* the conclusion of an international legal instrument or instruments on adequate security assurances to non-nuclear-weapon States;

17. *Also calls for* the early entry into force and strict observance of the Comprehensive Nuclear-Test-Ban Treaty;[7]

18. *Expresses its regret* that the 2005 Review Conference of the Parties to the Treaty on the Non-Proliferation of Nuclear Weapons was unable to achieve any substantive result and that the 2005 World Summit Outcome adopted by

---

[14] *2000 Review Conference of the Parties to the Treaty on the Non-Proliferation of Nuclear Weapons, Final Document*, vol. I (NPT/CONF.2000/28 (Parts I and II)), part I, section entitled "Article VI and eighth to twelfth preambular paragraphs", para. 15:6.
[15] Ibid., section entitled "Article VII and the security of non-nuclear-weapon States", para. 2.
[16] CD/1299.

the General Assembly[17] failed to make any reference to nuclear disarmament and nuclear non-proliferation;

19. *Also expresses its regret* that the Conference on Disarmament was unable to establish an ad hoc committee to deal with nuclear disarmament early in 2007, as called for by the General Assembly in its resolution 61/78;

20. *Reiterates its call upon* the Conference on Disarmament to establish, on a priority basis, an ad hoc committee to deal with nuclear disarmament early in 2008 and to commence negotiations on a phased programme of nuclear disarmament leading to the eventual total elimination of nuclear weapons;

21. *Calls for* the convening of an international conference on nuclear disarmament in all its aspects at an early date to identify and deal with concrete measures of nuclear disarmament;

22. *Requests* the Secretary-General to submit to the General Assembly at its sixty-third session a report on the implementation of the present resolution;

23. *Decides* to include in the provisional agenda of its sixty-third session the item entitled "Nuclear disarmament".

Action by the General Assembly

Date: 5 December 2007   Meeting: 61st meeting
Vote: 117-47-17   Report: A/62/391

Sponsors

Algeria, Bangladesh, Bhutan, Brunei Darussalam, Burkina Faso, Cambodia, Central African Republic, Congo, Cuba, Guinea, Haiti, Indonesia, Iran (Islamic Republic of), Jordan, Kenya, Lao People's Democratic Republic, Madagascar, Malaysia, Mongolia, **Myanmar**, Namibia, Nepal, Philippines, Samoa, Saudi Arabia, Sierra Leone, Sri Lanka, Suriname, Thailand, Uganda, Venezuela (Bolivarian Republic of), Viet Nam, Zimbabwe

Co-sponsors

Dominican Republic, Libyan Arab Jamahiriya, Singapore, Solomon Islands, Zambia

Recorded vote*

In favour:

Afghanistan, Algeria, Antigua and Barbuda, Argentina, Bahamas, Bahrain, Bangladesh, Barbados, Belize, Benin, Bhutan, Bolivia, Botswana, Brazil, Brunei Darussalam, Burkina Faso, Burundi, Cambodia, Cameroon, Cape

---

[17] See resolution 60/1.

* Subsequent to the voting, the delegation of Nauru advised the Secretariat that it had intended to vote in favour. The voting tally above does not reflect this information.

Verde, Central African Republic, Chile, China, Colombia, Comoros, Congo, Costa Rica, Côte d'Ivoire, Cuba, Democratic People's Republic of Korea, Djibouti, Dominica, Dominican Republic, Ecuador, Egypt, El Salvador, Equatorial Guinea, Eritrea, Ethiopia, Fiji, Gabon, Gambia, Ghana, Grenada, Guatemala, Guinea, Guinea-Bissau, Guyana, Haiti, Honduras, Indonesia, Iran (Islamic Republic of), Iraq, Jamaica, Jordan, Kenya, Kuwait, Lao People's Democratic Republic, Lebanon, Lesotho, Liberia, Libyan Arab Jamahiriya, Madagascar, Malawi, Malaysia, Maldives, Mali, Mauritania, Mexico, Mongolia, Morocco, Mozambique, Myanmar, Namibia, Nepal, New Zealand, Nicaragua, Niger, Nigeria, Oman, Panama, Papua New Guinea, Paraguay, Peru, Philippines, Qatar, Rwanda, Saint Kitts and Nevis, Saint Lucia, Saint Vincent and the Grenadines, Samoa, Sao Tome and Principe, Saudi Arabia, Senegal, Sierra Leone, Singapore, Solomon Islands, Somalia, South Africa, Sri Lanka, Sudan, Suriname, Swaziland, Syrian Arab Republic, Thailand, Togo, Tonga, Trinidad and Tobago, Tunisia, United Arab Emirates, United Republic of Tanzania, Uruguay, Venezuela (Bolivarian Republic of), Viet Nam, Yemen, Zambia, Zimbabwe

Against:
Albania, Andorra, Australia, Belgium, Bosnia and Herzegovina, Bulgaria, Canada, Croatia, Cyprus, Czech Republic, Denmark, Estonia, Finland, France, Georgia, Germany, Greece, Hungary, Iceland, Israel, Italy, Latvia, Liechtenstein, Lithuania, Luxembourg, Marshall Islands, Micronesia (Federated States of), Monaco, Montenegro, Netherlands, Norway, Palau, Poland, Portugal, Republic of Moldova, Romania, San Marino, Serbia, Slovakia, Slovenia, Spain, Switzerland, the former Yugoslav Republic of Macedonia, Turkey, Ukraine, United Kingdom of Great Britain and Northern Ireland, United States of America

Abstaining:
Armenia, Austria, Azerbaijan, Belarus, India, Ireland, Japan, Kazakhstan, Kyrgyzstan, Malta, Mauritius, Pakistan, Republic of Korea, Russian Federation, Sweden, Tajikistan, Uzbekistan

Action by the First Committee

Date: 30 October 2007 Meeting: 22nd meeting
Vote: 113-45-17 Draft resolution: A/C.1/62/L.40

Agenda item 98 (q)

62/43   Transparency and confidence-building measures in outer space activities

Text

The General Assembly,

Recalling its resolutions 60/66 of 8 December 2005 and 61/75 of 6 December 2006,

Reaffirming that the prevention of an arms race in outer space would avert a grave danger to international peace and security,

Conscious that further measures should be examined in the search for agreements to prevent an arms race in outer space, including the weaponization of outer space,

Recalling, in this context, its previous resolutions, including resolutions 45/55 B of 4 December 1990 and 48/74 B of 16 December 1993, which, inter alia, emphasize the need for increased transparency and confirm the importance of confidence-building measures as a means conducive to ensuring the attainment of the objective of the prevention of an arms race in outer space,

Recalling also the report of the Secretary-General of 15 October 1993 to the General Assembly at its forty-eighth session, the annex to which contains the study by governmental experts on the application of confidence-building measures in outer space,[1]

Noting the constructive debate which the Conference on Disarmament held on this subject in 2007,

Noting also the contribution of Member States which have submitted to the Secretary-General concrete proposals on international outer space transparency and confidence-building measures pursuant to paragraph 1 of resolution 61/75,

1.   *Takes note* of the report of the Secretary-General containing concrete proposals from Member States on international outer space transparency and confidence-building measures;[2]

2.   *Invites* all Member States to continue to submit to the Secretary-General concrete proposals on international outer space transparency and confidence-building measures in the interest of maintaining international peace and security and promoting international cooperation and the prevention of an arms race in outer space;

3.   *Requests* the Secretary-General to submit to the General Assembly at its sixty-third session a report with an annex containing concrete proposals from

---
[1] A/48/305 and Corr.1.
[2] A/62/114 and Add.1.

Member States on international outer space transparency and confidence-building measures;

4. *Decides* to include in the provisional agenda of its sixty-third session the item entitled "Transparency and confidence-building measures in outer space activities".

Action by the General Assembly

Date: 5 December 2007   Meeting: 61st meeting
Vote: 179-1-1   Report: A/62/391

Sponsors

Armenia, Austria, Belarus, China, Cyprus, Denmark, Germany, Greece, Ireland, Kazakhstan, Luxembourg, Mongolia, Netherlands, New Zealand, Romania, **Russian Federation**, Spain, Switzerland, Tajikistan, Uzbekistan, Venezuela (Bolivarian Republic of)

Co-sponsors

Belgium, Bulgaria, Cameroon, Chile, Costa Rica, Cuba, Finland, Guatemala, Indonesia, Italy, Kyrgyzstan, Malta, Myanmar, Norway, Pakistan, Portugal, Serbia, Slovenia, Sweden, the former Yugoslav Republic of Macedonia, Turkey, Turkmenistan, Viet Nam

Recorded vote

In favour:

Afghanistan, Albania, Algeria, Andorra, Antigua and Barbuda, Argentina, Armenia, Australia, Austria, Azerbaijan, Bahamas, Bahrain, Bangladesh, Barbados, Belarus, Belgium, Belize, Benin, Bhutan, Bolivia, Bosnia and Herzegovina, Botswana, Brazil, Brunei Darussalam, Bulgaria, Burkina Faso, Burundi, Cambodia, Cameroon, Canada, Cape Verde, Central African Republic, Chile, China, Colombia, Comoros, Congo, Costa Rica, Côte d'Ivoire, Croatia, Cuba, Cyprus, Czech Republic, Democratic People's Republic of Korea, Denmark, Djibouti, Dominican Republic, Ecuador, Egypt, El Salvador, Equatorial Guinea, Eritrea, Estonia, Ethiopia, Fiji, Finland, France, Gabon, Gambia, Georgia, Germany, Ghana, Greece, Grenada, Guatemala, Guinea, Guinea-Bissau, Guyana, Haiti, Honduras, Hungary, Iceland, India, Indonesia, Iran (Islamic Republic of), Iraq, Ireland, Italy, Jamaica, Japan, Jordan, Kazakhstan, Kenya, Kuwait, Kyrgyzstan, Lao People's Democratic Republic, Latvia, Lebanon, Lesotho, Liberia, Libyan Arab Jamahiriya, Liechtenstein, Lithuania, Luxembourg, Madagascar, Malawi, Malaysia, Maldives, Mali, Malta, Marshall Islands, Mauritania, Mauritius, Mexico, Micronesia (Federated States of), Monaco, Mongolia, Montenegro, Morocco, Mozambique, Myanmar, Namibia, Nepal, Netherlands, New Zealand, Nicaragua, Niger, Nigeria, Norway, Oman, Pakistan, Palau, Panama, Papua New

Guinea, Paraguay, Peru, Philippines, Poland, Portugal, Qatar, Republic of Korea, Republic of Moldova, Romania, Russian Federation, Rwanda, Saint Kitts and Nevis, Saint Lucia, Saint Vincent and the Grenadines, Samoa, San Marino, Sao Tome and Principe, Saudi Arabia, Senegal, Serbia, Sierra Leone, Singapore, Slovakia, Slovenia, Solomon Islands, Somalia, South Africa, Spain, Sri Lanka, Sudan, Suriname, Swaziland, Sweden, Switzerland, Syrian Arab Republic, Tajikistan, Thailand, the former Yugoslav Republic of Macedonia, Togo, Tonga, Trinidad and Tobago, Tunisia, Turkey, Turkmenistan, Ukraine, United Arab Emirates, United Kingdom of Great Britain and Northern Ireland, United Republic of Tanzania, Uruguay, Uzbekistan, Venezuela (Bolivarian Republic of), Viet Nam, Yemen, Zambia, Zimbabwe

Against:
United States of America

Abstaining:
Israel

Action by the First Committee

Date: 31 October 2007 Meeting: 23rd meeting
Vote: 168-1-1 Draft resolution: A/C.1/62/L.41

Agenda item 98 (v)

62/44   Conventional arms control at the regional and subregional levels

Text

The General Assembly,

Recalling its resolutions 48/75 J of 16 December 1993, 49/75 O of 15 December 1994, 50/70 L of 12 December 1995, 51/45 Q of 10 December 1996, 52/38 Q of 9 December 1997, 53/77 P of 4 December 1998, 54/54 M of 1 December 1999, 55/33 P of 20 November 2000, 56/24 I of 29 November 2001, 57/77 of 22 November 2002, 58/39 of 8 December 2003, 59/88 of 3 December 2004, 60/75 of 8 December 2005 and 61/82 of 6 December 2006,

Recognizing the crucial role of conventional arms control in promoting regional and international peace and security,

Convinced that conventional arms control needs to be pursued primarily in the regional and subregional contexts since most threats to peace and security in the post-cold-war era arise mainly among States located in the same region or subregion,

Aware that the preservation of a balance in the defence capabilities of States at the lowest level of armaments would contribute to peace and stability and should be a prime objective of conventional arms control,

Desirous of promoting agreements to strengthen regional peace and security at the lowest possible level of armaments and military forces,

Noting with particular interest the initiatives taken in this regard in different regions of the world, in particular the commencement of consultations among a number of Latin American countries and the proposals for conventional arms control made in the context of South Asia, and recognizing, in the context of this subject, the relevance and value of the Treaty on Conventional Armed Forces in Europe,[1] which is a cornerstone of European security,

Believing that militarily significant States and States with larger military capabilities have a special responsibility in promoting such agreements for regional security,

Believing also that an important objective of conventional arms control in regions of tension should be to prevent the possibility of military attack launched by surprise and to avoid aggression,

1.   *Decides* to give urgent consideration to the issues involved in conventional arms control at the regional and subregional levels;

---

[1] CD/1064.

2. *Requests* the Conference on Disarmament to consider the formulation of principles that can serve as a framework for regional agreements on conventional arms control, and looks forward to a report of the Conference on this subject;

3. *Requests* the Secretary-General, in the meantime, to seek the views of Member States on the subject and to submit a report to the General Assembly at its sixty-third session;

4. *Decides* to include in the provisional agenda of its sixty-third session the item entitled "Conventional arms control at the regional and subregional levels".

Action by the General Assembly

Date: 5 December 2007   Meeting: 61st meeting
Vote: 177-1-1   Report: A/62/391

Sponsors

Bangladesh, Belarus, Egypt, Malaysia, Nepal, **Pakistan**, Peru, Spain, the former Yugoslav Republic of Macedonia, Ukraine

Co-sponsors

Dominican Republic, Liberia, Syrian Arab Republic

*Recorded vote**

In favour:

Afghanistan, Albania, Algeria, Andorra, Antigua and Barbuda, Argentina, Armenia, Australia, Austria, Azerbaijan, Bahamas, Bahrain, Bangladesh, Barbados, Belarus, Belgium, Belize, Benin, Bolivia, Bosnia and Herzegovina, Botswana, Brazil, Brunei Darussalam, Bulgaria, Burkina Faso, Burundi, Cambodia, Cameroon, Canada, Cape Verde, Central African Republic, Chile, China, Colombia, Comoros, Congo, Costa Rica, Côte d'Ivoire, Croatia, Cyprus, Czech Republic, Democratic People's Republic of Korea, Denmark, Djibouti, Dominica, Dominican Republic, Ecuador, Egypt, El Salvador, Equatorial Guinea, Eritrea, Estonia, Ethiopia, Fiji, Finland, France, Gabon, Gambia, Georgia, Germany, Ghana, Greece, Grenada, Guatemala, Guinea, Guinea-Bissau, Guyana, Haiti, Honduras, Hungary, Iceland, Indonesia, Iran (Islamic Republic of), Iraq, Ireland, Israel, Italy, Jamaica, Japan, Jordan, Kazakhstan, Kenya, Kuwait, Kyrgyzstan, Latvia, Lebanon, Lesotho, Liberia, Libyan Arab Jamahiriya, Liechtenstein, Lithuania, Luxembourg, Madagascar, Malawi, Malaysia, Maldives, Mali, Malta, Marshall Islands, Mauritania, Mauritius, Mexico, Micronesia (Federated States of), Monaco, Mongolia, Montenegro,

---

* Subsequent to the voting, the delegation of Nauru advised the Secretariat that it had intended to vote in favour. The voting tally above does not reflect this information.

Morocco, Mozambique, Myanmar, Namibia, Nepal, Netherlands, New Zealand, Nicaragua, Niger, Nigeria, Norway, Oman, Pakistan, Palau, Panama, Papua New Guinea, Paraguay, Peru, Philippines, Poland, Portugal, Qatar, Republic of Korea, Republic of Moldova, Romania, Russian Federation, Rwanda, Saint Kitts and Nevis, Saint Lucia, Saint Vincent and the Grenadines, Samoa, San Marino, Sao Tome and Principe, Saudi Arabia, Senegal, Serbia, Sierra Leone, Singapore, Slovakia, Slovenia, Solomon Islands, Somalia, South Africa, Spain, Sri Lanka, Sudan, Suriname, Swaziland, Sweden, Switzerland, Syrian Arab Republic, Tajikistan, Thailand, the former Yugoslav Republic of Macedonia, Togo, Tonga, Trinidad and Tobago, Tunisia, Turkey, Turkmenistan, Ukraine, United Arab Emirates, United Kingdom of Great Britain and Northern Ireland, United Republic of Tanzania, United States of America, Uruguay, Uzbekistan, Venezuela (Bolivarian Republic of), Yemen, Zambia, Zimbabwe

Against:
India

Abstaining:
Bhutan

Action by the First Committee

Date: 30 October 2007   Meeting: 22nd meeting
Vote: 167-1-1   Draft resolution: A/C.1/62/L.42

Agenda item 98 (u)

62/45 Confidence-building measures in the regional and subregional context

Text

The General Assembly,

Guided by the purposes and principles enshrined in the Charter of the United Nations,

Recalling its resolutions 58/43 of 8 December 2003, 59/87 of 3 December 2004, 60/64 of 8 December 2005 and 61/81 of 6 December 2006,

Recalling also its resolution 57/337 of 3 July 2003 entitled "Prevention of armed conflict", in which it calls upon Member States to settle their disputes by peaceful means, as set out in Chapter VI of the Charter, inter alia, by any procedures adopted by the parties,

Recalling further the resolutions and guidelines adopted by consensus by the General Assembly and the Disarmament Commission relating to confidence-building measures and their implantation at the global, regional and subregional levels,

Considering the importance and effectiveness of confidence-building measures taken at the initiative and with the agreement of all States concerned and taking into account the specific characteristics of each region, since such measures can contribute to regional stability,

Convinced that resources released by disarmament, including regional disarmament, can be devoted to economic and social development and to the protection of the environment for the benefit of all peoples, in particular those of the developing countries,

Recognizing the need for meaningful dialogue among States concerned to avert conflict,

Welcoming the peace processes already initiated by States concerned to resolve their disputes through peaceful means bilaterally or through mediation, inter alia, by third parties, regional organizations or the United Nations,

Recognizing that States in some regions have already taken steps towards confidence-building measures at the bilateral, subregional and regional levels in the political and military fields, including arms control and disarmament, and noting that such confidence-building measures have improved peace and security in those regions and contributed to progress in the socio-economic conditions of their people,

Concerned that the continuation of disputes among States, particularly in the absence of an effective mechanism to resolve them through peaceful means, may contribute to the arms race and endanger the maintenance of international peace and security and the efforts of the international community to promote arms control and disarmament,

1. *Calls upon* Member States to refrain from the use or threat of use of force in accordance with the purposes and principles of the Charter of the United Nations;

2. *Reaffirms its commitment* to the peaceful settlement of disputes under Chapter VI of the Charter, in particular Article 33, which provides for a solution by negotiation, enquiry, mediation, conciliation, arbitration, judicial settlement, resort to regional agencies or arrangements or other peaceful means chosen by the parties;

3. *Reaffirms* the ways and means regarding confidence- and security-building measures set out in the report of the Disarmament Commission on its 1993 session;[1]

4. *Calls upon* Member States to pursue these ways and means through sustained consultations and dialogue, while at the same time avoiding actions that may hinder or impair such a dialogue;

5. *Urges* States to comply strictly with all bilateral, regional and international agreements, including arms control and disarmament agreements, to which they are party;

6. *Emphasizes* that the objective of confidence-building measures should be to help strengthen international peace and security and be consistent with the principle of undiminished security at the lowest level of armaments;

7. *Encourages* the promotion of bilateral and regional confidence-building measures, with the consent and participation of the parties concerned, to avoid conflict and prevent the unintended and accidental outbreak of hostilities;

8. *Requests* the Secretary-General to submit a report to the General Assembly at its sixty-third session containing the views of Member States on confidence-building measures in the regional and subregional context;

9. *Decides* to include in the provisional agenda of its sixty-third session the item entitled "Confidence-building measures in the regional and subregional context".

Action by the General Assembly

Date: 5 December 2007   Meeting: 61st meeting
Vote: Adopted without a vote   Report: A/62/391

---

[1] *Official Records of the General Assembly, Forty-eighth Session, Supplement No. 42* (A/48/42), annex II, sect. III.A.

Sponsors

Bangladesh, Colombia, Kazakhstan, Kuwait, Malaysia, **Pakistan**, Syrian Arab Republic, Ukraine

Co-sponsors

Germany, Sierra Leone

Action by the First Committee

Date: 31 October 2007 Meeting: 23rd meeting
Vote: Adopted without a vote Draft resolution: A/C.1/62/L.43

Agenda item 98 (e)

62/46 Preventing the acquisition by terrorists of radioactive materials and sources

Text

The General Assembly,

Recognizing the essential contribution of radioactive materials and sources to social and economic development, and the benefits drawn from their use for all States,

Recognizing also the determination of the international community to combat terrorism, as evident in relevant General Assembly and Security Council resolutions,

Deeply concerned by the threat of terrorism and the risk that terrorists may acquire, traffic in or use radioactive materials or sources in radiological dispersion devices,

Recalling the importance of international conventions aimed at preventing and suppressing such a risk, in particular the International Convention for the Suppression of Acts of Nuclear Terrorism, adopted on 13 April 2005,[1] and the Convention on the Physical Protection of Nuclear Material, adopted on 26 October 1979,[2] as well as its Amendment, adopted on 8 July 2005,

Noting that actions of the international community to combat the proliferation of weapons of mass destruction and prevent access by non-State actors to weapons of mass destruction and related material, notably Security Council resolution 1540 (2004) of 28 April 2004, constitute contributions to the protection against nuclear and radiological terrorism,

Stressing the importance of the role of the International Atomic Energy Agency in promoting and reinforcing the safety and security of radioactive materials and sources, in particular by supporting the improvement of national legal and regulatory infrastructure and by establishing technical guidance,

Taking note of the importance of the Joint Convention on the Safety of Spent Fuel Management and on the Safety of Radioactive Waste Management[3] with respect to the safety of the end of life of radioactive sources,

Taking note also of the importance of the Code of Conduct on the Safety and Security of Radioactive Sources[4] as a valuable instrument for enhancing the safety and security of radioactive sources, while recognizing that the Code

---

[1] Resolution 59/290, annex.
[2] United Nations, *Treaty Series*, vol. 1456, No. 24631.
[3] Ibid., vol. 2153, No. 37605.
[4] International Atomic Energy Agency, *Code of Conduct on the Safety and Security of Radioactive Sources* (IAEA/CODEOC/2004).

is not a legally binding instrument, and of the International Atomic Energy Agency Revised Action Plan for the Safety and Security of Radioactive Sources[5] and its Nuclear Security Plan for 2006-2009,[6]

Taking note further of resolutions GC(51)/RES/11 and GC(51)/RES/12, adopted by the General Conference of the International Atomic Energy Agency at its fifty-first regular session, which address measures to strengthen international cooperation in nuclear, radiation and transport safety and waste management and measures to protect against nuclear and radiological terrorism,[7]

Welcoming the ongoing individual and collective efforts of Member States to take into account in their deliberations the dangers posed by the lack or insufficiency of control over radioactive materials and sources, and recognizing the need for States to take more effective measures to strengthen those controls in accordance with their national legal authorities and legislation and consistent with international law,

Welcoming also the fact that Member States have taken multilateral actions to address this issue, as reflected in General Assembly resolution 61/8 of 30 October 2006,

Welcoming further the contribution of the International Atomic Energy Agency International Conference on the Safety and Security of Radioactive Sources: Towards a Global System for the Continuous Control of Sources throughout Their Life Cycle, held in Bordeaux, France, from 27 June to 1 July 2005, to the activities of the Agency on these issues,

Mindful of the responsibilities of every Member State, in accordance with international obligations, to maintain effective nuclear safety and security, asserting that responsibility for nuclear security within a State rests entirely with that State, and noting the important contribution of international cooperation in supporting the efforts of States to fulfil their responsibilities,

Mindful also of the urgent need for addressing, within the United Nations framework and through international cooperation, this rising concern for international security,

1. *Calls upon* Member States to support international efforts to prevent the acquisition and use by terrorists of radioactive materials and sources, and, if necessary, suppress such acts, in accordance with their national legal authorities and legislation and consistent with international law;

2. *Urges* Member States to take and strengthen national measures, as appropriate, to prevent the acquisition and use by terrorists of radioactive

---

[5] GOV/2001/29-GC(45)/12, attachment.
[6] See GC(49)/17.
[7] See International Atomic Energy Agency, *Resolutions and Other Decisions of the General Conference, Fifty-first Regular Session, 17-21 September 2007* (GC(51)/RES/DEC(2007)).

materials and sources, as well as terrorist attacks on nuclear plants and facilities which would result in radioactive releases, and, if necessary, suppress such acts, in particular by taking effective measures to account for, secure and physically protect such materials and sources in accordance with their international obligations;

3. *Encourages* Member States to enhance their national capacities with appropriate means of detection and related architecture or systems, including through international cooperation and assistance in conformity with international law and regulations, with a view to reflecting and preventing the illicit trafficking of radioactive materials and sources;

4. *Welcomes* the entry into force on 7 July 2007 of the International Convention for the Suppression of Acts of Nuclear Terrorism,[1] and invites all Member States that have not yet done so to sign and ratify this instrument as soon as possible, in accordance with their legal and constitutional processes;

5. *Invites* Member States, in particular those producing and distributing radioactive sources, to support and endorse the efforts of the International Atomic Energy Agency to enhance the safety and security of radioactive sources, as described in General Conference resolution GC(51)/RES/11 and to enhance the security of radioactive sources as described in the Agency's Nuclear Security Plan for 2006-2009,[6] urges all States to work towards following the guidance contained in the Agency's Code of Conduct on the Safety and Security of Radioactive Sources,[4] including, as appropriate, the guidance on the import and export of radioactive sources, noting that the guidance is supplementary to the Code, and encourages Member States to notify the Director General of the Agency of their intention to do so pursuant to General Conference resolution GC(48)/RES/10;[8]

6. *Recognizes* the value of information exchange on national approaches to controlling radioactive sources, and takes note of the endorsement by the Board of Governors of the International Atomic Energy Agency of a proposal for a formalized process for a voluntary periodic exchange on information and lessons learned and for the evaluation of progress made by States towards implementing the provisions of the Code of Conduct on the Safety and Security of Radioactive Sources;

7. *Welcomes* the efforts undertaken by Member States, including through international cooperation under the auspices of the International Atomic Energy Agency, to search for, locate and secure unsecured and/or uncontrolled ("orphan") radioactive sources within their State jurisdiction or territory;

8. *Encourages* cooperation among and between Member States and through relevant international and, where appropriate, regional organizations aimed at strengthening national capacities in this regard;

---

[8] Ibid., *Forty-eighth Regular Session, 20-24 September 2004* (GC(48)/RES/DEC(2004)).

9. *Decides* to include in the provisional agenda of its sixty-fourth session an item entitled "Preventing the acquisition by terrorists of radioactive materials and sources".

Action by the General Assembly

Date: 5 December 2007 Meeting: 61st meeting
Vote: Adopted without a vote Report: A/62/391

Sponsors

Albania, Armenia, Austria, Belgium, Bulgaria, Chile, Croatia, Cyprus, Czech Republic, Denmark, Estonia, Finland, **France**, Germany, Greece, Hungary, Ireland, Italy, Latvia, Lithuania, Luxembourg, Malta, Monaco, Netherlands, Norway, Poland, Portugal, Romania, Serbia, Slovakia, Slovenia, Spain, Sweden, Switzerland, the former Yugoslav Republic of Macedonia, Togo, United Kingdom of Great Britain and Northern Ireland

Co-sponsors

Canada, Montenegro, Republic of Moldova, Turkey

Action by the First Committee

Date: 2 November 2007 Meeting: 25th meeting
Vote: Adopted without a vote Draft resolution: A/C.1/62/L.46/Rev.1

Agenda item 98 (l)

62/47 The illicit trade in small arms and light weapons in all its aspects

Text

The General Assembly,

Recalling its resolutions 56/24 V of 24 December 2001, 57/72 of 22 November 2002, 58/241 of 23 December 2003, 59/86 of 3 December 2004, 60/81 of 8 December 2005 and 61/66 of 6 December 2006,

Emphasizing the importance of the continued and full implementation of the Programme of Action to Prevent, Combat and Eradicate the Illicit Trade in Small Arms and Light Weapons in All Its Aspects, adopted by the United Nations Conference on the Illicit Trade in Small Arms and Light Weapons in All Its Aspects,[1]

Welcoming the efforts by Member States to submit, on a voluntary basis, national reports on their implementation of the Programme of Action,

Noting with satisfaction regional and subregional efforts being undertaken in support of the implementation of the Programme of Action, and commending the progress that has already been made in this regard, including tackling both supply and demand factors that are relevant to addressing the illicit trade in small arms and light weapons,

Recognizing the efforts undertaken by non-governmental organizations in the provision of assistance to States for the implementation of the Programme of Action,

Recalling that, as part of the follow-up to the United Nations Conference on the Illicit Trade in Small Arms and Light Weapons in All Its Aspects, it was agreed that meetings of States should be convened on a biennial basis to consider the national, regional and global implementation of the Programme of Action,[2]

Recognizing that illicit brokering in small arms and light weapons is a serious problem that the international community should address urgently,

Bearing in mind the importance of regular national reporting, which could greatly facilitate the rendering of international cooperation and assistance to affected States,

---

[1] See *Report of the United Nations Conference on the Illicit Trade in Small Arms and Light Weapons in All Its Aspects, New York, 9-20 July 2001* (A/CONF.192/15), chap. IV, para. 24.

[2] Ibid., sect. IV, para. 1 (*b*).

Taking note of the report of the Secretary-General on the implementation of resolution 61/66,[3]

Welcoming the fact that the United Nations Conference to Review Progress Made in the Implementation of the Programme of Action to Prevent, Combat and Eradicate the Illicit Trade in Small Arms and Light Weapons in All Its Aspects, held from 26 June to 7 July 2006, highlighted the commitment of States to the Programme of Action as the main framework for measures within the activities of the international community to prevent, combat and eradicate the illicit trade in small arms and light weapons in all its aspects, beyond 2006,[4]

Taking note of the reports submitted to the General Assembly by the Secretary-General dealing with the issue of the illicit trade in small arms and light weapons in all its aspects,[5]

1. *Encourages* all initiatives, including those of the United Nations, other international organizations, regional and subregional organizations, non-governmental organizations and civil society, for the successful implementation of the Programme of Action to Prevent, Combat and Eradicate the Illicit Trade in Small Arms and Light Weapons in All Its Aspects,[1] and calls upon all Member States to contribute towards the continued implementation of the Programme of Action at the national, regional and global levels;

2. *Calls upon* all States to implement the International Instrument to Enable States to Identify and Trace, in a Timely and Reliable Manner, Illicit Small Arms and Light Weapons,[6] among others, through the provision of information to the Secretary-General on the name and contact information of the national points of contact and on national marking practices related to markings used to indicate country of manufacture and/or country of import, as applicable;

3. *Takes note* of the report submitted to the General Assembly by the Group of Governmental Experts established pursuant to resolution 60/81 to consider further steps to enhance international cooperation in preventing, combating and eradicating illicit brokering in small arms and light weapons,[7] and encourages States to implement its recommendations;

4. *Decides* that, in conformity with the follow-up to the Programme of Action, the next biennial meeting of States to consider the national, regional and global implementation of the Programme of Action shall be held from 14 to 18 July 2008, in New York;

---

[3] See A/62/162.
[4] See A/CONF.192/2006/RC/9.
[5] A/62/162 and A/62/163.
[6] A/60/88 and Corr.2, annex; see also decision 60/519.
[7] See A/62/163.

5. *Recalls* that the meeting of States to consider the implementation of the International Instrument to Enable States to Identify and Trace, in a Timely and Reliable Manner, Illicit Small Arms and Light Weapons, shall be held within the framework of the biennial meeting of States;

6. *Encourages* States to submit, well in advance of the next biennial meeting of States, national reports on their implementation of the Programme of Action and the International Instrument to Enable States to Identify and Trace, in a Timely and Reliable Manner, Illicit Small Arms and Light Weapons in accordance with these instruments, and requests the Secretary-General to collate and circulate such data and information provided by States;

7. *Also encourages* States to include in their national reports, on a voluntary basis, information on their efforts to prevent, combat and eradicate illicit brokering in small arms and light weapons, as well as on their actions aimed at enhancing international cooperation for this purpose;

8. *Calls upon* States, in considering the implementation of the Programme of Action, to take full advantage of the biennial meetings of States to identify priority issues or topics of relevance in the illicit trade in small arms and light weapons in all its aspects and to highlight their implementation challenges and opportunities;

9. *Underlines* the fact that the issue of the illicit trade in small arms and light weapons in all its aspects requires concerted efforts at the national, regional and international levels to prevent, combat and eradicate the illicit manufacture, transfer and circulation of small arms and light weapons and that their uncontrolled spread in many regions of the world has a wide range of humanitarian and socio-economic consequences and poses a serious threat to peace, reconciliation, safety, security, stability and sustainable development at the individual, local, national, regional and international levels;

10. *Emphasizes* the need to facilitate the implementation at the national level of the Programme of Action through the strengthening of national coordination agencies or bodies and institutional infrastructure;

11. *Also emphasizes* the fact that initiatives by the international community with respect to international cooperation and assistance remain essential and complementary to national implementation efforts, as well as to those at the regional and global levels;

12. *Recognizes* the necessity for interested States to develop effective coordination mechanisms, where they do not exist, in order to match the needs of States with existing resources to enhance the implementation of the Programme of Action and to make international cooperation and assistance more effective;

13. *Encourages* States to consider, among other mechanisms, the coherent identification of needs, priorities, national plans and programmes that

may require international cooperation and assistance from States and regional and international organizations in a position to do so;

14. *Encourages* civil society and relevant organizations to strengthen their cooperation and work with States at the respective national and regional levels to achieve the implementation of the Programme of Action;

15. *Requests* the Secretary-General to report to the General Assembly at its sixty-third session on the implementation of the present resolution;

16. *Decides* to include in the provisional agenda of its sixty-third session the item entitled "The illicit trade in small arms and light weapons in all its aspects".

Action by the General Assembly

Date: 5 December 2007 Meeting: 61st meeting
Vote: 179-1-0 Report: A/62/391

Sponsors

Afghanistan, Algeria, Andorra, Antigua and Barbuda, Argentina, Armenia, Azerbaijan, Belize, Bolivia, Brazil, Cameroon, Chile, **Colombia**, Congo, Costa Rica, Dominica, Dominican Republic, Ecuador, El Salvador, Eritrea, Finland, Germany, Guatemala, Haiti, Honduras, India, Jamaica, Japan, Kazakhstan, Lithuania, Mali, Nicaragua, Norway, Panama, Paraguay, Peru, Republic of Korea, Russian Federation, Samoa, San Marino, Sierra Leone, Solomon Islands, South Africa, Sri Lanka, Suriname, Switzerland, Thailand, Togo, Turkey, Ukraine, United Kingdom of Great Britain and Northern Ireland, Uruguay

Co-sponsors

Austria, Bangladesh, Belgium, Bulgaria, Czech Republic, Estonia, Ethiopia, Hungary, Iceland, Iraq, Ireland, Kyrgyzstan, Luxembourg, Mongolia, Morocco, Niger, Portugal, Romania, Slovakia, Slovenia, Spain, Sweden, Timor-Leste

Recorded vote

In favour:

Afghanistan, Albania, Algeria, Andorra, Antigua and Barbuda, Argentina, Armenia, Australia, Austria, Azerbaijan, Bahamas, Bahrain, Bangladesh, Barbados, Belarus, Belgium, Belize, Benin, Bhutan, Bolivia, Bosnia and Herzegovina, Botswana, Brazil, Brunei Darussalam, Bulgaria, Burkina Faso, Burundi, Cambodia, Cameroon, Canada, Cape Verde, Central African Republic, Chile, China, Colombia, Comoros, Congo, Costa Rica, Côte d'Ivoire, Croatia, Cuba, Cyprus, Czech Republic, Denmark, Djibouti, Dominican Republic, Ecuador, Egypt, El Salvador, Equatorial Guinea, Eritrea, Estonia, Ethiopia, Fiji, Finland, France, Gabon, Gambia,

Georgia, Germany, Ghana, Greece, Grenada, Guatemala, Guinea, Guinea-Bissau, Guyana, Haiti, Honduras, Hungary, Iceland, India, Indonesia, Iran (Islamic Republic of), Iraq, Ireland, Israel, Italy, Jamaica, Japan, Jordan, Kazakhstan, Kenya, Kuwait, Kyrgyzstan, Latvia, Lebanon, Lesotho, Liberia, Libyan Arab Jamahiriya, Liechtenstein, Lithuania, Luxembourg, Madagascar, Malawi, Malaysia, Maldives, Mali, Malta, Marshall Islands, Mauritania, Mauritius, Mexico, Micronesia (Federated States of), Monaco, Mongolia, Montenegro, Morocco, Mozambique, Myanmar, Namibia, Nauru, Nepal, Netherlands, New Zealand, Nicaragua, Niger, Nigeria, Norway, Oman, Pakistan, Palau, Panama, Papua New Guinea, Paraguay, Peru, Philippines, Poland, Portugal, Qatar, Republic of Korea, Republic of Moldova, Romania, Russian Federation, Rwanda, Saint Kitts and Nevis, Saint Lucia, Saint Vincent and the Grenadines, Samoa, San Marino, Sao Tome and Principe, Saudi Arabia, Senegal, Serbia, Sierra Leone, Singapore, Slovakia, Slovenia, Solomon Islands, Somalia, South Africa, Spain, Sri Lanka, Sudan, Suriname, Swaziland, Sweden, Switzerland, Syrian Arab Republic, Tajikistan, Thailand, the former Yugoslav Republic of Macedonia, Togo, Tonga, Trinidad and Tobago, Tunisia, Turkey, Turkmenistan, Ukraine, United Arab Emirates, United Kingdom of Great Britain and Northern Ireland, United Republic of Tanzania, Uruguay, Uzbekistan, Venezuela (Bolivarian Republic of), Viet Nam, Yemen, Zambia, Zimbabwe

Against:
United States of America

Abstaining:
None

Action by the First Committee

Date: 1 November 2007   Meeting: 24th meeting
Vote: 165-1-0   Draft resolution: A/C.1/62/L.49/Rev.1

Agenda item 98 (j)

62/48   Relationship between disarmament and development

Text

The General Assembly,

Recalling that the Charter of the United Nations envisages the establishment and maintenance of international peace and security with the least diversion for armaments of the world's human and economic resources,

Recalling also the provisions of the Final Document of the Tenth Special Session of the General Assembly concerning the relationship between disarmament and development,[1] as well as the adoption on 11 September 1987 of the Final Document of the International Conference on the Relationship between Disarmament and Development,[2]

Recalling further its resolutions 49/75 J of 15 December 1994, 50/70 G of 12 December 1995, 51/45 D of 10 December 1996, 52/38 D of 9 December 1997, 53/77 K of 4 December 1998, 54/54 T of 1 December 1999, 55/33 L of 20 November 2000, 56/24 E of 29 November 2001, 57/65 of 22 November 2002, 59/78 of 3 December 2004, 60/61 of 8 December 2005 and 61/64 of 6 December 2006, and its decision 58/520 of 8 December 2003,

Bearing in mind the Final Document of the Twelfth Conference of Heads of State or Government of Non-Aligned Countries, held in Durban, South Africa, from 29 August to 3 September 1998,[3] and the Final Document of the Thirteenth Ministerial Conference of the Movement of Non-Aligned Countries, held in Cartagena, Colombia, on 8 and 9 April 2000,[4]

Mindful of the changes in international relations that have taken place since the adoption on 11 September 1987 of the Final Document of the International Conference on the Relationship between Disarmament and Development, including the development agenda that has emerged over the past decade,

Bearing in mind the new challenges for the international community in the field of development, poverty eradication and the elimination of the diseases that afflict humanity,

Stressing the importance of the symbiotic relationship between disarmament and development and the important role of security in this connection, and concerned at increasing global military expenditure, which could otherwise be spent on development needs,

---

[1] See resolution S-10/2.
[2] United Nations publication, Sales No. E.87.IX.8.
[3] A/53/667-S/1998/1071, annex I.
[4] A/54/917-S/2000/580, annex.

Recalling the report of the Group of Governmental Experts on the relationship between disarmament and development[5] and its reappraisal of this significant issue in the current international context,

Taking note of the fact that 2007 marks the twentieth anniversary of the adoption in 1987 of the Final Document of the International Conference on the Relationship between Disarmament and Development,

Bearing in mind the importance of following up on the implementation of the action programme adopted at the 1987 International Conference on the Relationship between Disarmament and Development,[2]

1. *Stresses* the central role of the United Nations in the disarmament-development relationship, and requests the Secretary-General to strengthen further the role of the Organization in this field, in particular the high-level Steering Group on Disarmament and Development, in order to ensure continued and effective coordination and close cooperation between the relevant United Nations departments, agencies and sub-agencies;

2. *Requests* the Secretary-General to continue to take action, through appropriate organs and within available resources, for the implementation of the action programme adopted at the 1987 International Conference on the Relationship between Disarmament and Development;[2]

3. *Urges* the international community to devote part of the resources made available by the implementation of disarmament and arms limitation agreements to economic and social development, with a view to reducing the ever-widening gap between developed and developing countries;

4. *Encourages* the international community to achieve the Millennium Development Goals and to make reference to the contribution that disarmament could provide in meeting them when it reviews its progress towards this purpose in 2007, as well as to make greater efforts to integrate disarmament, humanitarian and development activities;

5. *Encourages* the relevant regional and subregional organizations and institutions, non-governmental organizations and research institutes to incorporate issues related to the relationship between disarmament and development in their agendas and, in this regard, to take into account the report of the Group of Governmental Experts on the relationship between disarmament and development;[5]

6. *Invites* Member States to provide the Secretary-General with information regarding measures and efforts to devote part of the resources made available by the implementation of disarmament and arms limitation agreements to economic and social development, with a view to reducing the ever-widening gap between developed and developing countries;

---

[5] See A/59/119.

7. *Requests* the Secretary-General to report to the General Assembly at its sixty-third session on the implementation of the present resolution, including the information provided by Member States pursuant to paragraph 6 above;

8. *Decides* to include in the provisional agenda of its sixty-third session the item entitled "Relationship between disarmament and development".

Action by the General Assembly

Date: 5 December 2007 Meeting: 61st meeting
Vote: 179-1-2 Report: A/62/391

Sponsors

Indonesia (on behalf of the States Members of the United Nations that are members of the Movement of Non-Aligned Countries)

Recorded vote

In favour:

Afghanistan, Albania, Algeria, Andorra, Antigua and Barbuda, Argentina, Armenia, Australia, Austria, Azerbaijan, Bahamas, Bahrain, Bangladesh, Barbados, Belarus, Belgium, Belize, Benin, Bhutan, Bolivia, Bosnia and Herzegovina, Botswana, Brazil, Brunei Darussalam, Bulgaria, Burkina Faso, Burundi, Cambodia, Cameroon, Canada, Cape Verde, Central African Republic, Chile, China, Colombia, Comoros, Congo, Costa Rica, Côte d'Ivoire, Croatia, Cuba, Cyprus, Czech Republic, Democratic People's Republic of Korea, Denmark, Djibouti, Dominican Republic, Ecuador, Egypt, El Salvador, Equatorial Guinea, Eritrea, Estonia, Ethiopia, Fiji, Finland, Gabon, Gambia, Georgia, Germany, Ghana, Greece, Grenada, Guatemala, Guinea, Guinea-Bissau, Guyana, Haiti, Honduras, Hungary, Iceland, India, Indonesia, Iran (Islamic Republic of), Iraq, Ireland, Italy, Jamaica, Japan, Jordan, Kazakhstan, Kenya, Kuwait, Kyrgyzstan, Lao People's Democratic Republic, Latvia, Lebanon, Lesotho, Liberia, Libyan Arab Jamahiriya, Liechtenstein, Lithuania, Luxembourg, Madagascar, Malawi, Malaysia, Maldives, Mali, Malta, Marshall Islands, Mauritania, Mauritius, Mexico, Micronesia (Federated States of), Monaco, Mongolia, Montenegro, Morocco, Mozambique, Myanmar, Namibia, Nauru, Nepal, Netherlands, New Zealand, Nicaragua, Niger, Nigeria, Norway, Oman, Pakistan, Palau, Panama, Papua New Guinea, Paraguay, Peru, Philippines, Poland, Portugal, Qatar, Republic of Korea, Republic of Moldova, Romania, Russian Federation, Rwanda, Saint Kitts and Nevis, Saint Lucia, Saint Vincent and the Grenadines, Samoa, San Marino, Sao Tome and Principe, Saudi Arabia, Senegal, Serbia, Sierra Leone, Singapore, Slovakia, Slovenia, Solomon Islands, Somalia, South Africa, Spain, Sri Lanka, Sudan, Suriname, Swaziland, Sweden, Switzerland, Syrian Arab Republic, Tajikistan, Thailand, the former Yugoslav Republic of Macedonia, Togo, Tonga, Trinidad and

Tobago, Tunisia, Turkey, Turkmenistan, Ukraine, United Arab Emirates, United Kingdom of Great Britain and Northern Ireland, United Republic of Tanzania, Uruguay, Uzbekistan, Venezuela (Bolivarian Republic of), Viet Nam, Yemen, Zambia, Zimbabwe

Against:
    United States of America

Abstaining:
    France, Israel

Action by the First Committee

    Date: 1 November 2007   Meeting: 24th meeting
    Vote: 166-1-2   Draft resolution: A/C.1/62/L.50

Agenda item 99 (b)

62/49 United Nations Regional Centre for Peace, Disarmament and Development in Latin America and the Caribbean

Text

The General Assembly,

Recalling its resolutions 41/60 J of 3 December 1986, 42/39 K of 30 November 1987 and 43/76 H of 7 December 1988 on the United Nations Regional Centre for Peace, Disarmament and Development in Latin America and the Caribbean, with headquarters in Lima,

Recalling also its resolutions 46/37 F of 9 December 1991, 48/76 E of 16 December 1993, 49/76 D of 15 December 1994, 50/71 C of 12 December 1995, 52/220 of 22 December 1997, 53/78 F of 4 December 1998, 54/55 F of 1 December 1999, 55/34 E of 20 November 2000, 56/25 E of 29 November 2001, 57/89 of 22 November 2002, 58/60 of 8 December 2003, 59/99 of 3 December 2004, 60/84 of 8 December 2005 and 61/92 of 6 December 2006,

Welcoming the twentieth anniversary of the Regional Centre,

Recognizing that the Regional Centre has continued to provide substantive support for the implementation of regional and subregional initiatives and has intensified its contribution to the coordination of United Nations efforts towards peace and disarmament and for the promotion of economic and social development,

Welcoming the report of the Secretary-General,[1] which, inter alia, concludes that the Regional Centre has continued to provide assistance to States in the Latin American and Caribbean region in the implementation of regional initiatives in the areas of peace and disarmament and development and that during the period under review such assistance was provided in the areas of practical disarmament measures, capacity-building and awareness-raising, in the preparation of national reports on weapons-related instruments and in the provision of forums for discussion among States to facilitate their reaching common positions on disarmament and non-proliferation issues, and welcoming also the Centre's initiation of the process of transferring to the African region its knowledge and best practices in the area of training courses for the law enforcement community on the prevention of illicit firearms trafficking,

Recalling the report of the Group of Governmental Experts on the relationship between disarmament and development,[2] referred to in General Assembly resolution 59/78 of 3 December 2004, which is of utmost interest with regard to the role that the Regional Centre plays in promoting the issue in the

---
[1] A/62/130.
[2] See A/59/119.

region in pursuit of its mandate to promote economic and social development related to peace and disarmament,

Noting that security and disarmament issues have always been recognized as significant topics in Latin America and the Caribbean, the first inhabited region in the world to be declared a nuclear-weapon-free zone,

Welcoming the support provided by the Regional Centre to strengthening the nuclear-weapon-free zone established by the Treaty for the Prohibition of Nuclear Weapons in Latin America and the Caribbean (Treaty of Tlatelolco),[3] as well as to promoting and assisting the ratification and implementation of existing multilateral agreements related to weapons of mass destruction and to promoting peace and disarmament education projects during the period under review,

Bearing in mind the important role of the Regional Centre in promoting confidence-building measures, arms control and limitation, disarmament and development at the regional level,

Bearing in mind also the importance of information, research, education and training for peace, disarmament and development in order to achieve understanding and cooperation among States,

Recognizing the need to provide the three United Nations regional centres for peace and disarmament with sufficient financial resources and cooperation for the planning and implementation of their programmes of activities,

1. *Reiterates its strong support* for the role of the United Nations Regional Centre for Peace, Disarmament and Development in Latin America and the Caribbean in the promotion of United Nations activities at the regional level to strengthen peace, stability, security and development among its member States;

2. *Expresses its satisfaction and congratulates* the Regional Centre for the activities carried out in the last year in the areas of peace, disarmament and development, and requests the Centre to take into account the proposals to be submitted by the countries of the region in promoting confidence-building measures, arms control and limitation, transparency, disarmament and development at the regional level;

3. *Expresses its appreciation* for the political support and financial contributions to the Regional Centre, which are essential for its continued operation;

4. *Appeals* to Member States, in particular those within the Latin American and Caribbean region, and to international governmental and non-governmental organizations and foundations to make and to increase voluntary contributions to strengthen the Regional Centre, its programme of activities and the implementation thereof;

---

[3] United Nations, *Treaty Series*, vol. 634, No. 9068.

5. *Invites* all States of the region to continue to take part in the activities of the Regional Centre, proposing items for inclusion in its programme of activities and making greater and better use of the potential of the Centre to meet the current challenges facing the international community with a view to fulfilling the aims of the Charter of the United Nations in the areas of peace, disarmament and development;

6. *Recognizes* that the Regional Centre has an important role in the promotion and development of regional initiatives agreed upon by the countries of Latin America and the Caribbean in the field of weapons of mass destruction, in particular nuclear weapons, and conventional arms, including small arms and light weapons, as well as in the relationship between disarmament and development;

7. *Encourages* the Regional Centre to further develop activities in the important area of disarmament and development;

8. *Highlights* the conclusion contained in the report of the Secretary-General to the sixty-first session of the General Assembly, that, through its activities, the Regional Centre has demonstrated its role as a viable regional actor in assisting States in the region to advance the cause of peace, disarmament and development in Latin America and the Caribbean;[4]

9. *Requests* the Secretary-General to provide the Regional Centre with all necessary support, within existing resources, so that it may carry out its programme of activities in accordance with its mandate;

10. *Also requests* the Secretary-General to report to the General Assembly at its sixty-third session on the implementation of the present resolution;

11. *Decides* to include in the provisional agenda of its sixty-third session the item entitled "United Nations Regional Centre for Peace, Disarmament and Development in Latin America and the Caribbean".

Action by the General Assembly

Date: 5 December 2007   Meeting: 61st meeting
Vote: Adopted without a vote Report: A/62/392

Sponsors

Peru (on behalf of the States Members of the United Nations that are members of the Group of Latin American and Caribbean States)

Action by the First Committee

Date: 31 October 2007   Meeting: 23rd meeting
Vote: Adopted without a vote Draft resolution: A/C.1/62/L.4

---

[4] See A/61/157, para. 49.

Agenda item 99 (a)

62/50   United Nations regional centres for peace and disarmament

Text

The General Assembly,

Recalling its resolutions 60/83 of 8 December 2005 and 61/90 of 6 December 2006 regarding the maintenance and revitalization of the three United Nations regional centres for peace and disarmament,

Recalling also the reports of the Secretary-General on the United Nations Regional Centre for Peace and Disarmament in Africa,[1] the United Nations Regional Centre for Peace and Disarmament in Asia and the Pacific[2] and the United Nations Regional Centre for Peace, Disarmament and Development in Latin America and the Caribbean,[3]

Reaffirming its decision, taken in 1982 at its twelfth special session, to establish the United Nations Disarmament Information Programme, the purpose of which is to inform, educate and generate public understanding and support for the objectives of the United Nations in the field of arms control and disarmament,[4]

Bearing in mind its resolutions 40/151 G of 16 December 1985, 41/60 J of 3 December 1986, 42/39 D of 30 November 1987 and 44/117 F of 15 December 1989 on the regional centres for peace and disarmament in Nepal, Peru and Togo,

Recognizing that the changes that have taken place in the world have created new opportunities as well as posed new challenges for the pursuit of disarmament, and, in this regard, bearing in mind that the regional centres for peace and disarmament can contribute substantially to understanding and cooperation among States in each particular region in the areas of peace, disarmament and development,

Noting that in paragraph 91 of the Final Document of the Fourteenth Conference of Heads of State or Government of Non-Aligned Countries, held in Havana, on 15 and 16 September 2006, the Heads of State or Government emphasized the importance of the United Nations activities at the regional level to increase the stability and security of its Member States, which could be

---

[1] A/62/140.
[2] A/62/153.
[3] A/62/130.
[4] See *Official Records of the General Assembly, Twelfth Special Session, Plenary Meetings,* 1st meeting, paras. 110 and 111.

promoted in a substantive manner by the maintenance and revitalization of the three regional centres for peace and disarmament,[5]

1. *Reiterates* the importance of the United Nations activities at the regional level to advancement in disarmament and to increase the stability and security of its Member States, which could be promoted in a substantive manner by the maintenance and revitalization of the three regional centres for peace and disarmament;

2. *Reaffirms* that, in order to achieve positive results, it is useful for the three regional centres to carry out dissemination and educational programmes that promote regional peace and security that are aimed at changing basic attitudes with respect to peace and security and disarmament so as to support the achievement of the purposes and principles of the United Nations;

3. *Appeals* to Member States in each region and those that are able to do so, as well as to international governmental and non-governmental organizations and foundations, to make voluntary contributions to the regional centres in their respective regions to strengthen their activities and initiatives;

4. *Emphasizes* the importance of the activities of the regional disarmament branch of the Office for Disarmament Affairs of the Secretariat;

5. *Requests* the Secretary-General to provide all necessary support, within existing resources, to the regional centres in carrying out their programmes of activities;

6. *Decides* to include in the provisional agenda of its sixty-third session the item entitled "United Nations regional centres for peace and disarmament".

Action by the General Assembly

Date: 5 December 2007   Meeting: 61st meeting
Vote: Adopted without a vote   Report: A/62/392

Sponsors

Indonesia (on behalf of the States Members of the United Nations that are members of the Movement of Non-Aligned Countries)

Action by the First Committee

Date: 1 November 2007   Meeting: 24th meeting
Vote: Adopted without a vote   Draft resolution: A/C.1/62/L.15

---

[5] See A/61/472-S/2006/780, annex I.

Agenda item 99 (f)

62/51 Convention on the Prohibition of the Use of Nuclear Weapons

Text

The General Assembly,

Convinced that the use of nuclear weapons poses the most serious threat to the survival of mankind,

Bearing in mind the advisory opinion of the International Court of Justice of 8 July 1996 on the *Legality of the Threat or Use of Nuclear Weapons*,[1]

Convinced that a multilateral, universal and binding agreement prohibiting the use or threat of use of nuclear weapons would contribute to the elimination of the nuclear threat and to the climate for negotiations leading to the ultimate elimination of nuclear weapons, thereby strengthening international peace and security,

Conscious that some steps taken by the Russian Federation and the United States of America towards a reduction of their nuclear weapons and the improvement in the international climate can contribute towards the goal of the complete elimination of nuclear weapons,

Recalling that paragraph 58 of the Final Document of the Tenth Special Session of the General Assembly[2] states that all States should actively participate in efforts to bring about conditions in international relations among States in which a code of peaceful conduct of nations in international affairs could be agreed upon and that would preclude the use or threat of use of nuclear weapons,

Reaffirming that any use of nuclear weapons would be a violation of the Charter of the United Nations and a crime against humanity, as declared in its resolutions 1653 (XVI) of 24 November 1961, 33/71 B of 14 December 1978, 34/83 G of 11 December 1979, 35/152 D of 12 December 1980 and 36/92 I of 9 December 1981,

Determined to achieve an international convention prohibiting the development, production, stockpiling and use of nuclear weapons, leading to their ultimate destruction,

Stressing that an international convention on the prohibition of the use of nuclear weapons would be an important step in a phased programme towards the complete elimination of nuclear weapons, with a specified framework of time,

---

[1] A/51/218, annex; see also *Legality of the Threat or Use of Nuclear Weapons, Advisory Opinion, I.C.J. Reports 1996*, p. 226.

[2] See resolution S-10/2.

Noting with regret that the Conference on Disarmament, during its 2007 session, was unable to undertake negotiations on this subject as called for in General Assembly resolution 61/97 of 6 December 2006,

1. *Reiterates its request* to the Conference on Disarmament to commence negotiations in order to reach agreement on an international convention prohibiting the use or threat of use of nuclear weapons under any circumstances;

2. *Requests* the Conference on Disarmament to report to the General Assembly on the results of those negotiations.

Action by the General Assembly

Date: 5 December 2007   Meeting: 61st meeting
Vote: 120-52-10   Report: A/62/392

Sponsors

Bangladesh, Cuba, **India**, Indonesia, Iran (Islamic Republic of), Kuwait, Madagascar, Malaysia, Mauritius, Nepal, Viet Nam

Co-sponsors

Bhutan, Bolivia, Botswana, Brunei Darussalam, Burkina Faso, Cambodia, Colombia, Egypt, El Salvador, Haiti, Jamaica, Jordan, Libyan Arab Jamahiriya, Myanmar, Nicaragua, Philippines, Samoa

Recorded vote

In favour:

Afghanistan, Algeria, Antigua and Barbuda, Argentina, Bahamas, Bahrain, Bangladesh, Barbados, Belize, Benin, Bhutan, Bolivia, Botswana, Brazil, Brunei Darussalam, Burkina Faso, Burundi, Cambodia, Cameroon, Cape Verde, Central African Republic, Chile, China, Colombia, Comoros, Congo, Costa Rica, Côte d'Ivoire, Cuba, Democratic People's Republic of Korea, Djibouti, Dominica, Dominican Republic, Ecuador, Egypt, El Salvador, Equatorial Guinea, Eritrea, Ethiopia, Fiji, Gabon, Gambia, Ghana, Grenada, Guatemala, Guinea, Guinea-Bissau, Guyana, Haiti, Honduras, India, Indonesia, Iran (Islamic Republic of), Iraq, Jamaica, Jordan, Kenya, Kuwait, Lao People's Democratic Republic, Lebanon, Lesotho, Liberia, Libyan Arab Jamahiriya, Madagascar, Malawi, Malaysia, Maldives, Mali, Mauritania, Mauritius, Mexico, Mongolia, Morocco, Mozambique, Myanmar, Namibia, Nauru, Nepal, Nicaragua, Niger, Nigeria, Oman, Pakistan, Panama, Papua New Guinea, Paraguay, Peru, Philippines, Qatar, Saint Kitts and Nevis, Saint Lucia, Saint Vincent and the Grenadines, Samoa, Sao Tome and Principe, Saudi Arabia, Senegal, Sierra Leone, Singapore, Solomon Islands, Somalia, South Africa, Sri Lanka, Sudan, Suriname, Swaziland, Syrian Arab Republic, Thailand,

Togo, Tonga, Trinidad and Tobago, Tunisia, Turkmenistan, United Arab Emirates, United Republic of Tanzania, Uruguay, Venezuela (Bolivarian Republic of), Viet Nam, Yemen, Zambia, Zimbabwe

Against:
Albania, Andorra, Australia, Austria, Belgium, Bosnia and Herzegovina, Bulgaria, Canada, Croatia, Cyprus, Czech Republic, Denmark, Estonia, Finland, France, Georgia, Germany, Greece, Hungary, Iceland, Ireland, Israel, Italy, Latvia, Liechtenstein, Lithuania, Luxembourg, Malta, Marshall Islands, Micronesia (Federated States of), Monaco, Montenegro, Netherlands, New Zealand, Norway, Palau, Poland, Portugal, Republic of Moldova, Romania, San Marino, Serbia, Slovakia, Slovenia, Spain, Sweden, Switzerland, the former Yugoslav Republic of Macedonia, Turkey, Ukraine, United Kingdom of Great Britain and Northern Ireland, United States of America

Abstaining:
Armenia, Azerbaijan, Belarus, Japan, Kazakhstan, Kyrgyzstan, Republic of Korea, Russian Federation, Tajikistan, Uzbekistan

Action by the First Committee

Date: 30 October 2007   Meeting: 22nd meeting
Vote: 115-50-11   Draft resolution: A/C.1/62/L.23

Agenda item 99 (d)

62/52   United Nations Regional Centre for Peace and Disarmament in Asia and the Pacific

Text

The General Assembly,

Recalling its resolutions 42/39 D of 30 November 1987 and 44/117 F of 15 December 1989, by which it established the United Nations Regional Centre for Peace and Disarmament in Asia and renamed it the United Nations Regional Centre for Peace and Disarmament in Asia and the Pacific, with headquarters in Kathmandu and with the mandate of providing, on request, substantive support for the initiatives and other activities mutually agreed upon by the Member States of the Asia-Pacific region for the implementation of measures for peace and disarmament, through appropriate utilization of available resources,

Taking note of the report of the Secretary-General,[1] in which he expresses his belief that the mandate of the Regional Centre remains valid and that the Centre has been a useful instrument for fostering a climate of cooperation for peace and disarmament in the region,

Noting that trends in the post-cold-war era have emphasized the function of the Regional Centre in assisting Member States as they deal with new security concerns and disarmament issues emerging in the region,

Commending the useful activities carried out by the Regional Centre in encouraging regional and subregional dialogue for the enhancement of openness, transparency and confidence-building, as well as the promotion of disarmament and security through the organization of regional meetings, which has come to be widely known within the Asia-Pacific region as "the Kathmandu process",

Expressing its appreciation to the Regional Centre for its organization of meetings, conferences and workshops in the region, held in Yokohama, Japan, from 21 to 23 August 2006 and Jeju Island, Republic of Korea, from 13 to 15 December 2006,

Welcoming the activities of the Regional Centre in the promotion of disarmament and non-proliferation education in the Asia-Pacific region, as recommended in the United Nations study on disarmament and non-proliferation education,[2]

Noting the important role of the Regional Centre in assisting region-specific initiatives of Member States,

---

[1] A/62/153.
[2] A/57/124.

Appreciating highly the overall support that Nepal has extended as the host nation of the headquarters of the Regional Centre,

1. *Reaffirms its strong support* for the forthcoming operation and further strengthening of the United Nations Regional Centre for Peace and Disarmament in Asia and the Pacific;

2. *Underlines* the importance of the Kathmandu process as a powerful vehicle for the development of the practice of region-wide security and disarmament dialogue;

3. *Expresses its appreciation* for the continuing political support and voluntary financial contributions to the Regional Centre, which are essential for its continued operation;

4. *Appeals* to Member States, in particular those within the Asia-Pacific region, as well as to international governmental and non-governmental organizations and foundations, to make voluntary contributions, the only resources of the Regional Centre, to strengthen the programme of activities of the Centre and the implementation thereof;

5. *Requests* the Secretary-General, taking note of paragraph 5 of General Assembly resolution 49/76 D of 15 December 1994, to provide the Regional Centre with the necessary support, within existing resources, in carrying out its programme of activities;

6. *Welcomes* the signing of the host country agreement and the memorandum of understanding by the High Representative for Disarmament Affairs and the Permanent Representative of Nepal on 20 July 2007 for the relocation of the Centre to Kathmandu;

7. *Requests* the Secretary-General to expedite the necessary preparations with a view to ensuring physical operation of the Regional Centre from Kathmandu within six months to enable the Centre to function effectively;

8. *Also requests* the Secretary-General to report to the General Assembly at its sixty-third session on the implementation of the present resolution;

9. *Decides* to include in the provisional agenda of its sixty-third session the item entitled "United Nations Regional Centre for Peace and Disarmament in Asia and the Pacific".

Action by the General Assembly

Date: 5 December 2007　　Meeting: 61st meeting
Vote: Adopted without a vote　　Report: A/62/392

Sponsors

Afghanistan, Bangladesh, China, Democratic People's Republic of Korea, India, Indonesia, Japan, Kazakhstan, Micronesia (Federated States of),

Myanmar, Nauru, **Nepal**, New Zealand, Pakistan, Sri Lanka, Thailand, Viet Nam

Co-sponsors

Barbados, Dominica, Kyrgyzstan, Lao People's Democratic Republic, Maldives, Mongolia, Samoa, Solomon Islands

Action by the First Committee

Date: 31 October 2007   Meeting: 23rd meeting
Vote: Adopted without a vote   Draft resolution: A/C.1/62/L.35

Agenda item 99 (e)

62/53 Regional confidence-building measures: activities of the United Nations Standing Advisory Committee on Security Questions in Central Africa

Text

The General Assembly,

Recalling its previous relevant resolutions, in particular resolution 61/96 of 6 December 2006,

Recalling also the guidelines for general and complete disarmament adopted at its tenth special session, the first special session devoted to disarmament,

Bearing in mind the establishment by the Secretary-General on 28 May 1992 of the United Nations Standing Advisory Committee on Security Questions in Central Africa, the purpose of which is to encourage arms limitation, disarmament, non-proliferation and development in the subregion,

Convinced that the resources released by disarmament, including regional disarmament, can be devoted to economic and social development and to the protection of the environment for the benefit of all peoples, in particular those of the developing countries,

Considering the importance and effectiveness of confidence-building measures taken on the initiative and with the participation of all States concerned and taking into account the specific characteristics of each region, since such measures can contribute to regional stability and to international peace and security,

Convinced that development can be achieved only in a climate of peace, security and mutual confidence both within and among States,

Recalling the Brazzaville Declaration on Cooperation for Peace and Security in Central Africa,[1] the Bata Declaration for the Promotion of Lasting Democracy, Peace and Development in Central Africa[2] and the Yaoundé Declaration on Peace, Security and Stability in Central Africa,[3]

Bearing in mind resolutions 1196 (1998) and 1197 (1998), adopted by the Security Council on 16 and 18 September 1998 respectively, following its consideration of the report of the Secretary-General on the causes of conflict and the promotion of durable peace and sustainable development in Africa,[4]

---

[1] A/50/474, annex I.
[2] A/53/258-S/1998/763, annex II, appendix I.
[3] A/53/868-S/1999/303, annex II.
[4] A/52/871-S/1998/318.

Emphasizing the need to strengthen the capacity for conflict prevention and peacekeeping in Africa,

1. *Reaffirms its support* for efforts aimed at promoting confidence-building measures at the regional and subregional levels in order to ease tensions and conflicts in Central Africa and to further peace, stability and sustainable development in the subregion;

2. *Reaffirms* the importance of disarmament, demobilization and reintegration programmes, and encourages the United Nations Peacebuilding Commission to support efforts for the political stabilization and reconstruction of post-conflict countries;

3. *Notes with satisfaction* the revitalization of the work of the United Nations Standing Advisory Committee on Security Questions in Central Africa following the decision of the twenty-fourth ministerial meeting of the Standing Advisory Committee, held at Kigali from 25 to 29 September 2006;

4. *Welcomes* the adoption by the twenty-fifth ministerial meeting of the Standing Advisory Committee, held at Sao Tome from 14 to 18 May 2007, of the "Sao Tome Initiative", which provides for the drafting of a legal instrument on the control of small arms and light weapons in Central Africa and of a code of conduct for defence and security forces in Central Africa, and encourages interested countries to provide their financial support for the development of these two projects;

5. *Also welcomes* the holding at Yaoundé, from 4 to 6 September 2007, of a special conference of the Standing Advisory Committee on cross-border security issues in Central Africa, and takes note of its recommendations, particularly the recommendation relating to the project for the establishment of an international school in Cameroon to train African gendarmes and police in peacekeeping operations;

6. *Encourages* the States members of the Economic Community of Central African States to continue their efforts to promote peace and security in their subregion;

7. *Requests* the Secretary-General, pursuant to Security Council resolution 1197 (1998), to provide the States members of the Standing Advisory Committee with the necessary support for the smooth functioning of the Council for Peace and Security in Central Africa;

8. *Encourages* the States members of the Economic Community of Central African States to pursue their efforts to render the early-warning mechanism for Central Africa fully operational as an instrument for analysing and monitoring the political situation in the subregion within the framework of the prevention of crises and armed conflicts, and requests the Secretary-General to provide the necessary assistance for its smooth functioning;

9. *Reaffirms its support* for the programme of work of the Standing Advisory Committee, adopted at the organizational meeting of the Committee, held in Yaoundé from 27 to 31 July 1992;

10. *Notes with satisfaction* the progress made by the Standing Advisory Committee in implementing its programme of work for the period 2006-2007;[5]

11. *Emphasizes* the importance of providing the States members of the Standing Advisory Committee with the essential support they need to carry out the full programme of activities which they adopted at their ministerial meetings;

12. *Appeals* to the international community to support the efforts undertaken by the States concerned to implement disarmament, demobilization and reintegration programmes;

13. *Requests* the Secretary-General and the Office of the United Nations High Commissioner for Refugees to continue their assistance to the countries of Central Africa in tackling the problems of refugees and displaced persons in their territories;

14. *Requests* the Secretary-General and the United Nations High Commissioner for Human Rights to continue to provide their full assistance for the proper functioning of the Subregional Centre for Human Rights and Democracy in Central Africa;

15. *Urges* Member States and intergovernmental and non-governmental organizations to support the activities of the Standing Advisory Committee effectively through voluntary contributions to the Trust Fund for the United Nations Standing Advisory Committee on Security Questions in Central Africa;

16. *Encourages* the States members of the Standing Advisory Committee to implement resolution 1540 (2004), adopted by the Security Council on 28 April 2004, which deals with combating the use of and trafficking in nuclear, biological or chemical weapons and their means of delivery by non-State actors;

17. *Requests* the Secretary-General to continue to provide assistance to the States members of the Standing Advisory Committee to ensure the continuation of their efforts;

18. *Calls upon* the Secretary-General to submit to the General Assembly at its sixty-third session a report on the implementation of the present resolution;

19. *Decides* to include in the provisional agenda of its sixty-third session the item entitled "Regional confidence-building measures: activities

---

[5] A/62/129.

of the United Nations Standing Advisory Committee on Security Questions in Central Africa".

Action by the General Assembly

    Date: 5 December 2007   Meeting: 61st meeting
    Vote: Adopted without a vote   Report: A/62/392

Sponsors

    Cameroon (on behalf of the States Members of the United Nations that are members of the Economic Community of Central African Sates)

Action by the First Committee

    Date: 2 November 2007   Meeting: 25th meeting
    Vote: Adopted without a vote   Draft resolution: A/C.1/62/L.52/Rev.1

Agenda item 100 (a)

62/54 Report of the Disarmament Commission

Text

The General Assembly,

Having considered the report of the Disarmament Commission,[1]

Recalling its resolutions 47/54 A of 9 December 1992, 47/54 G of 8 April 1993, 48/77 A of 16 December 1993, 49/77 A of 15 December 1994, 50/72 D of 12 December 1995, 51/47 B of 10 December 1996, 52/40 B of 9 December 1997, 53/79 A of 4 December 1998, 54/56 A of 1 December 1999, 55/35 C of 20 November 2000, 56/26 A of 29 November 2001, 57/95 of 22 November 2002, 58/67 of 8 December 2003, 59/105 of 3 December 2004, 60/91 of 8 December 2005 and 61/98 of 6 December 2006,

Considering the role that the Disarmament Commission has been called upon to play and the contribution that it should make in examining and submitting recommendations on various problems in the field of disarmament and in the promotion of the implementation of the relevant decisions adopted by the General Assembly at its tenth special session,

1. *Takes note* of the report of the Disarmament Commission;[1]

2. *Reaffirms* the validity of its decision 52/492 of 8 September 1998, concerning the efficient functioning of the Disarmament Commission;

3. *Recalls* its resolution 61/98, by which it adopted additional measures for improving the effectiveness of the Commission's methods of work;

4. *Reaffirms* the mandate of the Disarmament Commission as the specialized, deliberative body within the United Nations multilateral disarmament machinery that allows for in-depth deliberations on specific disarmament issues, leading to the submission of concrete recommendations on those issues;

5. *Also reaffirms* the importance of further enhancing the dialogue and cooperation among the First Committee, the Disarmament Commission and the Conference on Disarmament;

6. *Requests* the Disarmament Commission to continue its work in accordance with its mandate, as set forth in paragraph 118 of the Final Document of the Tenth Special Session of the General Assembly,[2] and with paragraph 3 of Assembly resolution 37/78 H of 9 December 1982, and to that end to make every effort to achieve specific recommendations on the items on its agenda,

---

[1] *Official Records of the General Assembly, Sixty-second Session, Supplement No. 42* (A/62/42).
[2] Resolution S-10/2.

taking into account the adopted "Ways and means to enhance the functioning of the Disarmament Commission";[3]

7. *Recommends* that the Disarmament Commission continue the consideration of the following items at its 2008 substantive session:

(*a*) Recommendations for achieving the objective of nuclear disarmament and non-proliferation of nuclear weapons;

(*b*) Practical confidence-building measures in the field of conventional weapons;

8. *Requests* the Disarmament Commission to meet for a period not exceeding three weeks during 2008, namely from 7 to 24 April, and to submit a substantive report to the General Assembly at its sixty-third session;

9. *Requests* the Secretary-General to transmit to the Disarmament Commission the annual report of the Conference on Disarmament,[4] together with all the official records of the sixty-second session of the General Assembly relating to disarmament matters, and to render all assistance that the Commission may require for implementing the present resolution;

10. *Also requests* the Secretary-General to ensure full provision to the Disarmament Commission and its subsidiary bodies of interpretation and translation facilities in the official languages and to assign, as a matter of priority, all the necessary resources and services, including verbatim records, to that end;

11. *Decides* to include in the provisional agenda of its sixty-third session the item entitled "Report of the Disarmament Commission".

Action by the General Assembly

Date: 5 December 2007   Meeting: 61st meeting
Vote: Adopted without a vote   Report: A/62/393

Sponsors

Uruguay (on behalf of the members of the extended Bureau of the Disarmament Commission)

Co-sponsors

Kazakhstan

Action by the First Committee

Date: 31 October 2007   Meeting: 23rd meeting
Vote: Adopted without a vote   Draft resolution: A/C.1/62/L.3

---

[3] A/CN.10/137.
[4] *Official Records of the General Assembly, Sixty-second Session, Supplement No. 27* (A/62/27).

Agenda item 100 (b)

62/55 Report of the Conference on Disarmament

Text

The General Assembly,

Having considered the report of the Conference on Disarmament,[1]

Convinced that the Conference on Disarmament, as the sole multilateral disarmament negotiating forum of the international community, has the primary role in substantive negotiations on priority questions of disarmament,

Recognizing the need to conduct multilateral negotiations with the aim of reaching agreement on concrete issues,

Recalling, in this respect, that the Conference has a number of urgent and important issues for negotiation,

Taking note of active discussions held on the programme of work during the 2007 session of the Conference, as duly reflected in the report and the records of the plenary meetings,

Taking note also of the increased deliberations of the Conference due to the constructive contribution of its member States, the work done under the authority of the Presidents of the Conference for the 2007 session, including focused structured debates on all substantive agenda items and with the participation of experts from capitals, and the cooperation among all six Presidents of the Conference,

Taking note further of significant contributions made during the 2007 session to promote substantive discussions on issues on the agenda, as well as of discussions held on other issues that could also be relevant to the current international security environment,

Stressing the urgent need for the Conference to commence its substantive work at the beginning of its 2008 session,

Recognizing the messages of the Secretary-General of the United Nations, as well as the addresses of Ministers for Foreign Affairs and other high-level officials, as expressions of support for the endeavours of the Conference and its role as the sole multilateral disarmament negotiating forum,

Bearing in mind the importance of efforts towards revitalization of the disarmament machinery, including the Conference,

Recognizing the importance of continuing consultations on the question of the expansion of the Conference membership,

---

[1] *Official Records of the General Assembly, Sixty-second Session, Supplement No. 27* (A/62/27).

1. *Reaffirms* the role of the Conference on Disarmament as the sole multilateral disarmament negotiating forum of the international community;

2. *Calls upon* the Conference to further intensify consultations and explore possibilities with a view to reaching an agreement on a programme of work;

3. *Takes note* of the strong collective interest of the Conference to build on the increased level and focus of its activities through 2007 and to commence substantive work as soon as possible during its 2008 session;

4. *Welcomes* the decision of the Conference to request its current President and the incoming President to conduct consultations during the intersessional period and, if possible, to make recommendations, taking into account all relevant proposals, past, present and future, including those submitted as documents of the Conference, views presented and discussions held, and to endeavour to keep the membership of the Conference informed, as appropriate, of their consultations, as contained in paragraph 57 of its report;[1]

5. *Requests* all States members of the Conference to cooperate with the current President and successive Presidents in their efforts to guide the Conference to the early commencement of substantive work in its 2008 session;

6. *Requests* the Secretary-General to continue to ensure the provision to the Conference of adequate administrative, substantive and conference support services;

7. *Requests* the Conference to submit a report on its work to the General Assembly at its sixty-third session;

8. *Decides* to include in the provisional agenda of its sixty-third session the item entitled "Report of the Conference on Disarmament".

Action by the General Assembly

Date: 5 December 2007   Meeting: 61st meeting
Vote: Adopted without a vote   Report: A/62/393

Sponsors

South Africa, Spain, Sri Lanka, Sweden, Switzerland, **Syrian Arab Republic**

Action by the First Committee

Date: 31 October 2007   Meeting: 23rd meeting
Vote: Adopted without a vote   Draft resolution: A/C.1/62/L.11

Agenda item 101

62/56 The risk of nuclear proliferation in the Middle East

Text

The General Assembly,

Bearing in mind its relevant resolutions,

Taking note of the relevant resolutions adopted by the General Conference of the International Atomic Energy Agency, the latest of which is resolution GC(51)/RES/17, adopted on 20 September 2007,[1]

Cognizant that the proliferation of nuclear weapons in the region of the Middle East would pose a serious threat to international peace and security,

Mindful of the immediate need for placing all nuclear facilities in the region of the Middle East under full-scope safeguards of the Agency,

Recalling the decision on principles and objectives for nuclear non-proliferation and disarmament adopted by the 1995 Review and Extension Conference of the Parties to the Treaty on the Non-Proliferation of Nuclear Weapons on 11 May 1995,[2] in which the Conference urged universal adherence to the Treaty[3] as an urgent priority and called upon all States not yet parties to the Treaty to accede to it at the earliest date, particularly those States that operate unsafeguarded nuclear facilities,

Recognizing with satisfaction that, in the Final Document of the 2000 Review Conference of the Parties to the Treaty on the Non-Proliferation of Nuclear Weapons, the Conference undertook to make determined efforts towards the achievement of the goal of universality of the Treaty, called upon those remaining States not parties to the Treaty to accede to it, thereby accepting an international legally binding commitment not to acquire nuclear weapons or nuclear explosive devices and to accept Agency safeguards on all their nuclear activities, and underlined the necessity of universal adherence to the Treaty and of strict compliance by all parties with their obligations under the Treaty,[4]

Recalling the resolution on the Middle East adopted by the 1995 Review and Extension Conference on 11 May 1995,[2] in which the Conference noted with concern the continued existence in the Middle East of unsafeguarded

---

[1] See International Atomic Energy Agency, *Resolutions and Other Decisions of the General Conference, Fifty-first Regular Session, 17-21 September 2007* (GC(51)/RES/DEC(2007)).

[2] See *1995 Review and Extension Conference of the Parties to the Treaty on the Non-Proliferation of Nuclear Weapons, Final Document, Part I* (NPT/CONF.1995/32 (Part I) and Corr.2), annex.

[3] United Nations, *Treaty Series*, vol. 729, No. 10485.

[4] See *2000 Review Conference of the Parties to the Treaty on the Non-Proliferation of Nuclear Weapons, Final Document*, vol. I (NPT/CONF.2000/28 (Parts I and II)), part I, section entitled "Article IX".

nuclear facilities, reaffirmed the importance of the early realization of universal adherence to the Treaty and called upon all States in the Middle East that had not yet done so, without exception, to accede to the Treaty as soon as possible and to place all their nuclear facilities under full-scope Agency safeguards,

Noting that Israel remains the only State in the Middle East that has not yet become party to the Treaty,

Concerned about the threats posed by the proliferation of nuclear weapons to the security and stability of the Middle East region,

Stressing the importance of taking confidence-building measures, in particular the establishment of a nuclear-weapon-free zone in the Middle East, in order to enhance peace and security in the region and to consolidate the global non-proliferation regime,

Emphasizing the need for all parties directly concerned to consider seriously taking the practical and urgent steps required for the implementation of the proposal to establish a nuclear-weapon-free zone in the region of the Middle East in accordance with the relevant resolutions of the General Assembly and, as a means of promoting this objective, inviting the countries concerned to adhere to the Treaty and, pending the establishment of the zone, to agree to place all their nuclear activities under Agency safeguards,

Noting that one hundred and seventy-seven States have signed the Comprehensive Nuclear-Test-Ban Treaty,[5] including a number of States in the region,

1. *Welcomes* the conclusions on the Middle East of the 2000 Review Conference of the Parties to the Treaty on the Non-Proliferation of Nuclear Weapons;[6]

2. *Reaffirms* the importance of Israel's accession to the Treaty on the Non-Proliferation of Nuclear Weapons[3] and placement of all its nuclear facilities under comprehensive International Atomic Energy Agency safeguards, in realizing the goal of universal adherence to the Treaty in the Middle East;

3. *Calls upon* that State to accede to the Treaty without further delay and not to develop, produce, test or otherwise acquire nuclear weapons, and to renounce possession of nuclear weapons, and to place all its unsafeguarded nuclear facilities under full-scope Agency safeguards as an important confidence-building measure among all States of the region and as a step towards enhancing peace and security;

4. *Requests* the Secretary-General to report to the General Assembly at its sixty-third session on the implementation of the present resolution;

---

[5] See resolution 50/245.
[6] See *2000 Review Conference of the Parties to the Treaty on the Non-Proliferation of Nuclear Weapons, Final Document*, vol. I (NPT/CONF.2000/28 (Parts I and II)), part I, section entitled "Article VII and the security of non-nuclear-weapon States", para. 16.

5. *Decides* to include in the provisional agenda of its sixty-third session the item entitled "The risk of nuclear proliferation in the Middle East".

Action by the General Assembly

Date: 5 December 2007   Meeting: 61st meeting
Vote: 170-5-7, as a whole   Report: A/62/394
166-3-6, p. para. 6

Sponsors

Algeria, Bahrain, Djibouti, **Egypt**, Iraq, Kuwait, Lebanon, Libyan Arab Jamahiriya, Morocco, Oman, Saudi Arabia, Sudan, Syrian Arab Republic, Tunisia, United Arab Emirates, Yemen

Co-sponsors

Jordan, Qatar

Recorded vote

As a whole

In favour:

Afghanistan, Albania, Algeria, Andorra, Antigua and Barbuda, Argentina, Armenia, Austria, Azerbaijan, Bahamas, Bahrain, Bangladesh, Barbados, Belarus, Belgium, Belize, Benin, Bhutan, Bolivia, Bosnia and Herzegovina, Botswana, Brazil, Brunei Darussalam, Bulgaria, Burkina Faso, Burundi, Cambodia, Cape Verde, Central African Republic, Chile, China, Colombia, Comoros, Congo, Costa Rica, Croatia, Cuba, Cyprus, Czech Republic, Democratic People's Republic of Korea, Denmark, Djibouti, Dominica, Dominican Republic, Ecuador, Egypt, El Salvador, Equatorial Guinea, Eritrea, Estonia, Fiji, Finland, France, Gabon, Gambia, Georgia, Germany, Ghana, Greece, Grenada, Guatemala, Guinea, Guinea-Bissau, Guyana, Haiti, Honduras, Hungary, Iceland, Indonesia, Iran (Islamic Republic of), Iraq, Ireland, Italy, Jamaica, Japan, Jordan, Kazakhstan, Kenya, Kuwait, Kyrgyzstan, Lao People's Democratic Republic, Latvia, Lebanon, Lesotho, Liberia, Libyan Arab Jamahiriya, Liechtenstein, Lithuania, Luxembourg, Madagascar, Malawi, Malaysia, Maldives, Mali, Malta, Mauritania, Mauritius, Mexico, Monaco, Mongolia, Montenegro, Morocco, Mozambique, Myanmar, Namibia, Nauru, Nepal, Netherlands, New Zealand, Nicaragua, Niger, Nigeria, Norway, Oman, Pakistan, Panama, Papua New Guinea, Paraguay, Peru, Philippines, Poland, Portugal, Qatar, Republic of Korea, Republic of Moldova, Romania, Russian Federation, Saint Kitts and Nevis, Saint Lucia, Saint Vincent and the Grenadines, Samoa, San Marino, Sao Tome and Principe, Saudi Arabia, Senegal, Serbia, Sierra Leone, Singapore, Slovakia, Slovenia, Solomon Islands, Somalia, South Africa, Spain, Sri Lanka, Sudan, Suriname, Swaziland, Sweden, Switzerland, Syrian Arab Republic, Tajikistan, Thailand, the former Yugoslav Republic of Macedonia, Togo, Trinidad and Tobago, Tunisia, Turkey, Turkmenistan, Ukraine, United Arab Emirates, United Kingdom of Great Britain and Northern Ireland, United Republic of Tanzania, Uruguay, Uzbekistan, Venezuela (Bolivarian Republic of), Viet Nam, Yemen, Zambia, Zimbabwe

Against:
Israel, Marshall Islands, Micronesia (Federated States of), Palau, United States of America

Abstaining:
Australia, Cameroon, Canada, Côte d'Ivoire, Ethiopia, India, Tonga

Preambular paragraph 6

In favour:
Afghanistan, Albania, Algeria, Andorra, Antigua and Barbuda, Argentina, Armenia, Australia, Austria, Azerbaijan, Bahamas, Bahrain, Bangladesh, Barbados, Belarus, Belgium, Belize, Benin, Bolivia, Bosnia and Herzegovina, Botswana, Brazil, Brunei Darussalam, Bulgaria, Burkina Faso, Burundi, Cambodia, Cameroon, Canada, Cape Verde, Central African Republic, Chile, China, Colombia, Comoros, Congo, Costa Rica, Croatia, Cuba, Cyprus, Czech Republic, Denmark, Djibouti, Dominica, Dominican Republic, Ecuador, Egypt, El Salvador, Eritrea, Estonia, Fiji, Finland, France, Gabon, Gambia, Germany, Ghana, Greece, Grenada, Guatemala, Guinea, Guinea-Bissau, Guyana, Haiti, Honduras, Hungary, Iceland, Indonesia, Iran (Islamic Republic of), Iraq, Ireland, Italy, Jamaica, Japan, Jordan, Kazakhstan, Kenya, Kuwait, Kyrgyzstan, Lao People's Democratic Republic, Latvia, Lebanon, Lesotho, Liberia, Libyan Arab Jamahiriya, Liechtenstein, Lithuania, Luxembourg, Madagascar, Malawi, Malaysia, Maldives, Mali, Malta, Mauritania, Mexico, Monaco, Mongolia, Montenegro, Morocco, Mozambique, Myanmar, Namibia, Nepal, Netherlands, New Zealand, Nicaragua, Niger, Nigeria, Norway, Oman, Panama, Papua New Guinea, Paraguay, Peru, Philippines, Poland, Portugal, Qatar, Republic of Korea, Republic of Moldova, Romania, Russian Federation, Saint Kitts and Nevis, Saint Lucia, Saint Vincent and the Grenadines, Samoa, San Marino, Sao Tome and Principe, Saudi Arabia, Senegal, Serbia, Sierra Leone, Singapore, Slovakia, Slovenia, Solomon Islands, Somalia, South Africa, Spain, Sri Lanka, Sudan, Suriname, Swaziland, Sweden, Switzerland, Syrian Arab Republic, Tajikistan, Thailand, the former Yugoslav Republic of Macedonia, Togo, Trinidad and Tobago, Tunisia, Turkey, Turkmenistan, Ukraine, United Arab Emirates, United Kingdom of Great Britain and Northern Ireland, United Republic of Tanzania, Uruguay, Uzbekistan, Venezuela (Bolivarian Republic of), Viet Nam, Yemen, Zambia, Zimbabwe

Against:
> India, Israel, United States of America

Abstaining:
> Bhutan, Equatorial Guinea, Ethiopia, Mauritius, Pakistan, Tonga

Action by the First Committee

Date: 30 October 2007	Meeting: 22nd meeting
Vote: 164-3-6, as a whole	Draft resolution: A/C.1/62/L.2
161-3-6, p. para. 6	

Agenda item 102

62/57 Convention on Prohibitions or Restrictions on the Use of Certain Conventional Weapons Which May Be Deemed to Be Excessively Injurious or to Have Indiscriminate Effects

Text

The General Assembly,

Recalling its resolution 61/100 of 6 December 2006,

Recalling with satisfaction the adoption and the entry into force of the Convention on Prohibitions or Restrictions on the Use of Certain Conventional Weapons Which May Be Deemed to Be Excessively Injurious or to Have Indiscriminate Effects,[1] and its amended article 1,[2] and the Protocol on Non-Detectable Fragments (Protocol I),[1] the Protocol on Prohibitions or Restrictions on the Use of Mines, Booby Traps and Other Devices (Protocol II)[1] and its amended version,[3] the Protocol on Prohibitions or Restrictions on the Use of Incendiary Weapons (Protocol III),[1] the Protocol on Blinding Laser Weapons (Protocol IV),[4] and the Protocol on Explosive Remnants of War (Protocol V),[5]

Welcoming the results of the Third Review Conference of the States Parties to the Convention on Prohibitions or Restrictions on the Use of Certain Conventional Weapons Which May Be Deemed to Be Excessively Injurious or to Have Indiscriminate Effects, and commending the efforts of the President of the Conference,

Welcoming also the decision of the Third Review Conference to commission follow-up work under the oversight of the Chairman-designate of a meeting of States Parties to the Convention to be held from 7 to 13 November 2007 in Geneva,[6] and the decision to convene, as a matter of urgency, an intersessional meeting of governmental experts to consider further the application and implementation of existing humanitarian law to specific munitions that may cause explosive remnants of war, with particular focus on cluster munitions, including the factors affecting their reliability and their technical and design characteristics, with a view to minimizing the humanitarian impact of the use of these munitions,[7]

---

[1] United Nations, *Treaty Series*, vol. 1342, No. 22495.
[2] See CCW/CONF.II/2 and Corr.1, part II.
[3] CCW/CONF.I/16 (Part I), annex B.
[4] Ibid., annex A.
[5] See CCW/MSP/2003/3, annex V, appendix II.
[6] See CCW/CONF.III/11 (Part II).
[7] Ibid.

Welcoming further the holding, on 18 June 2007, of the meeting of the Preparatory Committee for the First Conference of the States Parties to Protocol V to be held on 5 November 2007 in Geneva for the purpose of consultations and cooperation on all issues related to the operation of the Protocol,

Recalling the role played by the International Committee of the Red Cross in the elaboration of the Convention and the Protocols thereto, and welcoming the particular efforts of various international, non-governmental and other organizations in raising awareness of the humanitarian consequences of explosive remnants of war,

1. *Calls upon* all States that have not yet done so to take all measures to become parties, as soon as possible, to the Convention on Prohibitions or Restrictions on the Use of Certain Conventional Weapons Which May Be Deemed to Be Excessively Injurious or to Have Indiscriminate Effects[1] and the Protocols thereto, as amended, with a view to achieving the widest possible adherence to these instruments at an early date, and so as to ultimately achieve their universality;

2. *Calls upon* all States parties to the Convention that have not yet done so to express their consent to be bound by the Protocols to the Convention and the amendment extending the scope of the Convention and the Protocols thereto to include armed conflicts of a non-international character;

3. *Welcomes* the adoption by the Third Review Conference of a Plan of Action to promote universality of the Convention and its annexed Protocols,[8] and expresses appreciation for the efforts of the Secretary-General, as depositary of the Convention and its annexed Protocols, and the President of the Third Review Conference, on behalf of the High Contracting Parties, to achieve the goal of universality;

4. *Also welcomes* the decision of the Third Review Conference to establish a Compliance Mechanism in order to promote compliance and the full implementation of the obligations contained in the Convention and its annexed Protocols;[9]

5. *Further welcomes* the decision of the Third Review Conference to establish a Sponsorship Programme within the framework of the Convention,[10] and encourages States to contribute to the programme;

6. *Welcomes* the commitment by States parties to continue to address the humanitarian problems caused by certain specific types of munitions in all their aspects, including cluster munitions, with a view to minimizing the humanitarian impact of these munitions;

---

[8] Ibid., annex III.
[9] Ibid., annex II.
[10] Ibid., annex IV.

7. *Expresses support* for the work conducted by the Group of Governmental Experts and the decision of the Group, based on the substantive discussion on the application and implementation of existing humanitarian law at its intersessional meeting held in June 2007, without prejudice to the outcome, to recommend to the 2007 Meeting of the States Parties to the Convention to decide how best to address the humanitarian impact of cluster munitions as a matter of urgency, including the possibility of a new instrument;[11]

8. *Notes* the decision of the Third Review Conference to dedicate up to two days at the next Meeting of the States Parties in 2007 to the issue of mines other than anti-personnel mines;[6]

9. *Emphasizes* the importance of universalization of the Protocol on Explosive Remnants of War (Protocol V), and welcomes the commitment of States parties to the Protocol to the effective and efficient implementation of the Protocol;

10. *Notes* that, in conformity with article 8 of the Convention, conferences may be convened to examine amendments to the Convention or to any of the Protocols thereto, to examine additional protocols concerning other categories of conventional weapons not covered by existing Protocols or to review the scope and application of the Convention and the Protocols thereto and to examine any proposed amendments or additional protocols;

11. *Requests* the Secretary-General to render the necessary assistance and to provide such services, including summary records, as may be required for the Ninth Annual Conference of the High Contracting Parties to Amended Protocol II to the Convention to be held on 6 November 2007, for the First Conference of the States Parties to Protocol V to be held on 5 November 2007, and for the Meeting of the States Parties to the Convention to be held from 7 to 13 November 2007, as well as for any possible continuation of work after the Meetings, should the States parties deem it appropriate;

12. *Also requests* the Secretary-General, in his capacity as depositary of the Convention and the Protocols thereto, to continue to inform the General Assembly periodically, by electronic means, of ratifications and acceptances of and accessions to the Convention, its amended article 1,[2] and the Protocols thereto;

13. *Decides* to include in the provisional agenda of its sixty-third session the item entitled "Convention on Prohibitions or Restrictions on the Use of Certain Conventional Weapons Which May Be Deemed to Be Excessively Injurious or to Have Indiscriminate Effects".

---

[11] See CCW/GGE/2007/3, annex III.

Action by the General Assembly

Date: 5 December 2007   Meeting: 61st meeting
Vote: Adopted without a vote Report: A/62/395

Sponsors

Austria, Belgium, Bulgaria, Chile, Croatia, Cyprus, Czech Republic, Denmark, Ecuador, Estonia, Finland, France, Germany, Greece, Guatemala, Hungary, Iceland, India, Ireland, Italy, Latvia, Lithuania, Luxembourg, Malta, Netherlands, New Zealand, Peru, Poland, Portugal, Romania, Serbia, Sierra Leone, Slovakia, Slovenia, South Africa, Spain, **Sweden**, Switzerland, the former Yugoslav Republic of Macedonia, United Kingdom of Great Britain and Northern Ireland, Uruguay

Co-sponsors

Albania, Argentina, Bosnia and Herzegovina, Cameroon, Canada, Honduras, Israel, Kazakhstan, Liechtenstein, Monaco, Mongolia, Nicaragua, Norway, Panama, Republic of Moldova, Turkmenistan

Action by the First Committee

Date: 31 October 2007   Meeting: 23rd meeting
Vote: Adopted without a vote   Draft resolution: A/C.1/62/L.32

Agenda item 103

62/58   Strengthening of security and cooperation in the Mediterranean region

Text

The General Assembly,

Recalling its previous resolutions on the subject, including resolution 61/101 of 6 December 2006,

Reaffirming the primary role of the Mediterranean countries in strengthening and promoting peace, security and cooperation in the Mediterranean region,

Welcoming the efforts deployed by the Euro-Mediterranean countries to strengthen their cooperation in combating terrorism, in particular by the adoption of the Euro-Mediterranean Code of Conduct on Countering Terrorism by the Euro-Mediterranean Summit, held in Barcelona, Spain, on 27 and 28 November 2005,

Bearing in mind all the previous declarations and commitments, as well as all the initiatives taken by the riparian countries at the recent summits, ministerial meetings and various forums concerning the question of the Mediterranean region,

Recognizing the indivisible character of security in the Mediterranean and that the enhancement of cooperation among Mediterranean countries with a view to promoting the economic and social development of all peoples of the region will contribute significantly to stability, peace and security in the region,

Recognizing also the efforts made so far and the determination of the Mediterranean countries to intensify the process of dialogue and consultations with a view to resolving the problems existing in the Mediterranean region and to eliminating the causes of tension and the consequent threat to peace and security, and their growing awareness of the need for further joint efforts to strengthen economic, social, cultural and environmental cooperation in the region,

Recognizing further that prospects for closer Euro-Mediterranean cooperation in all spheres can be enhanced by positive developments worldwide, in particular in Europe, in the Maghreb and in the Middle East,

Reaffirming the responsibility of all States to contribute to the stability and prosperity of the Mediterranean region and their commitment to respecting the purposes and principles of the Charter of the United Nations as well as the provisions of the Declaration on Principles of International Law concerning

Friendly Relations and Cooperation among States in accordance with the Charter of the United Nations,[1]

Noting the peace negotiations in the Middle East, which should be of a comprehensive nature and represent an appropriate framework for the peaceful settlement of contentious issues in the region,

Expressing its concern at the persistent tension and continuing military activities in parts of the Mediterranean that hinder efforts to strengthen security and cooperation in the region,

Taking note of the report of the Secretary-General,[2]

1. *Reaffirms* that security in the Mediterranean is closely linked to European security as well as to international peace and security;

2. *Expresses its satisfaction* at the continuing efforts by Mediterranean countries to contribute actively to the elimination of all causes of tension in the region and to the promotion of just and lasting solutions to the persistent problems of the region through peaceful means, thus ensuring the withdrawal of foreign forces of occupation and respecting the sovereignty, independence and territorial integrity of all countries of the Mediterranean and the right of peoples to self-determination, and therefore calls for full adherence to the principles of non-interference, non-intervention, non-use of force or threat of use of force and the inadmissibility of the acquisition of territory by force, in accordance with the Charter and the relevant resolutions of the United Nations;

3. *Commends* the Mediterranean countries for their efforts in meeting common challenges through coordinated overall responses, based on a spirit of multilateral partnership, towards the general objective of turning the Mediterranean basin into an area of dialogue, exchanges and cooperation, guaranteeing peace, stability and prosperity, encourages them to strengthen such efforts through, inter alia, a lasting multilateral and action-oriented cooperative dialogue among States of the region, and recognizes the role of the United Nations in promoting regional and international peace and security;

4. *Recognizes* that the elimination of the economic and social disparities in levels of development and other obstacles as well as respect and greater understanding among cultures in the Mediterranean area will contribute to enhancing peace, security and cooperation among Mediterranean countries through the existing forums;

5. *Calls upon* all States of the Mediterranean region that have not yet done so to adhere to all the multilaterally negotiated legal instruments related to the field of disarmament and non-proliferation, thus creating the necessary conditions for strengthening peace and cooperation in the region;

6. *Encourages* all States of the region to favour the necessary conditions for strengthening the confidence-building measures among them by promoting

---

[1] Resolution 2625 (XXV), annex.
[2] A/62/111.

genuine openness and transparency on all military matters, by participating, inter alia, in the United Nations system for the standardized reporting of military expenditures and by providing accurate data and information to the United Nations Register of Conventional Arms;[3]

7. *Encourages* the Mediterranean countries to strengthen further their cooperation in combating terrorism in all its forms and manifestations, including the possible resort by terrorists to weapons of mass destruction, taking into account the relevant resolutions of the United Nations, and in combating international crime and illicit arms transfers and illicit drug production, consumption and trafficking, which pose a serious threat to peace, security and stability in the region and therefore to the improvement of the current political, economic and social situation and which jeopardize friendly relations among States, hinder the development of international cooperation and result in the destruction of human rights, fundamental freedoms and the democratic basis of pluralistic society;

8. *Requests* the Secretary-General to submit a report on means to strengthen security and cooperation in the Mediterranean region;

9. *Decides* to include in the provisional agenda of its sixty-third session the item entitled "Strengthening of security and cooperation in the Mediterranean region".

Action by the General Assembly

Date: 5 December 2007 Meeting: 61st meeting
Vote: Adopted without a vote Report: A/62/396

Sponsors

Albania, **Algeria**, Andorra, Austria, Belgium, Bosnia and Herzegovina, Bulgaria, Croatia, Cyprus, Czech Republic, Denmark, Egypt, Finland, France, Germany, Greece, Ireland, Jordan, Latvia, Lithuania, Luxembourg, Malta, Morocco, Poland, Portugal, Republic of Moldova, Serbia, Spain, Tunisia, Turkey, United Kingdom of Great Britain and Northern Ireland, Yemen, Zimbabwe

Co-sponsors

Estonia, Hungary, Iceland, Italy, Monaco, Montenegro, Netherlands, Norway, Romania, San Marino, Slovakia, Slovenia, Sweden, the former Yugoslav Republic of Macedonia

Action by the First Committee

Date: 30 October 2007 Meeting: 22nd meeting
Vote: Adopted without a vote Draft resolution: A/C.1/62/L.48

---

[3] See resolution 46/36 L.

Agenda item 104

62/59 Comprehensive Nuclear-Test-Ban Treaty

Text

The General Assembly,

Reiterating that the cessation of nuclear-weapon test explosions or any other nuclear explosions constitutes an effective nuclear disarmament and non-proliferation measure, and convinced that this is a meaningful step in the realization of a systematic process to achieve nuclear disarmament,

Recalling that the Comprehensive Nuclear-Test-Ban Treaty, adopted by its resolution 50/245 of 10 September 1996, was opened for signature on 24 September 1996,

Stressing that a universal and effectively verifiable Treaty constitutes a fundamental instrument in the field of nuclear disarmament and non-proliferation and that after more than ten years, its entry into force is more urgent than ever before,

Encouraged by the signing of the Treaty by one hundred and seventy-seven States, including forty-one of the forty-four needed for its entry into force, and welcoming the ratification of one hundred and forty States, including thirty-four of the forty-four needed for its entry into force, among which there are three nuclear-weapon States,

Recalling its resolution 61/104 of 6 December 2006,

Welcoming the Final Declaration of the Fifth Conference on Facilitating the Entry into Force of the Comprehensive Nuclear-Test-Ban Treaty, held in Vienna on 17 and 18 September 2007,[1] pursuant to article XIV of the Treaty,

1. *Stresses* the vital importance and urgency of signature and ratification, without delay and without conditions, to achieve the earliest entry into force of the Comprehensive Nuclear-Test-Ban Treaty;

2. *Welcomes* the contributions by the States signatories to the work of the Preparatory Commission for the Comprehensive Nuclear-Test-Ban Treaty Organization, in particular its efforts to ensure that the Treaty's verification regime will be capable of meeting the verification requirements of the Treaty upon its entry into force, in accordance with article IV of the Treaty;

3. *Underlines* the need to maintain momentum towards completion of all elements of the verification regime;

4. *Urges* all States not to carry out nuclear-weapon test explosions or any other nuclear explosions, to maintain their moratoriums in this regard and to refrain from acts that would defeat the object and purpose of the Treaty,

---

[1] CTBT-Art.XIV/2007/6, annex.

while stressing that these measures do not have the same permanent and legally binding effect as the entry into force of the Treaty;

5. *Calls for* a peaceful solution of the nuclear issues on the Korean Peninsula through successful implementation of the Joint Statement, and the initial and second-phase actions to implement it, agreed upon in the framework of the Six-Party Talks;

6. *Urges* all States that have not yet signed the Treaty to sign and ratify it as soon as possible;

7. *Urges* all States that have signed but not yet ratified the Treaty, in particular those whose ratification is needed for its entry into force, to accelerate their ratification processes with a view to ensuring their earliest successful conclusion;

8. *Urges* all States to remain seized of the issue at the highest political level and, where in a position to do so, to promote adherence to the Treaty through bilateral and joint outreach, seminars and other means;

9. *Requests* the Secretary-General, in consultation with the Preparatory Commission for the Comprehensive Nuclear-Test-Ban Treaty Organization, to prepare a report on the efforts of States that have ratified the Treaty towards its universalization and possibilities for providing assistance on ratification procedures to States that so request it, and to submit such a report to the General Assembly at its sixty-third session;

10. *Decides* to include in the provisional agenda of its sixty-third session the item entitled "Comprehensive Nuclear-Test-Ban Treaty".

Action by the General Assembly

Date: 5 December 2007   Meeting: 61st meeting
Vote: 176-1-4   Report: A/62/397

Sponsors

Australia, Latvia, Lithuania, Luxembourg, Malta, Mexico, **New Zealand**, Turkey

Co-sponsors

Afghanistan, Andorra, Argentina, Armenia, Austria, Belgium, Benin, Bolivia, Bosnia and Herzegovina, Brazil, Bulgaria, Cameroon, Canada, Chile, China, Costa Rica, Croatia, Cyprus, Czech Republic, Denmark, El Salvador, Eritrea, Estonia, Finland, France, Germany, Greece, Iceland, Ireland, Italy, Japan, Kazakhstan, Liechtenstein, Monaco, Mongolia, Netherlands, Norway, Peru, Philippines, Poland, Portugal, Republic of Korea, Republic of Moldova, Romania, Russian Federation, Samoa, San Marino, Serbia, Sierra Leone, Slovakia, Slovenia, South Africa, Suriname, Sweden, Switzerland, Thailand, the former Yugoslav Republic of Macedonia, Timor-Leste, Ukraine, United Kingdom of Great Britain and Northern Ireland, Uruguay

Recorded vote

In favour:
Afghanistan, Albania, Algeria, Andorra, Antigua and Barbuda, Argentina, Armenia, Australia, Austria, Azerbaijan, Bahamas, Bahrain, Bangladesh, Barbados, Belarus, Belgium, Belize, Benin, Bhutan, Bolivia, Bosnia and Herzegovina, Botswana, Brazil, Brunei Darussalam, Bulgaria, Burkina Faso, Burundi, Cambodia, Cameroon, Canada, Cape Verde, Central African Republic, Chile, China, Comoros, Congo, Costa Rica, Côte d'Ivoire, Croatia, Cuba, Cyprus, Czech Republic, Denmark, Djibouti, Dominican Republic, Ecuador, Egypt, El Salvador, Equatorial Guinea, Eritrea, Estonia, Ethiopia, Fiji, Finland, France, Gabon, Gambia, Georgia, Germany, Ghana, Greece, Grenada, Guatemala, Guinea, Guinea-Bissau, Guyana, Haiti, Honduras, Hungary, Iceland, Indonesia, Iran (Islamic Republic of), Iraq, Ireland, Israel, Italy, Jamaica, Japan, Jordan, Kazakhstan, Kenya, Kuwait, Kyrgyzstan, Lao People's Democratic Republic, Latvia, Lebanon, Lesotho, Liberia, Libyan Arab Jamahiriya, Liechtenstein, Lithuania, Luxembourg, Madagascar, Malawi, Malaysia, Maldives, Mali, Malta, Marshall Islands, Mauritania, Mexico, Micronesia (Federated States of), Monaco, Mongolia, Montenegro, Morocco, Mozambique, Myanmar, Namibia, Nauru, Nepal, Netherlands, New Zealand, Nicaragua, Niger, Nigeria, Norway, Oman, Pakistan, Palau, Panama, Papua New Guinea, Paraguay, Peru, Philippines, Poland, Portugal, Qatar, Republic of Korea, Republic of Moldova, Romania, Russian Federation, Rwanda, Saint Kitts and Nevis, Saint Lucia, Saint Vincent and the Grenadines, Samoa, San Marino, Sao Tome and Principe, Saudi Arabia, Senegal, Serbia, Sierra Leone, Singapore, Slovakia, Slovenia, Solomon Islands, Somalia, South Africa, Spain, Sri Lanka, Sudan, Suriname, Swaziland, Sweden, Switzerland, Tajikistan, Thailand, the former Yugoslav Republic of Macedonia, Togo, Tonga, Trinidad and Tobago, Tunisia, Turkey, Turkmenistan, Ukraine, United Arab Emirates, United Kingdom of Great Britain and Northern Ireland, United Republic of Tanzania, Uruguay, Uzbekistan, Venezuela (Bolivarian Republic of), Viet Nam, Yemen, Zambia, Zimbabwe

Against:
United States of America

Abstaining:
Colombia, India, Mauritius, Syrian Arab Republic

Action by the First Committee

Date: 31 October 2007 Meeting: 23rd meeting
Vote: 166-1-4 Draft resolution: A/C.1/62/L.28

Agenda item 105

62/60 Convention on the Prohibition of the Development, Production and Stockpiling of Bacteriological (Biological) and Toxin Weapons and on Their Destruction

Text

The General Assembly,

Recalling its previous resolutions relating to the complete and effective prohibition of bacteriological (biological) and toxin weapons and to their destruction,

Noting with satisfaction that there are one hundred and fifty-nine States parties to the Convention on the Prohibition of the Development, Production and Stockpiling of Bacteriological (Biological) and Toxin Weapons and on Their Destruction,[1] including all of the permanent members of the Security Council,

Bearing in mind its call upon all States parties to the Convention to participate in the implementation of the recommendations of the Review Conferences, including the exchange of information and data agreed to in the Final Declaration of the Third Review Conference of the Parties to the Convention,[2] and to provide such information and data in conformity with standardized procedure to the Secretary-General on an annual basis and no later than 15 April,

Welcoming the reaffirmation made in the Final Declaration of the Fourth Review Conference[3] that under all circumstances the use of bacteriological (biological) and toxin weapons and their development, production and stockpiling are effectively prohibited under article I of the Convention,

Welcoming also the successful outcome of the Sixth Review Conference, which adopted a Final Document[4] after a gap of ten years,[5] conducted a consensus article-by-article review of the operation of the Convention and reached decisions on the continuity of the intersessional meetings of experts and States parties,

Recalling the decision reached at the Sixth Review Conference to hold four annual meetings of the States parties of one week's duration each year commencing in 2007, prior to the Seventh Review Conference, which is to be

---

[1] United Nations, *Treaty Series*, vol. 1015, No. 14860.
[2] BWC/CONF.III/23, part II.
[3] BWC/CONF.IV/9, part II.
[4] BWC/CONF.VI/6.
[5] The previous full review was conducted at the Fourth Review Conference in 1996.

held not later than the end of 2011, and to hold a one-week meeting of experts to prepare for each meeting of the States parties,[6]

1. *Notes with satisfaction* the increase in the number of States parties to the Convention on the Prohibition of the Development, Production and Stockpiling of Bacteriological (Biological) and Toxin Weapons and on Their Destruction,[1] reaffirms the call upon all signatory States that have not yet ratified the Convention to do so without delay, and calls upon those States that have not signed the Convention to become parties thereto at an early date, thus contributing to the achievement of universal adherence to the Convention;

2. *Welcomes* the information and data provided to date, and reiterates its call upon all States parties to the Convention to participate in the exchange of information and data agreed to in the Final Declaration of the Third Review Conference of the Parties to the Convention;[2]

3. *Takes note* of the decision of the Sixth Review Conference, taking into account the importance of providing administrative support to meetings agreed by the Review Conference as well as comprehensive implementation and universalization of the Convention and the exchange of confidence-building measures, to establish an Implementation Support Unit, funded by States parties, for the period from 2007-2011,[7] within the framework defined by the Review Conference;

4. *Notes with satisfaction* that the Sixth Review Conference agreed on several measures to update the mechanism for the transmission of information in the framework of the confidence-building measures;

5. *Recalls* the decisions reached at the Sixth Review Conference,[8] and calls upon States parties to the Convention to participate in their implementation;

6. *Requests* the Secretary-General to continue to render the necessary assistance to the depositary Governments of the Convention and to provide such services as may be required for the implementation of the decisions and recommendations of the Review Conferences, including all assistance to the annual meetings of the States parties and the meetings of experts;

7. *Decides* to include in the provisional agenda of its sixty-third session the item entitled "Convention on the Prohibition of the Development, Production and Stockpiling of Bacteriological (Biological) and Toxin Weapons and on Their Destruction".

---

[6] BWC/CONF.VI/6, part III, para. 7.
[7] Ibid., part III, paras. 5 and 6.
[8] Ibid., part III, paras. 1 and 7.

Action by the General Assembly

Date: 5 December 2007 Meeting: 61st meeting
Vote: Adopted without a vote Report: A/62/398

Sponsors

Hungary

Action by the First Committee

Date: 31 October 2007 Meeting: 23rd meeting
Vote: Adopted without a vote Draft resolution: A/C.1/62/L.37

Agenda item 99 (c)

62/216 United Nations Regional Centre for Peace and Disarmament in Africa

Text

The General Assembly,

Mindful of the provisions of Article 11, paragraph 1, of the Charter of the United Nations stipulating that a function of the General Assembly is to consider the general principles of cooperation in the maintenance of international peace and security, including the principles governing disarmament and arms limitation,

Recalling its resolutions 40/151 G of 16 December 1985, 41/60 D of 3 December 1986, 42/39 J of 30 November 1987 and 43/76 D of 7 December 1988 on the United Nations Regional Centre for Peace and Disarmament in Africa, and its resolutions 46/36 F of 6 December 1991 and 47/52 G of 9 December 1992 on regional disarmament, including confidence-building measures,

Recalling also its resolutions 48/76 E of 16 December 1993, 49/76 D of 15 December 1994, 50/71 C of 12 December 1995, 51/46 E of 10 December 1996, 52/220 of 22 December 1997, 53/78 C of 4 December 1998, 54/55 B of 1 December 1999, 55/34 D of 20 November 2000, 56/25 D of 29 November 2001, 57/91 of 22 November 2002, 58/61 of 8 December 2003, 59/101 of 3 December 2004, 60/86 of 8 December 2005 and 61/93 of 6 December 2006,

Aware of the important role that the Regional Centre can play in promoting confidence-building and arms-limitation measures at the regional level, thereby promoting progress in the area of sustainable development,

Taking into account the need to establish close cooperation between the Regional Centre and the Peace and Security Council of the African Union, in particular its institutions in the field of peace, disarmament and security, as well as with relevant United Nations bodies and programmes in Africa for greater effectiveness,

Taking note of the report of the Secretary-General,[1] in which he stated that the Regional Centre's ability to fulfil its mandate continued to be hampered by the lack of funding, in particular core funding,

Deeply concerned that, as noted in the report of the Secretary-General, voluntary contributions continued to decline and remained insufficient for the Regional Centre to fulfil its mandate effectively and efficiently, and that there is no foreseeable reliable source of funding that would ensure its operational sustainability,

---

[1] A/62/140.

Recalling that the General Assembly, in its resolution 60/86, requested the Secretary-General to establish, within existing resources, a Consultative Mechanism of interested States, in particular African States, for the reorganization of the Regional Centre,

1. *Notes with satisfaction* the conclusion of the work of the Consultative Mechanism for the Reorganization of the United Nations Regional Centre for Peace and Disarmament in Africa, which made concrete recommendations on the Centre's future work programme, as well as on its staffing and funding;[2]

2. *Notes with appreciation* the recommendations of the Consultative Mechanism on the Regional Centre's future work programme, as well as on its staffing and funding;

3. *Invites* the Regional Centre, taking into account the availability of financial resources, to focus its actions on the priorities identified in the recommendations of the Consultative Mechanism;

4. *Recommends* that three posts (one Professional at the P-3 level and two General Service (Other level)) be established and added to the structure of the Regional Centre, and funded from the regular budget, as recommended by the Consultative Mechanism;

5. *Also recommends* that the operating costs of the Regional Centre be funded from the regular budget;

6. *Urges* all States, as well as international governmental and non-governmental organizations and foundations, to make voluntary contributions in order to strengthen the programmes and activities of the Regional Centre and facilitate their implementation;

7. *Requests* the Secretary-General to continue to provide the necessary support to the Regional Centre for better achievements and results;

8. *Also requests* the Secretary-General to facilitate close cooperation between the Regional Centre and the African Union, in particular in the areas of peace, security and development, and to continue to provide assistance towards stabilizing the financial situation of the Centre;

9. *Further requests* the Secretary-General to report to the General Assembly at its sixty-third session on the implementation of the present resolution;

10. *Decides* to include in the provisional agenda of its sixty-third session the item entitled "United Nations Regional Centre for Peace and Disarmament in Africa".

---

[2] See A/62/167.

Action by the General Assembly

Date: 21 December 2007   Meeting: 79th meeting
Vote: 150-0-5   Report: A/62/392

Sponsors

Nigeria (on behalf of the States Members of the United Nations that are members of the Group of African States)

Co-sponsors

Barbados, Dominica

*Recorded vote**

In favour:
Afghanistan, Algeria, Andorra, Angola, Antigua and Barbuda, Argentina, Armenia, Austria, Azerbaijan, Bahamas, Bahrain, Bangladesh, Barbados, Belarus, Belgium, Belize, Benin, Bosnia and Herzegovina, Botswana, Brazil, Brunei Darussalam, Bulgaria, Burkina Faso, Burundi, Cambodia, Chile, China, Colombia, Congo, Costa Rica, Croatia, Cuba, Cyprus, Czech Republic, Democratic People's Republic of Korea, Denmark, Djibouti, Dominican Republic, Ecuador, Egypt, El Salvador, Eritrea, Estonia, Finland, France, Gabon, Georgia, Germany, Ghana, Greece, Guatemala, Guinea, Guyana, Haiti, Honduras, Hungary, Iceland, India, Indonesia, Iraq, Ireland, Italy, Jamaica, Jordan, Kazakhstan, Kenya, Kuwait, Kyrgyzstan, Lao People's Democratic Republic, Latvia, Lebanon, Lesotho, Libyan Arab Jamahiriya, Liechtenstein, Lithuania, Luxembourg, Madagascar, Malawi, Malaysia, Maldives, Mali, Malta, Marshall Islands, Mauritania, Mauritius, Mexico, Micronesia (Federated States of), Monaco, Mongolia, Montenegro, Morocco, Mozambique, Myanmar, Namibia, Nauru, Nepal, Netherlands, New Zealand, Nicaragua, Niger, Nigeria, Norway, Oman, Pakistan, Panama, Peru, Philippines, Poland, Portugal, Qatar, Republic of Korea, Republic of Moldova, Romania, Russian Federation, Rwanda, Saint Lucia, San Marino, Saudi Arabia, Senegal, Serbia, Sierra Leone, Singapore, Slovakia, Slovenia, South Africa, Spain, Sri Lanka, Sudan, Swaziland, Sweden, Switzerland, Syrian Arab Republic, Thailand, the former Yugoslav Republic of Macedonia, Timor-Leste, Togo, Trinidad and Tobago, Tunisia, Turkey, Uganda, Ukraine, United Arab Emirates, United Republic of Tanzania, Uruguay, Uzbekistan, Venezuela (Bolivarian Republic of), Viet Nam, Yemen, Zambia, Zimbabwe

Against:
None

---

* Subsequent to the voting, the delegation of the Islamic Republic of Iran advised the Secretariat that it had intended to vote in favour. The voting tally above does not reflect this information.

Abstaining:
>Australia, Canada, Japan, United Kingdom of Great Britain and Northern Ireland, United States of America

Action by the First Committee
>Date: 2 November 2007 Meeting: 25th meeting
>Vote: 164-1-5 Draft resolution: A/C.1/62/L.24/Rev.1

Decisions

Agenda item 92

62/512 Review of the implementation of the Declaration on the Strengthening of International Security

Text

The General Assembly decides to include in the provisional agenda of its sixty-fourth session the item entitled "Review of the implementation of the Declaration on the Strengthening of International Security".

Action by the General Assembly

Date: 5 December 2007　　Meeting: 61st meeting
Vote: Adopted without a vote　　Report: A/62/385

Sponsors

Indonesia (on behalf of the States Members of the United Nations that are members of the Movement of Non-Aligned Countries)

Action by the First Committee

Date: 1 November 2007　　Meeting: 24th meeting
Vote: Adopted without a vote　　Draft resolution: A/C.1/62/L.51

Agenda item 98 (bb)

62/513 United Nations conference to identify appropriate ways of eliminating nuclear dangers in the context of nuclear disarmament

Text

The General Assembly decides to include in the provisional agenda of its sixty-third session the item entitled "United Nations conference to identify appropriate ways of eliminating nuclear dangers in the context of nuclear disarmament".

Action by the General Assembly

Date: 5 December 2007 Meeting: 61st meeting
Vote: 133-3-43 Report: A/62/391

Sponsors

Mexico*

Recorded vote

In favour:
Afghanistan, Algeria, Antigua and Barbuda, Argentina, Armenia, Bahamas, Bahrain, Bangladesh, Barbados, Belarus, Belize, Benin, Bhutan, Bolivia, Botswana, Brazil, Brunei Darussalam, Burkina Faso, Burundi, Cambodia, Cameroon, Cape Verde, Central African Republic, Chile, China, Colombia, Comoros, Congo, Costa Rica, Côte d'Ivoire, Cuba, Cyprus, Democratic People's Republic of Korea, Djibouti, Dominica, Dominican Republic, Ecuador, Egypt, El Salvador, Equatorial Guinea, Eritrea, Ethiopia, Fiji, Gabon, Gambia, Ghana, Grenada, Guatemala, Guinea, Guinea-Bissau, Guyana, Haiti, Honduras, India, Indonesia, Iran (Islamic Republic of), Iraq, Ireland, Jamaica, Japan, Jordan, Kazakhstan, Kenya, Kuwait, Kyrgyzstan, Lao People's Democratic Republic, Lebanon, Lesotho, Liberia, Libyan Arab Jamahiriya, Madagascar, Malawi, Malaysia, Maldives, Mali, Malta, Marshall Islands, Mauritania, Mauritius, Mexico, Mongolia, Morocco, Mozambique, Myanmar, Namibia, Nepal, New Zealand, Nicaragua, Niger, Nigeria, Oman, Pakistan, Panama, Papua New Guinea, Paraguay, Peru, Philippines, Qatar, Rwanda, Saint Kitts and Nevis, Saint Lucia, Saint Vincent and the Grenadines, Samoa, Sao Tome and Principe, Saudi Arabia, Senegal, Sierra Leone, Singapore, Solomon Islands, Somalia, South Africa, Sri Lanka, Sudan, Suriname, Swaziland, Sweden, Syrian Arab Republic, Tajikistan, Thailand, Togo, Tonga, Trinidad and Tobago, Tunisia, Ukraine, United Arab Emirates, United Republic of Tanzania,

---

* The draft resolution was submitted by Mexico.

Uruguay, Uzbekistan, Venezuela (Bolivarian Republic of), Viet Nam, Yemen, Zambia, Zimbabwe

Against:
France, United Kingdom of Great Britain and Northern Ireland, United States of America

Abstaining:
Albania, Andorra, Australia, Austria, Azerbaijan, Belgium, Bosnia and Herzegovina, Bulgaria, Canada, Croatia, Czech Republic, Denmark, Estonia, Finland, Georgia, Germany, Greece, Hungary, Iceland, Israel, Italy, Latvia, Liechtenstein, Lithuania, Luxembourg, Montenegro, Netherlands, Norway, Palau, Poland, Portugal, Republic of Korea, Republic of Moldova, Romania, Russian Federation, San Marino, Serbia, Slovakia, Slovenia, Spain, Switzerland, the former Yugoslav Republic of Macedonia, Turkey

Action by the First Committee

Date: 30 October 2007	Meeting: 22nd meeting
Vote: 123-3-44	Draft resolution: A/C.1/62/L.6

Agenda item 98 (f)

62/514 Missiles

Text

The General Assembly, recalling its resolutions 54/54 F of 1 December 1999, 55/33 A of 20 November 2000, 56/24 B of 29 November 2001, 57/71 of 22 November 2002, 58/37 of 8 December 2003, 59/67 of 3 December 2004 and 61/59 of 6 December 2006 and its decision 60/515 of 8 December 2005, decides to include in the provisional agenda of its sixty-third session the item entitled "Missiles".

Action by the General Assembly

Date: 5 December 2007 Meeting: 61st meeting
Vote: 123-7-51 Report: A/62/391

Sponsors

Egypt, Indonesia, **Iran (Islamic Republic of)**

Co-sponsors

Zambia

Recorded vote

In favour:

Afghanistan, Algeria, Antigua and Barbuda, Argentina, Armenia, Bahamas, Bahrain, Bangladesh, Barbados, Belarus, Belize, Benin, Bhutan, Bolivia, Botswana, Brazil, Brunei Darussalam, Burkina Faso, Burundi, Cambodia, Cameroon, Cape Verde, Central African Republic, Chile, China, Colombia, Comoros, Congo, Costa Rica, Côte d'Ivoire, Cuba, Democratic People's Republic of Korea, Djibouti, Dominica, Dominican Republic, Ecuador, Egypt, El Salvador, Equatorial Guinea, Eritrea, Ethiopia, Fiji, Gabon, Gambia, Ghana, Grenada, Guatemala, Guinea, Guinea-Bissau, Guyana, Haiti, Honduras, India, Indonesia, Iran (Islamic Republic of), Iraq, Jamaica, Jordan, Kazakhstan, Kenya, Kuwait, Kyrgyzstan, Lao People's Democratic Republic, Lebanon, Lesotho, Libyan Arab Jamahiriya, Madagascar, Malawi, Malaysia, Maldives, Mali, Mauritania, Mauritius, Mexico, Mongolia, Morocco, Mozambique, Myanmar, Namibia, Nepal, Nicaragua, Niger, Nigeria, Oman, Pakistan, Panama, Paraguay, Peru, Philippines, Qatar, Russian Federation, Saint Kitts and Nevis, Saint Lucia, Saint Vincent and the Grenadines, Sao Tome and Principe, Saudi Arabia, Senegal, Sierra Leone, Singapore, Solomon Islands, Somalia, South Africa, Sri Lanka, Sudan, Suriname, Swaziland, Syrian Arab Republic, Tajikistan, Thailand, Togo, Tonga, Trinidad and Tobago, Tunisia, Turkmenistan, United Arab Emirates, United Republic of Tanzania, Uruguay, Uzbekistan, Venezuela (Bolivarian Republic of), Viet Nam, Yemen, Zambia, Zimbabwe

Against:
Denmark, France, Israel, Netherlands, Palau, United Kingdom of Great Britain and Northern Ireland, United States of America

Abstaining:
Albania, Andorra, Australia, Austria, Azerbaijan, Belgium, Bosnia and Herzegovina, Bulgaria, Canada, Croatia, Cyprus, Czech Republic, Estonia, Finland, Georgia, Germany, Greece, Hungary, Iceland, Ireland, Italy, Japan, Latvia, Liberia, Liechtenstein, Lithuania, Luxembourg, Malta, Marshall Islands, Monaco, Montenegro, New Zealand, Norway, Papua New Guinea, Poland, Portugal, Republic of Korea, Republic of Moldova, Romania, Rwanda, Samoa, San Marino, Serbia, Slovakia, Slovenia, Spain, Sweden, Switzerland, the former Yugoslav Republic of Macedonia, Turkey, Ukraine

Action by the First Committee

Date: 30 October 2007   Meeting: 22nd meeting
Vote: 117-6-51   Draft resolution: A/C.1/62/L.20

ANNEX

List of reports and notes of the Secretary-General

Agenda item 88	**Reduction of military budgets**
A/62/158, Add.1 and 2	Objective information on military matters, including transparency of mililtary expenditures
Agenda item 93	**Developments in the field of information and telecommunications in the context of international security**
A/62/98 and Add.1	Developments in the field of information and telecommunications in the context of international security
Agenda item 94	**Establishment of a nuclear-weapon-free zone in the region of the Middle East**
A/62/95 (Part I) and Add.1	Establishment of a nuclear-weapon-free zone in the region of the Middle East
Agenda item 97	**Verification in all its aspects, including the role of the United Nations in the field of verification**
A/61/1028	Verification in all its aspects, including the role of the United Nations in the field of verification
Agenda item 98	**General and complete disarmament**
A/62/93	Conventional arms control at the regional and subregional levels
A/62/99	Further measures in the field of disarmament for the prevention of an arms race on the seabed and the ocean floor and in the subsoil thereof
A/62/112	Relationship between disarmament and development
A/62/114 and Add.1	Transparency and confidence-building measures in outer space activities
A/62/115 and Add.1	Confidence-building measures in the regional and subregional context
A/62/133	Promotion of multilateralism in the area of disarmament and non-proliferation

A/62/134	Observance of environmental norms in the drafting and implementation of agreements on disarmament and arms control
A/62/139	Implementation of the Convention on the Prohibition of the Development, Production, Stockpiling and Use of Chemical Weapons and on Their Destruction
A/62/156	Measures to prevent terrorists from acquiring weapons of mass destruction
A/62/162	The illicit trade in small arms and light weapons in all its aspects — assistance to States for curbing the illicit traffic in small arms and light weapons and collecting them
A/62/163	The illicit trade in small arms and light weapons in all its aspects
A/62/165 and Add.1	Nuclear disarmament — follow-up to the advisory opinion of the International Court of Justice on the *Legality of the Threat or Use of Nuclear Weapons* — reducing nuclear danger
A/62/166 and Add.1	Problems arising from the accumulation of conventional ammunition stockpiles in surplus
A/62/170, Add.1 and 2	United Nations Register of Conventional Arms
A/62/278 (Parts I and II), Add.1 and 2	Towards an arms trade treaty: establishing common international standards for the import, export and transfer of conventional arms

Agenda item 99 — **Review and implementation of the Concluding Document of the Twelfth Special Session of the General Assembly**

A/62/129	Regional confidence-building measures: activities of the United Nations Standing Advisory Committee on Security Questions in Central Africa
A/62/130	United Nations Regional Centre for Peace, Disarmament and Development in Latin America and the Caribbean
A/62/140	United Nations Regional Centre for Peace and Disarmament in Africa
A/62/153	United Nations Regional Centre for Peace and Disarmament in Asia and the Pacific

Agenda item 100	**Review of the implementation of the recommendations and decisions adopted by the General Assembly at its tenth special session**
A/62/152	United Nations Institute for Disarmament Research
A/62/309	Work of the Advisory Board on Disarmament Matters
Agenda item 101	**The risk of nuclear proliferation in the Middle East**
A/62/95 (Part II)	The risk of nuclear proliferation in the Middle East
Agenda item 103	**Strengthening of security and cooperation in the Mediterranean region**
A/62/111	Strengthening of security and cooperation in the Mediterranean region
Agenda item 104	**Comprehensive Nuclear-Test-Ban Treaty**
A/62/113 and Add.1	Comprehensive Nuclear-Test-Ban Treaty
A/62/135	Comprehensive Nuclear-Test-Ban Treaty